Mom! I Learn Division Using Math-Chess-Puzzles Connection

棋谜式除法

Frank Ho   Amanda Ho

何数棋谜 培训

Ho Math Chess Learning Centre

Mom! I Learn Division Using Math-Chess-Puzzles Connection

Ho Math Chess 何数棋谜 妈!我会棋谜式除法啦!

Frank Ho, Amanda Ho © 2004 – 2017, all rights reserved.

Student's Name _____ Date _____

Table of Contents

***** Part 1 Worksheets using math-chess-puzzles connection ***** 8
Chess pieces and their mathematical values 9
IQ math chess puzzles 10
Memory and computation training 11
Frankho Maze 何数棋谜宫 12
Trace the path from ⊠ to ✳ 12
Movement direction is shown by a darker line segment. 12
***** Review of times table ***** 13
Multiplication of 2 13
Multiplication of 3 14
Multiplication 4 15
Multiplication 5 16
Multiplication of 6 17
Multiplication of 7 18
Multiplication of 8 19
Multiplication of 9 20
Multiplication of 10 21
Learning multiplication and division 22
Numerical ability assessment 30
Frankho Eight Diagrams Math™ 31
Assessment of multiplication 32
Assessment of multiplication (order of operation) 34
Addition, subtraction, multiplication and division of 2 35
Addition, subtraction, multiplication and division of 3 36
Addition, subtraction, multiplication and division of 4 37
Addition, subtraction, multiplication and division of 5 38
Addition, subtraction, multiplication and division of 6 39
Addition, subtraction, multiplication and division of 7 40
Addition, subtraction, multiplication and division of 8 41
Addition, subtraction, multiplication and division of 9 42

No part of this publication can be copied, duplicated, or reproduced.

Mom! I Learn Division Using Math-Chess-Puzzles Connection

Ho Math Chess　何数棋谜　妈!我会棋谜式除法啦!

Frank Ho, Amanda Ho © 2004 – 2017, all rights reserved.

Student's Name _____　Date _____

Addition, subtraction, multiplication and division of 10's power or multiples of 10	43
Learning multiplication by pattern	44
Addition, subtraction, and division of 11	45
Addition, subtraction, and division of 12	46
Addition, subtraction, and division of 13	47
Addition, subtraction, and division of 14	48
Addition, subtraction, and division of 15	49
Addition, subtraction, and division of 16	50
Addition, subtraction, and division of 17	51
Addition, subtraction, and division of 18	52
Reverse Subtraction	53
Reverse Addition	54
Reverse Multiplication	55
Reverse Division	57
Learning division from multiplication (Concept used for % and getting one factor)	59
Paired whole numbers	61
Adding with convergent thinking	63
Intelligent math worksheet	67
Spatial relation and subtraction operation	74
Intelligent worksheets of division and remainder	83
Division with minimum quotient and no remainder	111
Reduce the following fractions.	113
dd divided by dd	122
***** Part 2 Multiplication Review *****	145
dd × dd multiplication concepts	146
dd × dd with carrying	148
ddd × dd with carrying	160
ddd	161
ddd × dd without carrying	164
d0d × dd	168
***** Part 3 Traditional worksheets *****	170

No part of this publication can be copied, duplicated, or reproduced.

Mom! I Learn Division Using Math-Chess-Puzzles Connection

Ho Math Chess 何数棋谜 妈!我会棋谜式除法啦!

Frank Ho, Amanda Ho © 2004 − 2017, all rights reserved.

Student's Name _____ Date _____

Less than or equal ≤	171
Division notations	172
Divisible by 2	173
Divisible by 3	174
Divisible by 4	175
Divisible by 5	176
Divisible by 6	177
Divisible by 9	178
Divisible by 10	179
Dividing by relating	183
Multiplying by relating	184
From multiplication to division procedure	185
From multiplication to division (d ÷ d)	186
dd ÷ d with 1-digit quotient and no remainder	188
From multiplication to division	190
dd ÷ d with 1-digit quotient and no remainder	195
dd ÷ d with remainder vs. no remainder	198
From multiplication to division	204
Multiplication and division facts	212
Use the following array	214
Division math minutes	216
dd ÷ d with 2-digit quotient and no remainder	218
dd ÷ d with 2-digit quotient and remainder	224
ddd ÷ d with three-digit quotient and no remainder	226
ddd ÷ d with three-digit quotient and remainder	230
Short Division	233
Rounding whole number (5 up, 4 down)	235
Trailing zeros in the dividend	239
Trailing zeros in the dividend and divisor	240
Dividend with trailing 0's (with no remainder)	241
Trailing zeros in the dividend and divisor	242
Zeros in the middle of quotient	244

No part of this publication can be copied, duplicated, or reproduced.

Mom! I Learn Division Using Math-Chess-Puzzles Connection

Ho Math Chess 何数棋谜 妈!我会棋谜式除法啦!

Frank Ho, Amanda Ho © 2004 – 2017, all rights reserved.

Student's Name _____ Date _____

Quotient with leading, middle, and training zeros	246
d0… d0.. ÷ d0… with no remainder	247
ddd ÷ dd with 2-digit quotient	250
Estimating ddd ÷ dd with 1-digit quotient	258
ddd ÷ dd with 1-digit quotient	259
ddd ÷ dd with 1-digit quotient and remainder	263
Estimating of 2-digit(s) quotient by rounding	267
Estimating quotient of 2-digit or more divisors by rounding	268
ddd ÷ dd = q with no remainder	270
ddd ÷ dd = qq with no remainder	271
ddddd ÷ ddd	276
Addition and subtraction	279
Multiplication and addition	285
Multiplication and subtraction	289
Division and addition	292
Division and subtraction	302
Multiplication and division	303
***** Part 4 Decimal division *****	304
ddd ÷ dd. Round the answers to the nearest hundredth.	307
ddd ÷ dd. Round the answers to the nearest hundredth.	308
dddd÷ dd. Round the answers to the nearest hundredth.	309
dddd÷ dd. Round the answers to the nearest hundredth.	310
ddd ÷ ddd. Round the answers to the nearest hundredth.	311
dddd÷ ddd. Round the answers to the nearest hundredth.	312

Mom! I Learn Division Using Math-Chess-Puzzles Connection

Ho Math Chess 何数棋谜 妈!我会棋谜式除法啦!

Frank Ho, Amanda Ho © 2004 – 2017, all rights reserved.

Student's Name _____ Date _____

About Ho Math Chess™ Math Workbooks

I have taught students from grade 1 to grade 12 since I opened the Vancouver **Ho Math Chess** Learning Centre in 1995. I have personally witnessed on how some students suffered because they could not master some very basic computational skills. I do not want to create a workbook, which is about practice, practice, and more practice of computational skills. This has motivated me to create a workbook that would be very different from the conventional ones in terms of the way the questions are presented to the students. I wanted students to learn basic computation skills by using the carefully designed worksheets so that students can master basic computation skills in an intuitive way. These worksheets were being designed while I actually watched student's work and modified accordingly to their responses.

I had an idea to create a computational workbook, which integrates chess knowledge, puzzles, and math in such a way that students could learn how to transfer abstract symbols into numerical values and then calculating the results by using puzzles-like problems. This idea may sound very simple but the result is much more profound – not only students learn to do math in multi-step, they also learn how to process information by converting abstract symbols into numerical values, which is important in learning critical thinking skill.

One very noticeable computation format in **Ho Math Chess** math workbooks is the way computation directions are presented - it is no longer just a linear fashion; instead, students work on computations in all kinds of directions: top-down, bottom up, left to eight, right to left, diagonally, and even circular motion. For example, the multiplication workbook computation format is designed in such a way that it takes the boredom out by using the format of multi-direction computation and multi-concept learning. Students could be introduced division computation procedure while working on multiplication and even equivalent fractions but without realizing that they are actually working on advanced math concepts and mechanic computation procedure beyond their grade level. One other example is that the factoring procedure is introduced while students are working on multiplication. These many embedded computational procedures included in the elementary level of math workbook will benefit students when they go to higher grades.

Mom! I Learn Division Using Math-Chess-Puzzles Connection
Ho Math Chess　何数棋谜　妈!我会棋谜式除法啦!
Frank Ho, Amanda Ho © 2004 – 2017, all rights reserved.
Student's Name _____ Date _____

My idea of using multi-direction, multi-operation, multi-procedure, multi-concept learning style is the very distinct and innovative way of creating these workbooks. Students found them less boring and even willing to do the same worksheets the second time if they did not master the first time.

I am hoping by working through these addition, subtraction, multiplication workbooks, the division would be just a matter of fine-tuning its computation procedure.

In 2014, all computation workbooks have taken major upgrades to include truly math and chess integrated material, this idea is a world first and these worksheets formats are also a world first. With these releases of many new and innovative workbooks, the math teaching and tutoring has taken the entire math tutoring to a revolutionary stage. Because of the creation of integrated math, chess, and puzzles integrated workbooks, Ho Math Chess has made the dream of fun math teaching becomes true.

Students at Ho Math Chess have enjoyed math even more than the previous workbooks and we see dramatic changes in student's attitude, they are happier and more willing to work on math.

Frank Ho
Amanda Ho

July 2014

Mom! I Learn Division Using Math-Chess-Puzzles Connection

Ho Math Chess 何数棋谜 妈!我会棋谜式除法啦!

Frank Ho, Amanda Ho © 2004 – 2017, all rights reserved.

Student's Name _____ Date _____

***** Part 1 Worksheets using math-chess-puzzles connection *****

Mom! I Learn Division Using Math-Chess-Puzzles Connection

Ho Math Chess 何数棋谜 妈!我会棋谜式除法啦!

Frank Ho, Amanda Ho © 2004 – 2017, all rights reserved.

Student's Name _____ Date _____

Chess pieces and their mathematical values

Symbols of chess pieces	Names of chess pieces	Mathematical values
♕ ♛	Queen	9
♖ ♜	Rook	5
♗ ♝	Bishop	3
♘ ♞	Knight	3
♙ ♟	Pawn	1
♔ ♚	King	0

No part of this publication can be copied, duplicated, or reproduced.

Mom! I Learn Division Using Math-Chess-Puzzles Connection

Ho Math Chess　何数棋谜　妈!我会棋谜式除法啦!

Frank Ho, Amanda Ho © 2004 − 2017, all rights reserved.

Student's Name _____ Date _____

IQ math chess puzzles

You are a chess piece ↙↖↑↗↘ located at (e, 5).

6	(a, 3)	(b, 3)	(c, 3)
5	(a, 2)	4 1 / 2 3	(c, 2)
4	(a, 1)	(b, 1)	(c, 1)
	d	e	f

Rule: All the digits 1 to 3 must appear exactly once in every row and column.

▨ + The least of ✦ = _____   ▨ + The least of ✦ = _____

▨ + The largest of ✦ = _____   ▨ + The largest of ✦ = _____

▨ + The sum of even numbers ✦ = _____   ▨ + The sum of odd numbers ✦ = _____

▨ + The range of odd numbers of ✦ = _____   ▨ + The average of the numbers of ✦ = _____

4+2=6, 12=3
3+3=6, 2+3=5
2+2=4, 4+5=9
1+2=3, $3+\frac{7}{4}=4\frac{3}{4}$

Page 10

Mom! I Learn Division Using Math-Chess-Puzzles Connection

Ho Math Chess 何数棋谜 妈!我会棋谜式除法啦!

Frank Ho, Amanda Ho © 2004 − 2017, all rights reserved.

Student's Name _____ Date _____

Memory and computation training

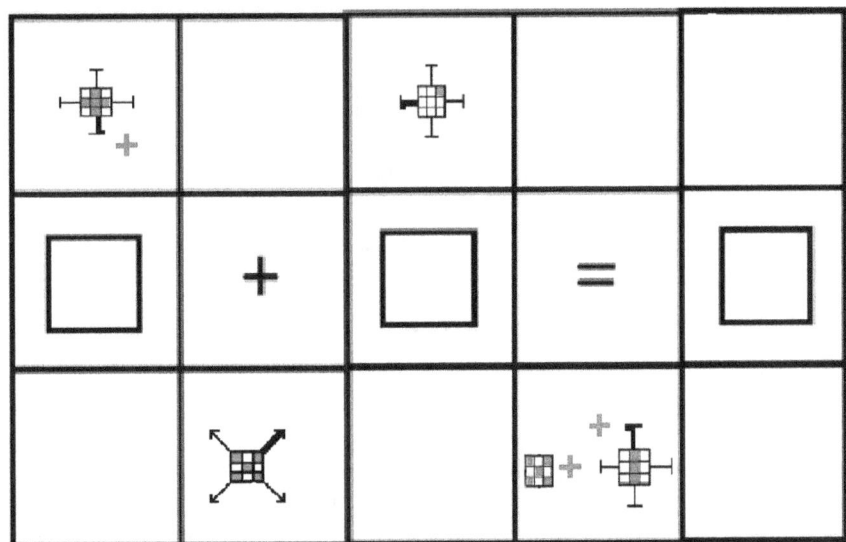

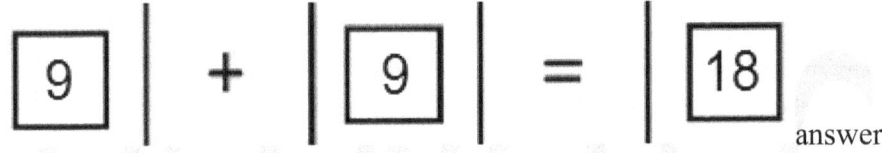

9 + 9 = 18   answer

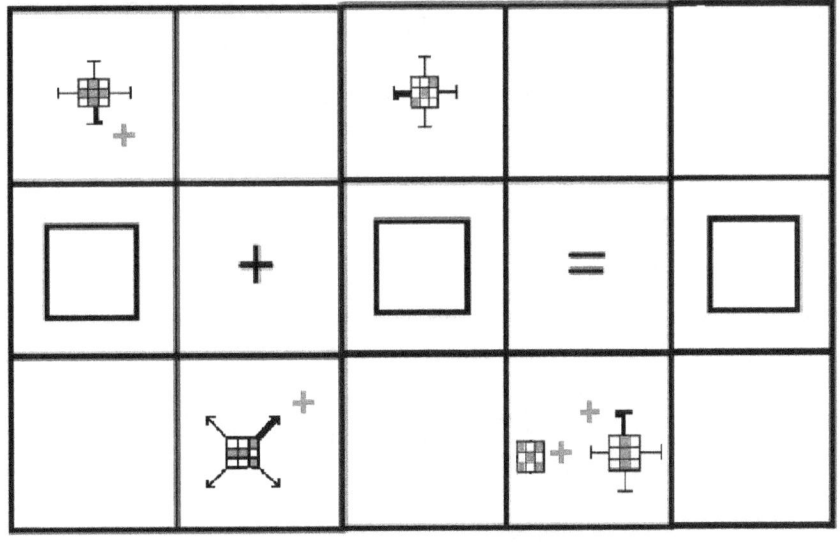

11 + 9 = 20   answer

Mom! I Learn Division Using Math-Chess-Puzzles Connection

Ho Math Chess 何数棋谜 妈!我会棋谜式除法啦!

Frank Ho, Amanda Ho © 2004 − 2017, all rights reserved.

Student's Name _____ Date _____

Frankho Maze 何数棋谜宫

Trace the path from ⊞ to ✻.

Movement direction is shown by a darker line segment.

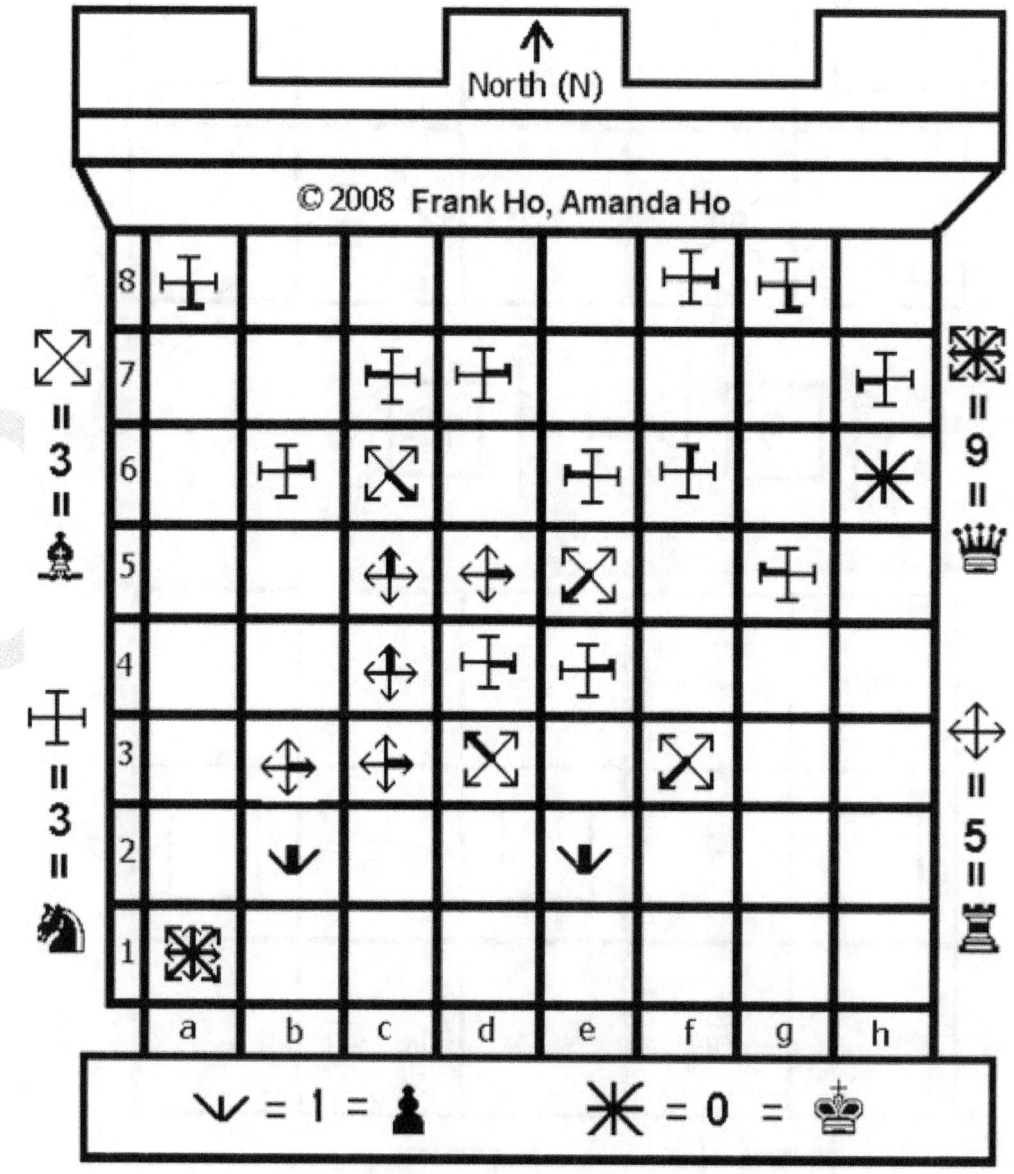

Mom! I Learn Division Using Math-Chess-Puzzles Connection

Ho Math Chess   何数棋谜   妈!我会棋谜式除法啦!

Frank Ho, Amanda Ho © 2004 − 2017, all rights reserved.

Student's Name _____ Date_____

***** Review of times table *****

Multiplication of 2

9	2	3
8	2	4
7	6	5

$2 \times 3=6$, $2 \times 6=12$
$2 \times 4=8$, $2 \times 7=14$
$2 \times 4=8$, $2 \times 8=16$
$2 \times 5=10$, $2 \times 9=18$

Page 13

Mom! I Learn Division Using Math-Chess-Puzzles Connection

Ho Math Chess 何数棋谜 妈!我会棋谜式除法啦!

Frank Ho, Amanda Ho © 2004 – 2017, all rights reserved.

Student's Name _____ Date _____

Multiplication of 3

9	2	3
8	3	4
7	6	5

6, 18
9, 21
12, 24
15, 27

Page 14

Mom! I Learn Division Using Math-Chess-Puzzles Connection

Ho Math Chess 何数棋谜 妈!我会棋谜式除法啦!

Frank Ho, Amanda Ho © 2004 − 2017, all rights reserved.

Student's Name _____ Date _____

Multiplication 4

9	2	3
8	4	4
7	6	5

8, 24
12, 28
16, 32
20, 36

Mom! I Learn Division Using Math-Chess-Puzzles Connection

Ho Math Chess 何数棋谜 妈!我会棋谜式除法啦!

Frank Ho, Amanda Ho © 2004 − 2017, all rights reserved.

Student's Name _____ Date _____

Multiplication 5

9	2	3
8	5	4
7	6	5

10, 30
15, 35
20, 40
25, 45

Page 16

Mom! I Learn Division Using Math-Chess-Puzzles Connection

Ho Math Chess   何数棋谜   妈!我会棋谜式除法啦!

Frank Ho, Amanda Ho © 2004 − 2017, all rights reserved.

Student's Name _____ Date_____

Multiplication of 6

9	2	3
8	6	4
7	6	5

12, 36
18, 42
24, 48
30, 54

Page 17

Mom! I Learn Division Using Math-Chess-Puzzles Connection

Ho Math Chess 何数棋谜 妈!我会棋谜式除法啦!

Frank Ho, Amanda Ho © 2004 – 2017, all rights reserved.

Student's Name_____ Date_____

Multiplication of 7

14, 42
21, 49
28, 56
35, 63

Mom! I Learn Division Using Math-Chess-Puzzles Connection

Ho Math Chess 何数棋谜 妈!我会棋谜式除法啦!

Frank Ho, Amanda Ho © 2004 − 2017, all rights reserved.

Student's Name _____ Date _____

Multiplication of 8

9	2	3
8	8	4
7	6	5

16, 48
24, 56
32, 64
40, 72

Page 19

Mom! I Learn Division Using Math-Chess-Puzzles Connection

Ho Math Chess 何数棋谜 妈!我会棋谜式除法啦!

Frank Ho, Amanda Ho © 2004 – 2017, all rights reserved.

Student's Name _____ Date _____

Multiplication of 9

9	2	3
8	9	4
7	6	5

18, 54
27, 63
36, 72
45, 81

Mom! I Learn Division Using Math-Chess-Puzzles Connection

Ho Math Chess 何数棋谜 妈!我会棋谜式除法啦!

Frank Ho, Amanda Ho © 2004 – 2017, all rights reserved.

Student's Name _____ Date _____

Multiplication of 10

9	2	3
8	10	4
7	6	5

9	2	3
8	10	4
7	6	5

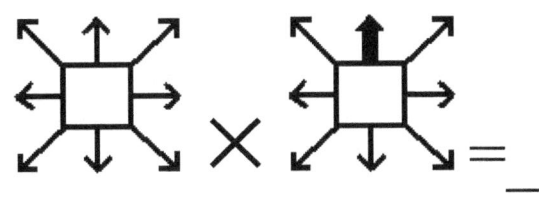 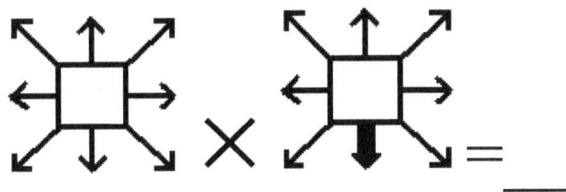

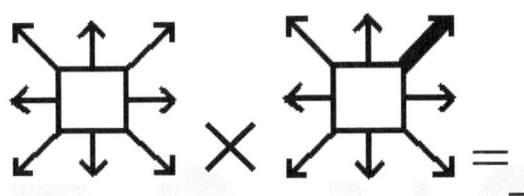 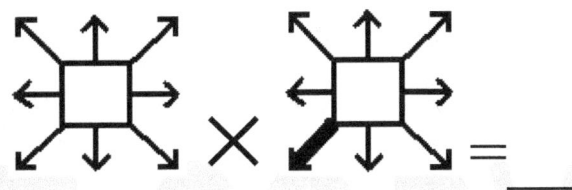

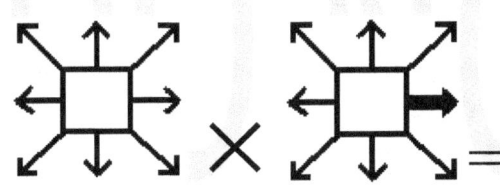 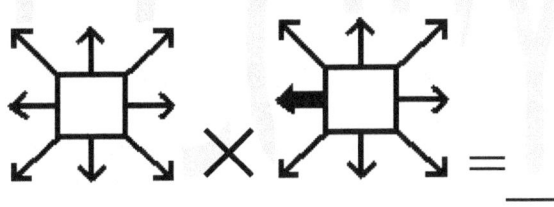

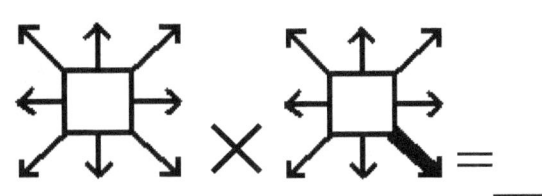 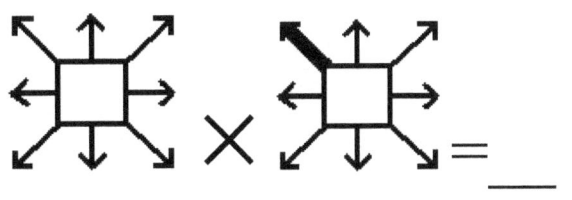

20, 60
30, 70
40, 80
50, 90

Mom! I Learn Division Using Math-Chess-Puzzles Connection

Ho Math Chess 何数棋谜 妈!我会棋谜式除法啦!

Frank Ho, Amanda Ho © 2004 – 2017, all rights reserved.

Student's Name _____ Date _____

Learning multiplication and division

5	2	3	4	6	6
4	9	6	3	5	8
3	5	7	7	2	4
2	2	4	9	3	5
1	7	4	3	6	6
	a	B	c	d	e

You are at c3 = ☐.

Find out all factors of 7 = _____ 1, 7

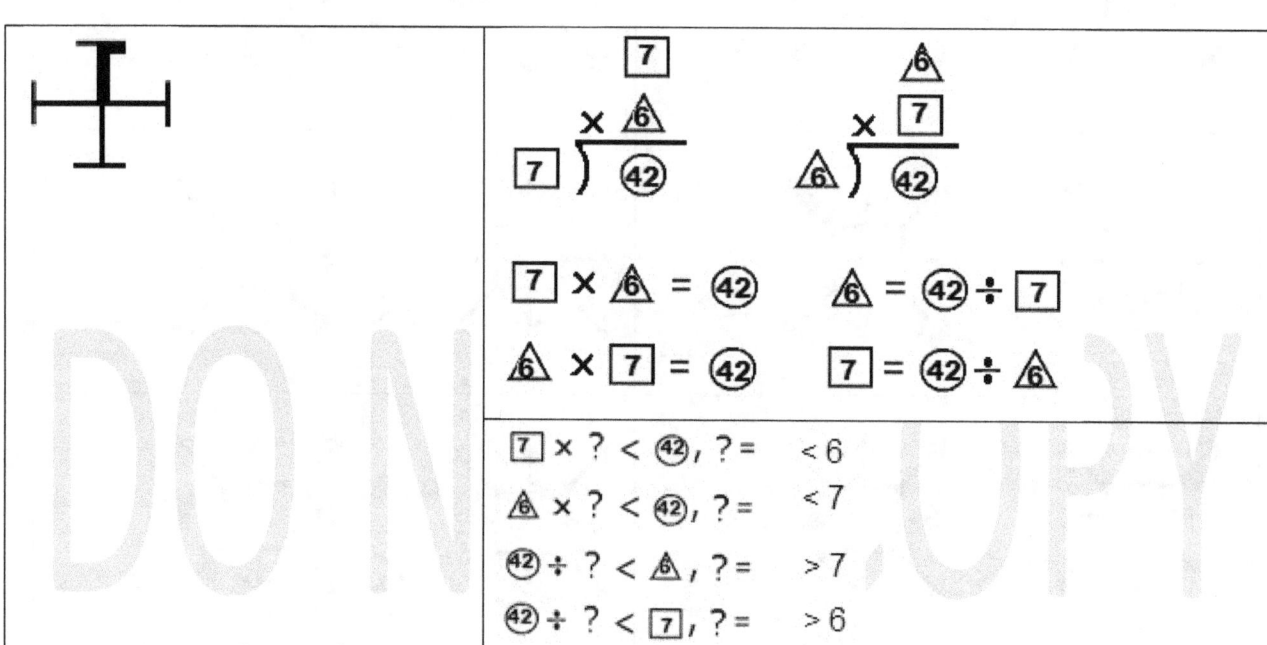

Mom! I Learn Division Using Math-Chess-Puzzles Connection

Ho Math Chess　何数棋谜　妈!我会棋谜式除法啦!

Frank Ho, Amanda Ho © 2004 − 2017, all rights reserved.

Student's Name _____ Date _____

Learning multiplication and division

5	2	3	4	7	6
4	9	6	3	5	8
3	5	7	7	2	4
2	2	4	9	3	5
1	7	4	3	6	6
	a	b	c	d	e

You are at c3 = □.

Find out all factors of 7 = _____.

$$\square \overline{)\stackrel{\times \triangle}{\bigcirc}} \qquad \triangle \overline{)\stackrel{\times \square}{\bigcirc}}$$

$$\square \times \triangle = \bigcirc \qquad \triangle = \bigcirc \div \square$$

$$\triangle \times \square = \bigcirc \qquad \square = \bigcirc \div \triangle$$

$\square \times ? < \bigcirc, ? = $ _____

$\triangle \times ? < \bigcirc, ? = $ _____

$\bigcirc \div ? < \triangle, ? = $ _____

$\bigcirc \div ? < \square, ? = $ _____

<8
<7
>7
>8

$7 \times 8 = 56$

Mom! I Learn Division Using Math-Chess-Puzzles Connection

Ho Math Chess   何数棋谜   妈!我会棋谜式除法啦!

Frank Ho, Amanda Ho © 2004 − 2017, all rights reserved.

Student's Name _____ Date _____

Learning multiplication and division

5	2	3	4	7	6
4	9	6	3	5	8
3	5	7	7	2	4
2	2	4	9	3	5
1	7	4	3	6	6
	a	b	c	d	e

You are at c3 = □.

Find out all factors of 7 = _____.

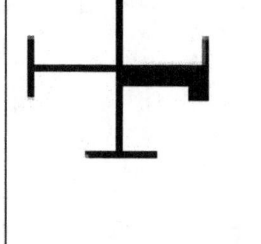

$\square \times \triangle$ over $\square) \overline{\bigcirc}$ $\triangle \times \square$ over $\triangle) \overline{\bigcirc}$

$\square \times \triangle = \bigcirc$ $\triangle = \bigcirc \div \square$

$\triangle \times \square = \bigcirc$ $\square = \bigcirc \div \triangle$

$\square \times ? < \bigcirc, ? = $ _____

$\triangle \times ? < \bigcirc, ? = $ _____

$\bigcirc \div ? < \triangle, ? = $ _____

$\bigcirc \div ? < \square, ? = $ _____

< 5
< 7
> 7
> 5

$7 \times 5 = 35$

Mom! I Learn Division Using Math-Chess-Puzzles Connection

Ho Math Chess   何数棋谜   妈!我会棋谜式除法啦!

Frank Ho, Amanda Ho © 2004 – 2017, all rights reserved.

Student's Name _____   Date _____

Learning multiplication and division

5	2	3	4	7	6
4	9	6	3	5	8
3	5	7	7	2	4
2	2	4	9	3	5
1	7	4	3	6	6
	a	b	c	d	e

You are at c3 = ☐.

Find out all factors of 7 = _____.

$$\square \overline{)\bigcirc}^{\times \triangle} \qquad \triangle \overline{)\bigcirc}^{\times \square}$$

$\square \times \triangle = \bigcirc \qquad \triangle = \bigcirc \div \square$

$\triangle \times \square = \bigcirc \qquad \square = \bigcirc \div \triangle$

$\square \times ? < \bigcirc, ? =$ _____

$\triangle \times ? < \bigcirc, ? =$ _____

$\bigcirc \div ? < \triangle, ? =$ _____

$\bigcirc \div ? < \square, ? =$ _____

< 6
< 7
> 7
> 6

7 × 6 = 42

Mom! I Learn Division Using Math-Chess-Puzzles Connection

Ho Math Chess   何数棋谜   妈!我会棋谜式除法啦!

Frank Ho, Amanda Ho © 2004 − 2017, all rights reserved.

Student's Name _____ Date _____

Learning multiplication and division

5	2	3	4	7	6
4	9	6	3	5	8
3	5	7	7	2	4
2	2	4	9	3	5
1	7	4	3	6	6
	a	b	c	d	e

You are at c3 = ☐.

Find out all factors of 7 = _____.

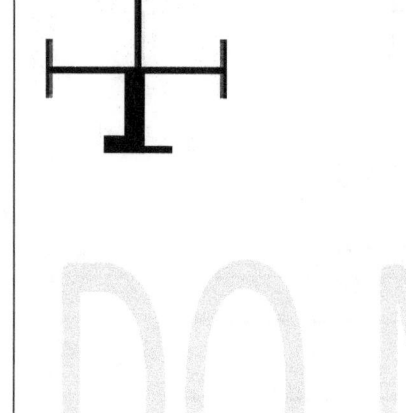

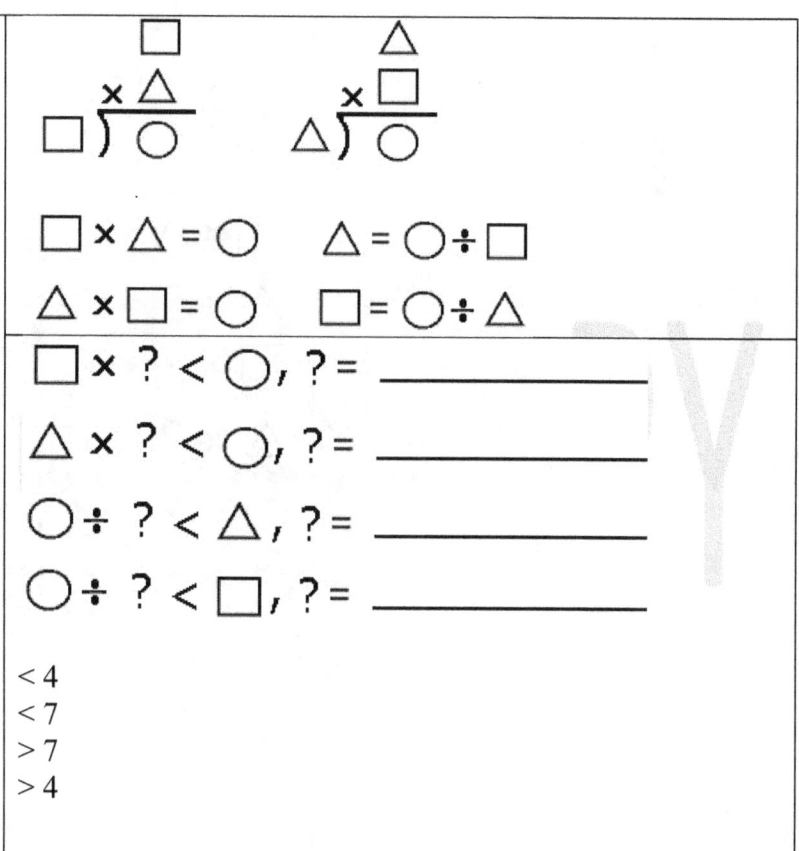

< 4
< 7
> 7
> 4

$7 \times 4 = 28$

Page 26

Mom! I Learn Division Using Math-Chess-Puzzles Connection

Ho Math Chess   何数棋谜   妈!我会棋谜式除法啦!

Frank Ho, Amanda Ho © 2004 – 2017, all rights reserved.

Student's Name _____ Date _____

Learning multiplication and division

5	2	3	4	7	6
4	9	6	3	5	8
3	5	7	7	2	4
2	2	4	9	3	5
1	7	4	3	6	6
	a	b	c	d	e

You are at c3 = ☐.

Find out all factors of 7 = _____.

□ × △ = ○   △ = ○ ÷ □
△ × □ = ○   □ = ○ ÷ △

□ × ? < ○, ? = _____
△ × ? < ○, ? = _____
○ ÷ ? < △, ? = _____
○ ÷ ? < □, ? = _____

< 2
< 7
> 7
> 2

$7 \times 4 = 28$

Mom! I Learn Division Using Math-Chess-Puzzles Connection

Ho Math Chess 何数棋谜 妈!我会棋谜式除法啦!

Frank Ho, Amanda Ho © 2004 − 2017, all rights reserved.

Student's Name _____ Date _____

Learning multiplication and division

5	2	3	4	7	6
4	9	6	3	5	8
3	5	7	7	2	4
2	2	4	9	3	5
1	7	4	3	6	6
	a	b	c	d	e

You are at c3 = ☐.

Find out all factors of 7 = _____.

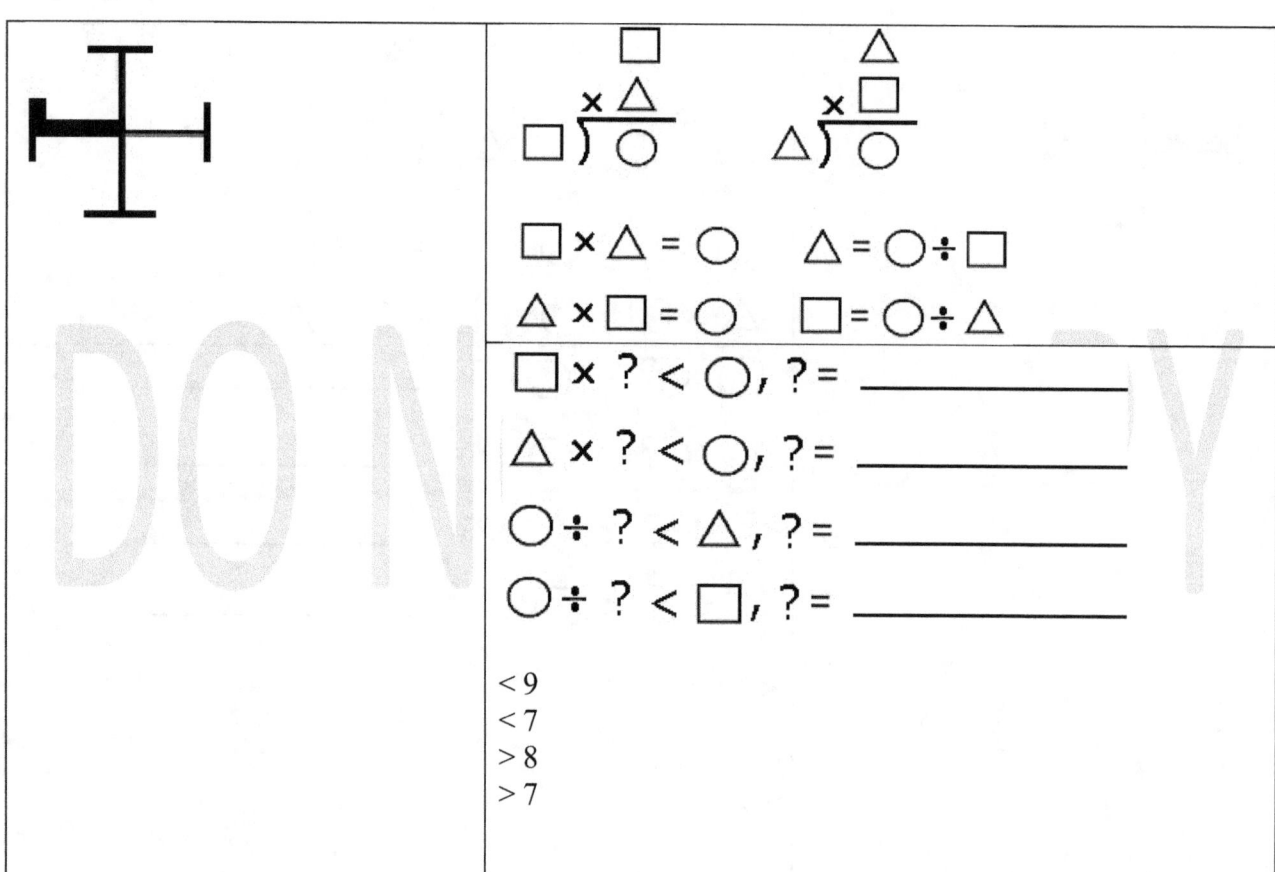

$\square \times \triangle = \bigcirc \qquad \triangle = \bigcirc \div \square$

$\triangle \times \square = \bigcirc \qquad \square = \bigcirc \div \triangle$

$\square \times ? < \bigcirc, ? =$ _____

$\triangle \times ? < \bigcirc, ? =$ _____

$\bigcirc \div ? < \triangle, ? =$ _____

$\bigcirc \div ? < \square, ? =$ _____

< 9
< 7
> 8
> 7

$7 \times 2 = 14$

Page 28

Mom! I Learn Division Using Math-Chess-Puzzles Connection

Ho Math Chess 何数棋谜 妈!我会棋谜式除法啦!

Frank Ho, Amanda Ho © 2004 − 2017, all rights reserved.

Student's Name _____ Date _____

Learning multiplication and division

5	2	3	4	7	6
4	9	6	3	5	8
3	5	7	7	2	4
2	2	4	9	3	5
1	7	4	3	6	6
	a	b	c	d	e

You are at c3 = ☐.

Find out all factors of 7 = _____.

$$\square \times \triangle = \bigcirc \qquad \triangle = \bigcirc \div \square$$

$$\triangle \times \square = \bigcirc \qquad \square = \bigcirc \div \triangle$$

☐ × ? < ○, ? = _____

△ × ? < ○, ? = _____

○ ÷ ? < △, ? = _____

○ ÷ ? < ☐, ? = _____

< 3
< 7
> 7
> 3

$7 \times 3 = 21$

Page 29

Mom! I Learn Division Using Math-Chess-Puzzles Connection

Ho Math Chess 何数棋谜 妈!我会棋谜式除法啦!

Frank Ho, Amanda Ho © 2004 − 2017, all rights reserved.

Student's Name _____ Date _____

Numerical ability assessment

#						
1	3 + 9	12	12 × 2	24	One hour is how many minutes	60
2	9 + 3	12	22 × 2	44	One hour 20 minutes is how many minutes	80
3	12 − 3	9	33 × 2	66	15 minutes is how many hours?	1/4
4	12 − 9	3	44 × 2	88	30 minutes is how many hours?	1/2
5	2 × 2	4	55 × 2	110	121 × 2	242
6	3 × 3	9	11 × 3	33	242 × 2	484
7	4 × 4	16	22 × 3	66	123 × 2	246
8	6 × 6	36	44 × 3	132	321 × 2	642
9	5 × 5	25	55 × 3	165	213 × 2	426
10	9 × 9	81	8 × 3	24	312 × 2	424
11	8 × 8	64	8 × 9	72	231 × 2	462
12	11 × 11	121	9 × 6	54	321 × 2	642
13	10 × 10	100	7 × 6	42	121 × 3	363
14	7 × 7	49	5 × 6	30	232 × 3	696
15	12 × 12	144	2 × 6	12	123 × 3	369
16	13 × 13	169	1 × 1 × 1 × 1	1	321 × 3	963
17	14 × 14	196	1 ÷ 1	1	213 × 3	639
18	15 × 15	225	23 ÷ 1	23	312 × 3	936
19	25 × 25	625	24 ÷ 2	12	231 × 3	693
20	35 × 35	1225	22 ÷ 1	22	321 × 3	963
21	55 × 55	3025	48 ÷ 2	24	121 × 3	363
22	19 − 2	17	48 ÷ 4	12	242 × 3	726
23	14 − 5	9	48 ÷ 3	16	25 ÷ 5	5
24	12 − 8	4	48 ÷ 12	4	2555 ÷ 5	511
25	13 − 6	7	48 ÷ 6	8	250 ÷ 5	50
26	11 − 4	7	48 ÷ 48	1	2500 ÷ 5	500
27	10 − 9	1	72 ÷ 2	36	2505 ÷ 5	501
28	10 − 4	6	72 ÷ 3	24	25050 ÷ 5	5010
29	18 − 9	9	72 ÷ 4	18	100 ÷ 5	20
30	17 − 8	9	72 ÷ 12	6	1000 ÷ 5	200
31	17 − 9	8	72 ÷ 6	12	500 ÷ 5	100
32	11 − 2	9	72 ÷ 36	2	100 ÷ 50	2
33	13 − 4	9	1 ÷ 2	1/2	100 ÷ 100	1
34	15 − 8	7	2 ÷ 4	1/2	100 ÷ 10	10
35	17 − 9	8	$\frac{1}{2} + \frac{1}{2}$	1	1000 ÷ 10	100
36	14 − 9	5	One dollar is how many cents?	100	1 ÷ 0.1	10
37	13 − 4	9	One dollar 10 cents is how many cents?	110	10 ÷ 0.1	100

Mom! I Learn Division Using Math-Chess-Puzzles Connection

Ho Math Chess 何数棋谜 妈!我会棋谜式除法啦!

Frank Ho, Amanda Ho © 2004 – 2017, all rights reserved.

Student's Name _____ Date _____

Frankho Eight Diagrams Math™

只见棋谜不见题 劝君迷路不哭涕 数学象棋加谜题 健脑思维真神奇

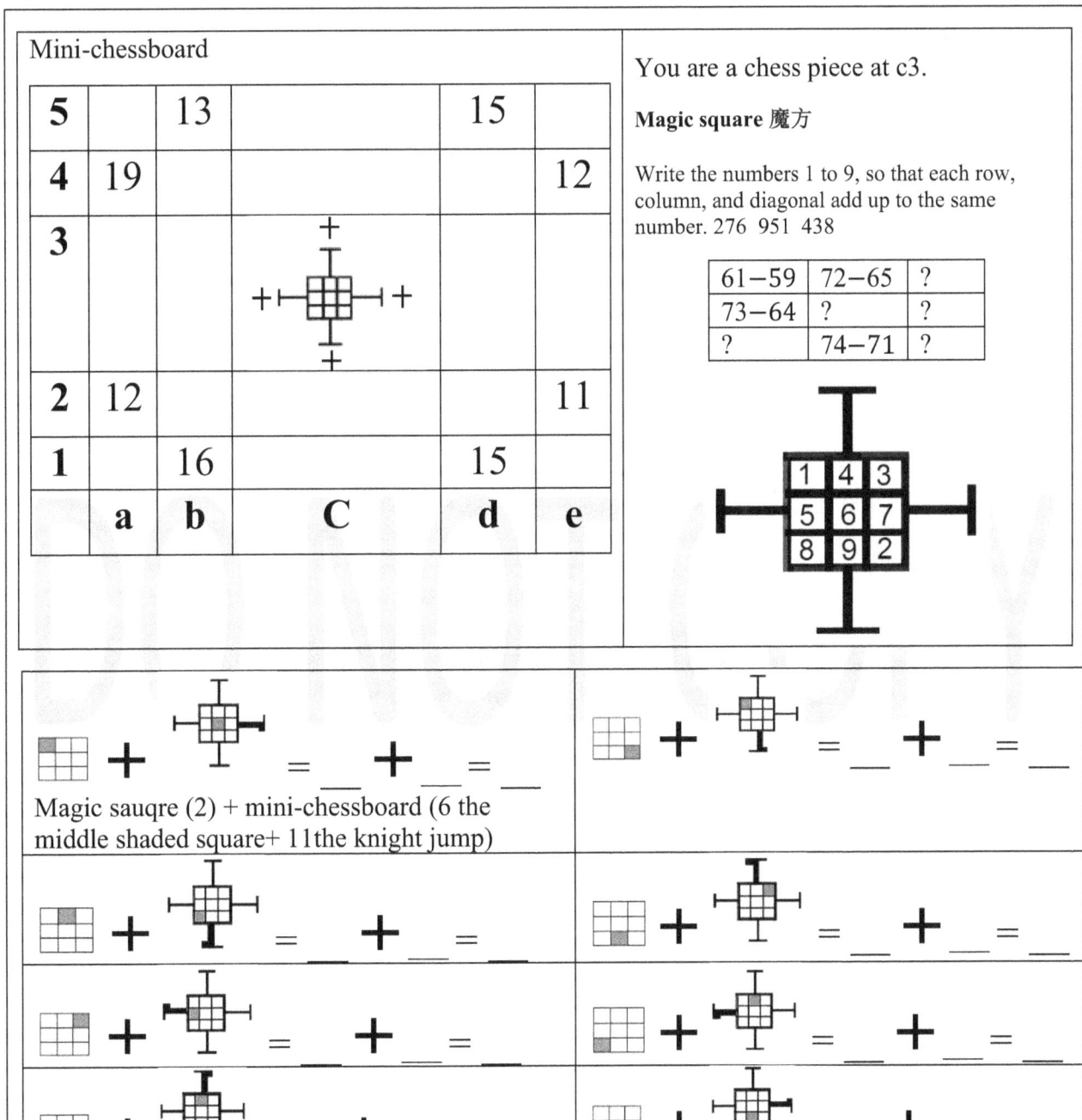

2+17=19,　8+16=24,
7+24=31,　3+16=19,
6+24=30,　4+16=20,
1+19=20,　9+21=30

No part of this publication can be copied, duplicated, or reproduced.

Mom! I Learn Division Using Math-Chess-Puzzles Connection

Ho Math Chess   何数棋谜   妈!我会棋谜式除法啦!

Frank Ho, Amanda Ho © 2004 − 2017, all rights reserved.

Student's Name _____ Date _____

Assessment of multiplication

Fill in each ? by a number such that $a_1 \times a_2 = a_3$ and $b_1 \times b_2 = b_3$.

✗ = $a_1 \times b_2$, ✗ = $b_1 \times a_2$.

Example

3	6	1
2	?2	?1
1	?3	?1
	a	b

$3 \times 2 = 6, 1 \times 1 = 1$

✗ + ✗ = _3_ + _2_ = 5

$3 \times 1 + 1 \times 2 = 5$

✗ − ✗ = _3_ − _2_ = 1

$3 \times 1 − 1 \times 2 = 3 − 2 = 1$

3	6	2
2	?	?
1	?	?
	a	b

✗ + ✗ = __ + __ = 13

✗ − ✗ = __ − __ = 11

3	6	2
2	?	?
1	?	?
	a	b

✗ + ✗ = __ + __ = 8

✗ − ✗ = __ − __ = 4

6 1
1 2
12 + 1 = 13
12 − 1 = 11

1 1
6 2
6 + 2 = 8
6 − 2 = 4

Mom! I Learn Division Using Math-Chess-Puzzles Connection

Ho Math Chess 何数棋谜 妈!我会棋谜式除法啦!

Frank Ho, Amanda Ho © 2004 – 2017, all rights reserved.

Student's Name _____ Date _____

Assessment of multiplication

Fill in each ? by a number such that $a1 \times a2 = a3$ and $b1 \times b2 = b3$.

$\searrow = a1 \times b2$, $\swarrow = b1 \times a2$.

	a	b
3	6	2
2	?	?
1	?	?

$\searrow + \swarrow = \_\_ + \_\_ = 7$

$\searrow - \swarrow = \_\_ - \_\_ = 1$

	a	b
3	6	3
2	?	?
1	?	?

$\searrow + \swarrow = \_\_ + \_\_ = 19$

$\searrow - \swarrow = \_\_ - \_\_ = 17$

	a	b
3	6	3
2	?	?
1	?	?

$\searrow + \swarrow = \_\_ + \_\_ = 11$

$\searrow - \swarrow = \_\_ - \_\_ = \_\_ - \_\_ = 7$

3 2
2 1
4 + 3 = 7
4 − 3 = 1

6 1
1 3
18 + 1 = 19
18 − 1 = 17

3 1
2 3
9 + 2 = 11
9 − 2 = 7

Page 33

Mom! I Learn Division Using Math-Chess-Puzzles Connection

Ho Math Chess　何数棋谜　妈!我会棋谜式除法啦!

Frank Ho, Amanda Ho © 2004 – 2017, all rights reserved.

Student's Name _____ Date _____

Assessment of multiplication (order of operation)

3	1	8	5
2	4	6	4
1	2	3	8
	a	b	c

You are at b2 = ☐ ..

☐ + ♔ × (☐ – 1) = ___ + ___ × ___ = ___

☐ + ♔ × (☐ – 1) = ___ + ___ × ___ = ___

☐ + ♔ × (☐ – 1) = ___ + ___ × ___ = ___

☐ + ♔ × (☐ – 1) = ___ + ___ × ___ = ___

☐ + ♗ × (☐ – 1) = ___ + ___ × ___ = ___

☐ + ♗ × (☐ – 1) = ___ + ___ × ___ = ___

☐ + ♗ × (☐ – 1) = ___ + ___ × ___ = ___

6 + 4 × (6 – 1) = 6 + 4 × 5 = 26

6 + 3 × (6 – 1) = 6 + 3 × 5 = 21

6 + 4 × (6 – 1) = 6 + 4 × 5 = 26

6 + 8 × (6 – 1) = 6 + 8 × 5 = 46

6 + 5 × (6 – 1) = 6 + 5 × 5 = 31

6 + 8 × (6 – 1) = 6 + 8 × 5 = 46

6 + 2 × (6 – 1) = 6 + 2 × 5 = 26

Mom! I Learn Division Using Math-Chess-Puzzles Connection

Ho Math Chess　何数棋谜　妈!我会棋谜式除法啦!

Frank Ho, Amanda Ho © 2004 − 2017, all rights reserved.

Student's Name _____　　　Date _____

Addition, subtraction, multiplication and division of 2

28 39 48 / 29 **2** 58 / 78 18 19	11 21 31 / 41 **2** 51 / 61 71 81	13 19 15 / 18 **2** 14 / 17 12 16	12 16 18 / 14 **2** 10 / 6 8 4
39 + 2 = 41	21 − 2 = 19	19 × 2 = 38	16 ÷ 2 = 8
__ + __ = __ 50	__ − __ = __ 29	__ × __ = __ 30	__ ÷ __ = __ 9
__ + __ = __ 60	__ − __ = __ 49	__ × __ = __ 28	__ ÷ __ = __ 5
__ + __ = __ 21	__ − __ = __ 79	__ × __ = __ 32	__ ÷ __ = __ 2
__ + __ = __ 20	__ − __ = __ 69	__ × __ = __ 24	__ ÷ __ = __ 4
__ + __ = __ 80	__ − __ = __ 59	__ × __ = __ 34	__ ÷ __ = __ 3
__ + __ = __ 31	__ − __ = __ 29	__ × __ = __ 36	__ ÷ __ = __ 7
__ + __ = __ 30	__ − __ = __ 9	__ × __ = __ 26	__ ÷ __ = __ 6

Mom! I Learn Division Using Math-Chess-Puzzles Connection

Ho Math Chess 何数棋谜 妈!我会棋谜式除法啦!

Frank Ho, Amanda Ho © 2004 – 2017, all rights reserved.

Student's Name _____ Date _____

Addition, subtraction, multiplication and division of 3

27	39	48
29	3	57
76	18	16

12	21	33
41	3	54
62	73	83

13	19	15
18	3	14
17	12	16

12	15	27
21	3	33
24	36	39

42 18 57 5
51 30 45 9
60 51 42 11
19 80 48 13
21 70 36 12
79 59 51 8
32 38 54 7
30 9 39 4

Page 36

Mom! I Learn Division Using Math-Chess-Puzzles Connection

Ho Math Chess 何数棋谜 妈!我会棋谜式除法啦!

Frank Ho, Amanda Ho © 2004 – 2017, all rights reserved.

Student's Name_____ Date_____

Addition, subtraction, multiplication and division of 4

27	39	48
29	4	57
76	18	16

12	21	33
41	4	54
62	73	83

13	19	15
18	4	14
17	12	16

12	16	28
20	4	32
24	28	36

43 17 76 4
52 29 60 7
61 50 56 8
20 79 64 9
22 69 48 7
80 58 68 6
33 37 72 5
31 8 52 3

Mom! I Learn Division Using Math-Chess-Puzzles Connection

Ho Math Chess 何数棋谜 妈!我会棋谜式除法啦!

Frank Ho, Amanda Ho © 2004 – 2017, all rights reserved.

Student's Name _____ Date _____

Addition, subtraction, multiplication and division of 5

28	39	46
27	5	58
76	19	17

12	21	34
44	5	53
61	73	82

13	19	15
18	5	14
17	12	16

10	15	20
35	5	40
30	35	45

44 16 95 3
51 29 75 4
63 48 70 8
22 77 80 9
24 68 60 7
81 56 85 6
32 39 90 7
33 7 65 2

Page 38

Mom! I Learn Division Using Math-Chess-Puzzles Connection

Ho Math Chess 何数棋谜 妈!我会棋谜式除法啦!

Frank Ho, Amanda Ho © 2004 – 2017, all rights reserved.

Student's Name _____ Date _____

Addition, subtraction, multiplication and division of 6

28	39	45
26	6	57
76	18	19

13	21	32
45	6	54
63	72	81

13	19	15
18	6	14
17	12	16

12	18	24
42	6	30
36	48	54

45 15 114 3
51 26 90 4
63 48 84 5
25 75 96 9
24 66 72 8
82 57 102 6
32 39 108 7
34 7 78 2

Page 39

Mom! I Learn Division Using Math-Chess-Puzzles Connection

Ho Math Chess 何数棋谜 妈!我会棋谜式除法啦!

Frank Ho, Amanda Ho © 2004 − 2017, all rights reserved.

Student's Name _____ Date _____

Addition, subtraction, multiplication and division of 7

28	39	45
26	7	57
74	18	19

13	21	36
45	7	54
63	72	80

13	19	15
18	7	14
17	12	16

14	21	28
42	7	35
49	56	63

46 14 133 3
52 29 105 4
64 47 98 5
26 73 112 9
25 65 84 8
81 56 119 7
33 38 126 6
35 6 91 2

Page 40

Mom! I Learn Division Using Math-Chess-Puzzles Connection

Ho Math Chess 何数棋谜 妈!我会棋谜式除法啦!

Frank Ho, Amanda Ho © 2004 − 2017, all rights reserved.

Student's Name _____ Date _____

Addition, subtraction, multiplication and division of 8

28	39	44
26	8	57
73	15	14

13	21	32
45	8	54
66	77	81

13	19	15
18	8	14
17	12	16

32	16	24
40	8	48
56	48	72

_39_ + _8_ = _47_   _21_ − _8_ = _13_   _19_ × _8_ = _152_   _16_ ÷ _8_ = _2_

47 13 152 2
52 24 120 3
65 46 112 6
22 73 128 9
23 69 96 6
81 58 136 7
34 37 144 5
36 5 104 4

Mom! I Learn Division Using Math-Chess-Puzzles Connection

Ho Math Chess 何数棋谜 妈!我会棋谜式除法啦!

Frank Ho, Amanda Ho © 2004 – 2017, all rights reserved.

Student's Name ______________________________ Date ______________

Addition, subtraction, multiplication and division of 9

28 39 44 26 9 57 73 15 14	13 21 32 45 9 54 66 77 81	13 19 15 18 9 14 17 12 16	36 18 27 45 9 24 33 11 32
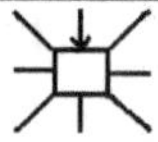 ___ + ___ = ___	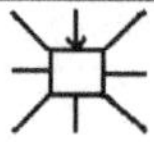 ___ − ___ = ___	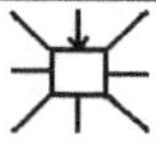 ___ × ___ = ___	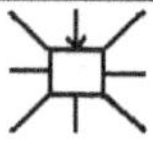 ___ ÷ ___ = ___
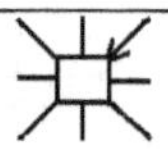 ___ + ___ = ___	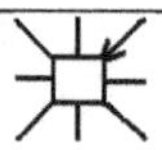 ___ − ___ = ___	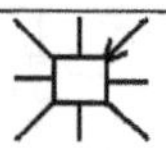 ___ × ___ = ___	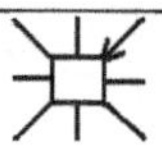 ___ ÷ ___ = ___
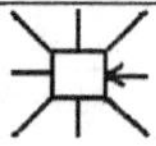 ___ + ___ = ___	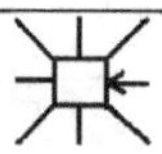 ___ − ___ = ___	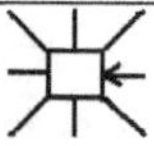 ___ × ___ = ___	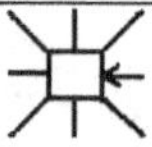 ___ ÷ ___ = ___
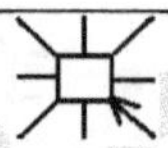 ___ + ___ = ___	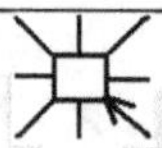 ___ − ___ = ___	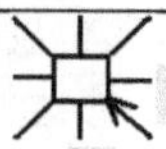 ___ × ___ = ___	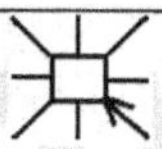 ___ ÷ ___ = ___
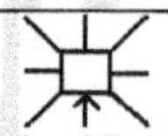 ___ + ___ = ___	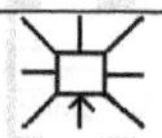 ___ − ___ = ___	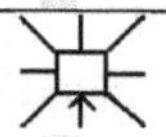 ___ × ___ = ___	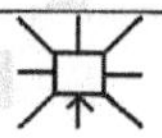 ___ ÷ ___ = ___
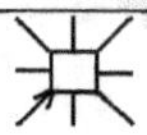 ___ + ___ = ___	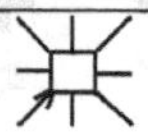 ___ − ___ = ___	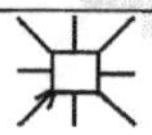 ___ × ___ = ___	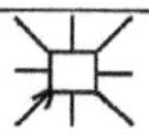 ___ ÷ ___ = ___
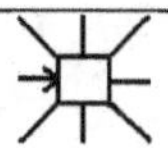 ___ + ___ = ___	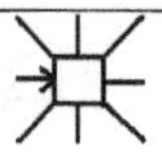 ___ − ___ = ___	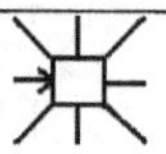 ___ × ___ = ___	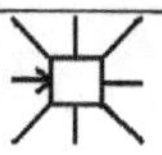 ___ ÷ ___ = ___
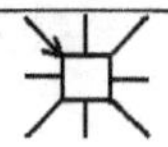 ___ + ___ = ___	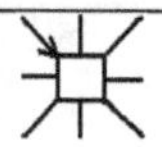 ___ − ___ = ___	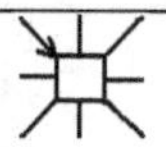 ___ × ___ = ___	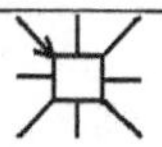 ___ ÷ ___ = ___

DO NOT COPY

48 12 171 2
53 23 135 3
66 45 126 6
23 72 144 8
24 68 108 9
82 57 153 7
35 34 162 5
37 4 117 4

Mom! I Learn Division Using Math-Chess-Puzzles Connection

Ho Math Chess 何数棋谜 妈!我会棋谜式除法啦!

Frank Ho, Amanda Ho © 2004 − 2017, all rights reserved.

Student's Name _____ Date _____

Addition, subtraction, multiplication, and division of 10's power or multiples of 10

8	9	4
6	10	7
3	5	1

13	21	32
45	100	54
66	77	81

13	19	15
18	30	14
17	12	16

36	18	27
45	50	24
33	11	32

_9_ + _1_ = 10   _21_ + _79_ = 100   _19_ + _11_ = 30   _18_ + _32_ = 50

1 79 11 32
6 68 15 23
3 46 16 26
9 19 14 18
5 23 18 39
3 34 13 17
4 55 12 5
7 87 17 14

Mom! I Learn Division Using Math-Chess-Puzzles Connection

Ho Math Chess　何数棋谜　妈!我会棋谜式除法啦!

Frank Ho, Amanda Ho © 2004 – 2017, all rights reserved.

Student's Name _____ Date _____

Learning multiplication by pattern

3	2	3	4
2	5	8	6
1	7	8	9
	a	b	c

The original square is at b2.

b2 × ✥ = _ × _ = ◯, ◯ ÷ b2 = △, △ × b2 = ◯, ◯ ÷ ✥ = _

b2 × ✥ = _ × _ = ◯, ◯ ÷ b2 = △, △ × b2 = ◯, ◯ ÷ ✥ = _

b2 × ✥ = _ × _ = ◯, ◯ ÷ b2 = △, △ × b2 = ◯, ◯ ÷ ✥ = _

b2 × ✥ = _ × _ = ◯, ◯ ÷ b2 = △, △ × b2 = ◯, ◯ ÷ ✥ = _

b2 × ✕ = _ × _ = ◯, ◯ ÷ b2 = △, △ × b2 = ◯, ◯ ÷ ✕ = _

b2 × ✕ = _ × _ = ◯, ◯ ÷ b2 = △, △ × b2 = ◯, ◯ ÷ ✕ = _

b2 × ✕ = _ × _ = ◯, ◯ ÷ b2 = △, △ × b2 = ◯, ◯ ÷ ✕ = _

b2 × ✕ = _ × _ = ◯, ◯ ÷ b2 = △, △ × b2 = ◯, ◯ ÷ ✕ = _

8 × 3=24, 8 × 6=48, 8 × 8=64, 8 × 5=40, 8 × 4=32, 8 × 9=72, 8 × 7=56, 8 × 2=16

Mom! I Learn Division Using Math-Chess-Puzzles Connection

Ho Math Chess 何数棋谜 妈!我会棋谜式除法啦!

Frank Ho, Amanda Ho © 2004 − 2017, all rights reserved.

Student's Name _____ Date _____

Addition, subtraction, and division of 11

2	3	4
5	11	6
7	8	9

$\underline{3} + \underline{8} = 11$

$11 - 3 = \underline{8}$

Division examples with quotient 3 (11, 9, 2), quotient 2 (11, 8, 3)

Problems: 6 1 5, 9 1 2, 8 1 3, 7 1 4, 5 2 1, 2 5 1

Answers:
7, 4
5, 6
2, 9
3, 8
4, 7
6, 5
9, 2

No part of this publication can be copied, duplicated, or reproduced.

Mom! I Learn Division Using Math-Chess-Puzzles Connection

Ho Math Chess 何数棋谜 妈!我会棋谜式除法啦!

Frank Ho, Amanda Ho © 2004 − 2017, all rights reserved.

Student's Name _____ Date _____

Addition, subtraction, and division of 12

4	3	4
5	12	6
7	8	9

4	3	4
5	12	6
7	8	9

4	3	4
5	12	6
7	8	9

4	3	4
5	12	6
7	8	9

3 + 9 = 12

12 − 3 = 9

9 3, 8 4, 6 6, 3 9, 4 8, 5 7, 7 5, 8 4
3 3 2, 4 2 3
6 1 5, 9 1 2
8 1 3, 2 1 4
5 2 1, 2 5 1

Page 46

Mom! I Learn Division Using Math-Chess-Puzzles Connection

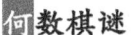 Math Chess   何数棋谜   妈!我会棋谜式除法啦!

Frank Ho, Amanda Ho © 2004 − 2017, all rights reserved.

Student's Name _____ Date _____

Addition, subtraction, and division of 13

4	5	6
5	13	6
7	8	9

4	5	6
5	13	6
7	8	9

4	5	6
5	13	6
7	8	9

4	5	6
5	13	6
7	8	9

$5 + 8 = 13$

$13 - 5 = 8$

8 5, 7 6, 7 6, 4 9, 5 8, 6 7, 8 5, 9 4
346 430
620 913
814 715
522 430

No part of this publication can be copied, duplicated, or reproduced.   Page 47

Mom! I Learn Division Using Math-Chess-Puzzles Connection

Ho Math Chess 何数棋谜 妈!我会棋谜式除法啦!

Frank Ho, Amanda Ho © 2004 − 2017, all rights reserved.

Student's Name _____ Date _____

Addition, subtraction, and division of 14

8	5	7
5	14	6
7	8	9

8	5	7
5	14	6
7	8	9

8	5	7
5	14	6
7	8	9

8	5	7
5	14	6
7	8	9

5 + 9 = 14

14 − 5 = 9

9 5, 7 7, 8 6, 5 9, 6 8, 7 7, 9 5, 6 8
523 621
621 914
815 716
523 431

No part of this publication can be copied, duplicated, or reproduced.   Page 48

Mom! I Learn Division Using Math-Chess-Puzzles Connection

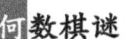 Math Chess 何数棋谜 妈!我会棋谜式除法啦!

Frank Ho, Amanda Ho © 2004 − 2017, all rights reserved.

Student's Name _____ Date _____

Addition, subtraction, and division of 15

6	7	8
9	15	6
7	8	9

6	7	8
9	15	6
7	8	9

6	7	8
9	15	6
7	8	9

6	7	8
9	15	6
7	8	9

$\underline{7} + \underline{8} = 15$

$15 - 7 = \underline{8}$

8 7, 7 8, 9 6, 6 9, 7 8, 8 7, 6 9, 9 6
524 720
622 915
816 720
524 816

Page 49

Mom! I Learn Division Using Math-Chess-Puzzles Connection

Ho Math Chess 何数棋谜 妈!我会棋谜式除法啦!

Frank Ho, Amanda Ho © 2004 − 2017, all rights reserved.

Student's Name _____ Date _____

Addition, subtraction, and division of 16

7	8	9
8	16	7
7	8	9

7	8	9
8	16	7
7	8	9

7	8	9
8	16	7
7	8	9

7	8	9
8	16	7
7	8	9

$\underline{8} + \underline{8} = 16$

$16 - 8 = \underline{8}$

$\underline{} + \underline{} = \underline{}$

$\underline{} - \underline{} = \underline{}$

8 8, 7 7, 9 7, 7 9, 8 9, 8 7, 8 8, 9 7

721 817
623 916
817 721
916 623

Page 50

Mom! I Learn Division Using Math-Chess-Puzzles Connection

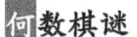 Math Chess   何数棋谜   妈!我会棋谜式除法啦!

Frank Ho, Amanda Ho © 2004 − 2017, all rights reserved.

Student's Name _____ Date _____

Addition, subtraction, and division of 17

8	9	8
9	17	8
9	8	9

8	9	8
9	17	8
9	8	9

8	9	8
9	17	8
9	8	9

8	9	8
9	17	8
9	8	9

$9 + 8 = 17$

$17 - 9 = 8$

8 8, 9 9, 9 9, 8 8, 9 9, 8 8, 8 8, 9 9

820 917
722 917
820 722
822 722

No part of this publication can be copied, duplicated, or reproduced.   Page 51

Mom! I Learn Division Using Math-Chess-Puzzles Connection

Ho Math Chess 何数棋谜 妈!我会棋谜式除法啦!

Frank Ho, Amanda Ho © 2004 – 2017, all rights reserved.

Student's Name _____ Date _____

Addition, subtraction, and division of 18

9	9	9
9	18	9
9	9	9

9	9	9
9	18	9
9	9	9

9	9	9
9	18	9
9	9	9

9	9	9
9	18	9
9	9	9

$9 + \underline{8} = 18$

$18 - 9 = \underline{9}$

All are pairs of 9, 9 for the first two columns.
All 9 2 0

No part of this publication can be copied, duplicated, or reproduced.

Mom! I Learn Division Using Math-Chess-Puzzles Connection

Ho Math Chess   何数棋谜   妈!我会棋谜式除法啦!

Frank Ho, Amanda Ho © 2004 – 2017, all rights reserved.

Student's Name _____ Date _____

Reverse Subtraction

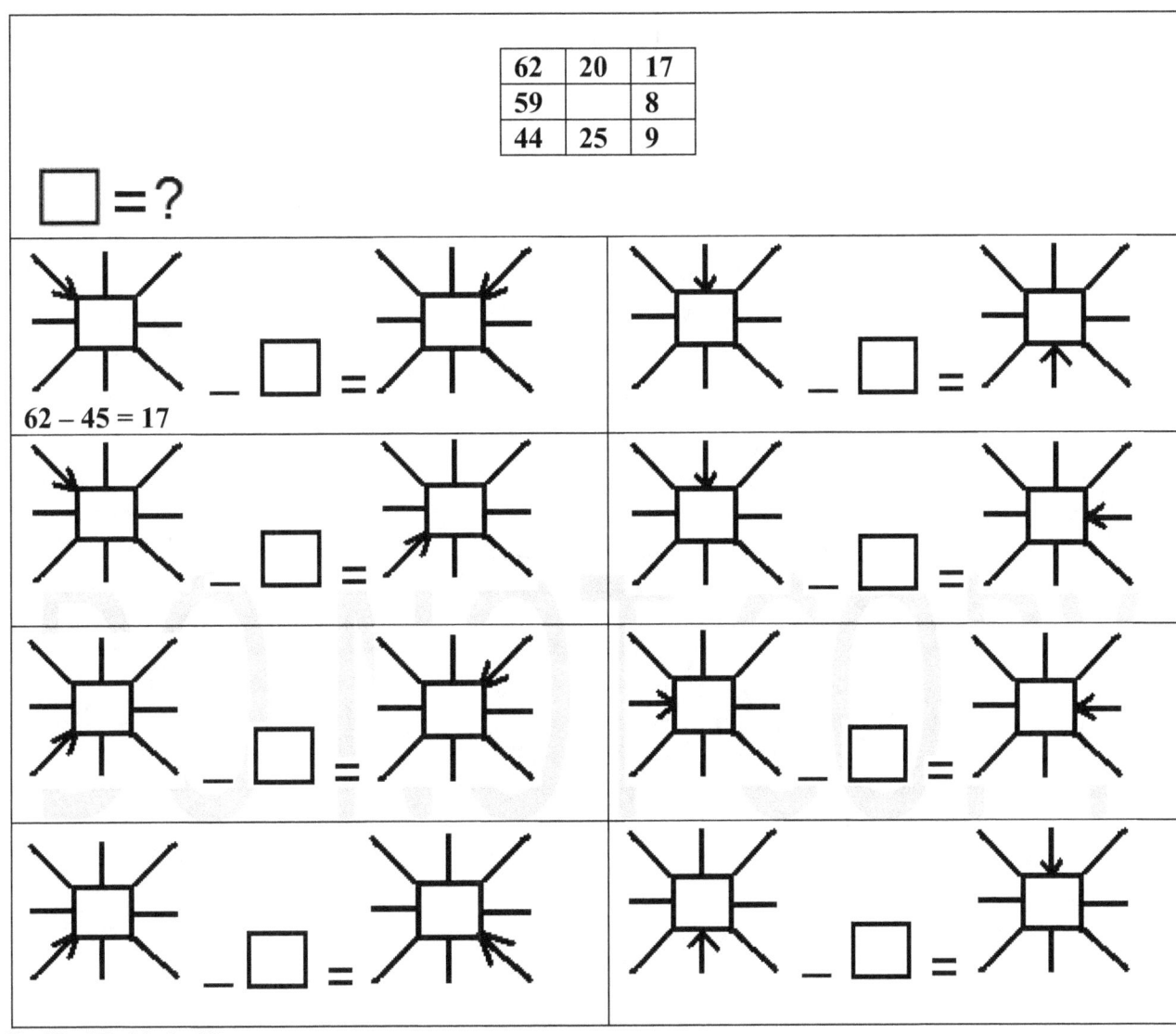

62-45=17, 33-8=25
62-18=44, 33-25=8
44-27=17, 59-51=8
44-35=9, 25-20=5

Mom! I Learn Division Using Math-Chess-Puzzles Connection

Ho Math Chess　何数棋谜　妈!我会棋谜式除法啦!

Frank Ho, Amanda Ho © 2004 – 2017, all rights reserved.

Student's Name _____ Date _____

Reverse Addition

62	33	17
59		8
44	25	9

□ = ?

79 – 17 = 62

62 – 45 = □

62-45=17, 33-8=25
62-18=44, 33-25=8
44-27=17, 59-51=8
44-35=9, 25-16=9

Mom! I Learn Division Using Math-Chess-Puzzles Connection

Ho Math Chess 何数棋谜 妈!我会棋谜式除法啦!

Frank Ho, Amanda Ho © 2004 — 2017, all rights reserved.

Student's Name _____ Date _____

Reverse Multiplication

18	12	14
10	2	6
8	4	16

□ = ?, ✶ = central square

□ × ✶ = ✶   9 × 2 = 18

9, 6
5, 7
4, 3
2, 8

Page 55

Mom! I Learn Division Using Math-Chess-Puzzles Connection

Ho Math Chess 何数棋谜 妈!我会棋谜式除法啦!

Frank Ho, Amanda Ho © 2004 – 2017, all rights reserved.

Student's Name _____ Date _____

Reverse Multiplication

18	12	14
10	2	6
8	4	16

□ = ?, ✳ = central square

Example: 2 × 9 = 18

9, 6
5, 7
4, 3
2, 8

Page 56

Mom! I Learn Division Using Math-Chess-Puzzles Connection

Reverse Division

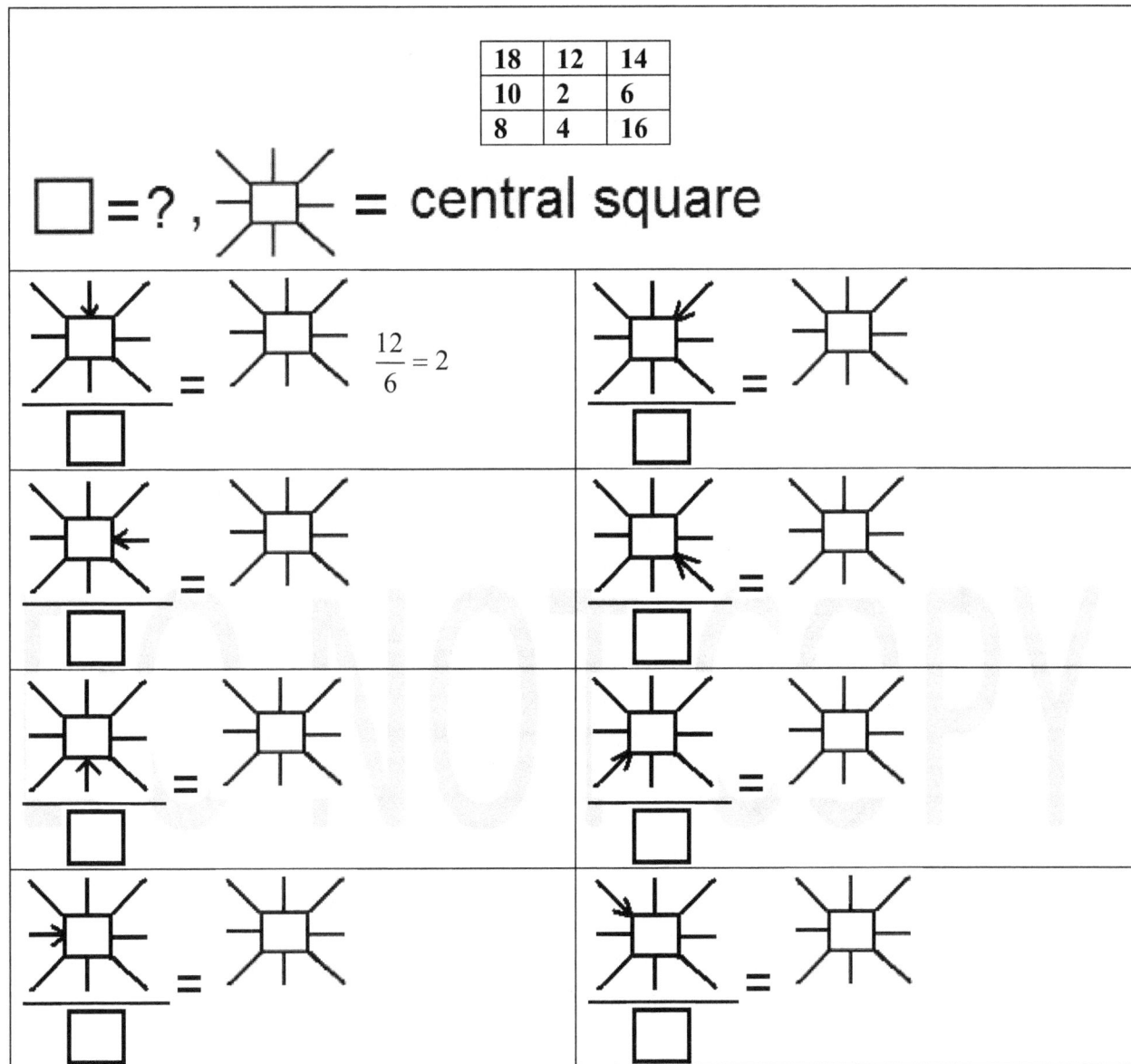

6, 2
3, 8
2, 4
5, 9

Mom! I Learn Division Using Math-Chess-Puzzles Connection

Ho Math Chess 何数棋谜 妈!我会棋谜式除法啦!

Frank Ho, Amanda Ho © 2004 – 2017, all rights reserved.

Student's Name _____ Date _____

Reverse Division

9	2	3
8	2	4
7	6	5

□ = ?, ✳ = central square

12, 6
8, 10
4, 14
16, 18

Page 58

Mom! I Learn Division Using Math-Chess-Puzzles Connection

Ho Math Chess 何数棋谜 妈!我会棋谜式除法啦!

Frank Ho, Amanda Ho © 2004 − 2017, all rights reserved.

Student's Name _____ Date _____

Learning division from multiplication (Concept used for % and getting one factor)

5		9		2	
4	8	9	2	3	3
3		8	6	4	
2	7	7	6	5	4
1		6		5	
	a	b	c	d	e

You are ⬕ at C3, □ = ?

⬕ × c_4 = □, □ ÷ c_4 = ⬕, □ ÷ ⬕ = c_4

⬕ × d_3 = □, □ ÷ d_3 = ⬕, □ ÷ ⬕ = d_3

⬕ × c_2 = □, □ ÷ c_2 = ⬕, □ ÷ ⬕ = c_2

⬕ × b_3 = □, □ ÷ b_3 = ⬕, □ ÷ ⬕ = b_3

⬕ × d_4 = □, □ ÷ d_4 = ⬕, □ ÷ ⬕ = d_4

⬕ × d_2 = □, □ ÷ d_2 = ⬕, □ ÷ ⬕ = d_2

⬕ × b_2 = □, □ ÷ b_2 = ⬕, □ ÷ ⬕ = b_2

⬕ × b_4 = □, □ ÷ b_4 = ⬕, □ ÷ ⬕ = b_4

12, 24, 36, 48, 18, 30, 42, 52

Mom! I Learn Division Using Math-Chess-Puzzles Connection

Ho Math Chess 何数棋谜 妈!我会棋谜式除法啦!

Frank Ho, Amanda Ho © 2004 − 2017, all rights reserved.

Student's Name _____ Date_____

Learning division from multiplication (Concept used for % and getting one factor)

5		9		2	
4	8	9	2	3	3
3		8	6	4	
2	7	7	6	5	4
1		6		5	
	a	b	c	d	e

You are ⊕ at C3, □ = ?

⊕ × d5 = □, □ ÷ d5 = ⊕, ⊕ ÷ ⊕ = d5

⊕ × b5 = □, □ ÷ b5 = ⊕, ⊕ ÷ ⊕ = b5

⊕ × e4 = □, □ ÷ e4 = ⊕, ⊕ ÷ ⊕ = e4

⊕ × e2 = □, □ ÷ e2 = ⊕, ⊕ ÷ ⊕ = e2

⊕ × d1 = □, □ ÷ d1 = ⊕, ⊕ ÷ ⊕ = d1

⊕ × b1 = □, □ ÷ b1 = ⊕, ⊕ ÷ ⊕ = b1

⊕ × a4 = □, □ ÷ a4 = ⊕, ⊕ ÷ ⊕ = a4

⊕ × a2 = □, □ ÷ a2 = ⊕, ⊕ ÷ ⊕ = a2

12, 54, 18, 24, 30, 36, 48, 42

Mom! I Learn Division Using Math-Chess-Puzzles Connection

Ho Math Chess 何数棋谜 妈!我会棋谜式除法啦!

Frank Ho, Amanda Ho © 2004 − 2017, all rights reserved.

Student's Name _____ Date _____

Paired whole numbers

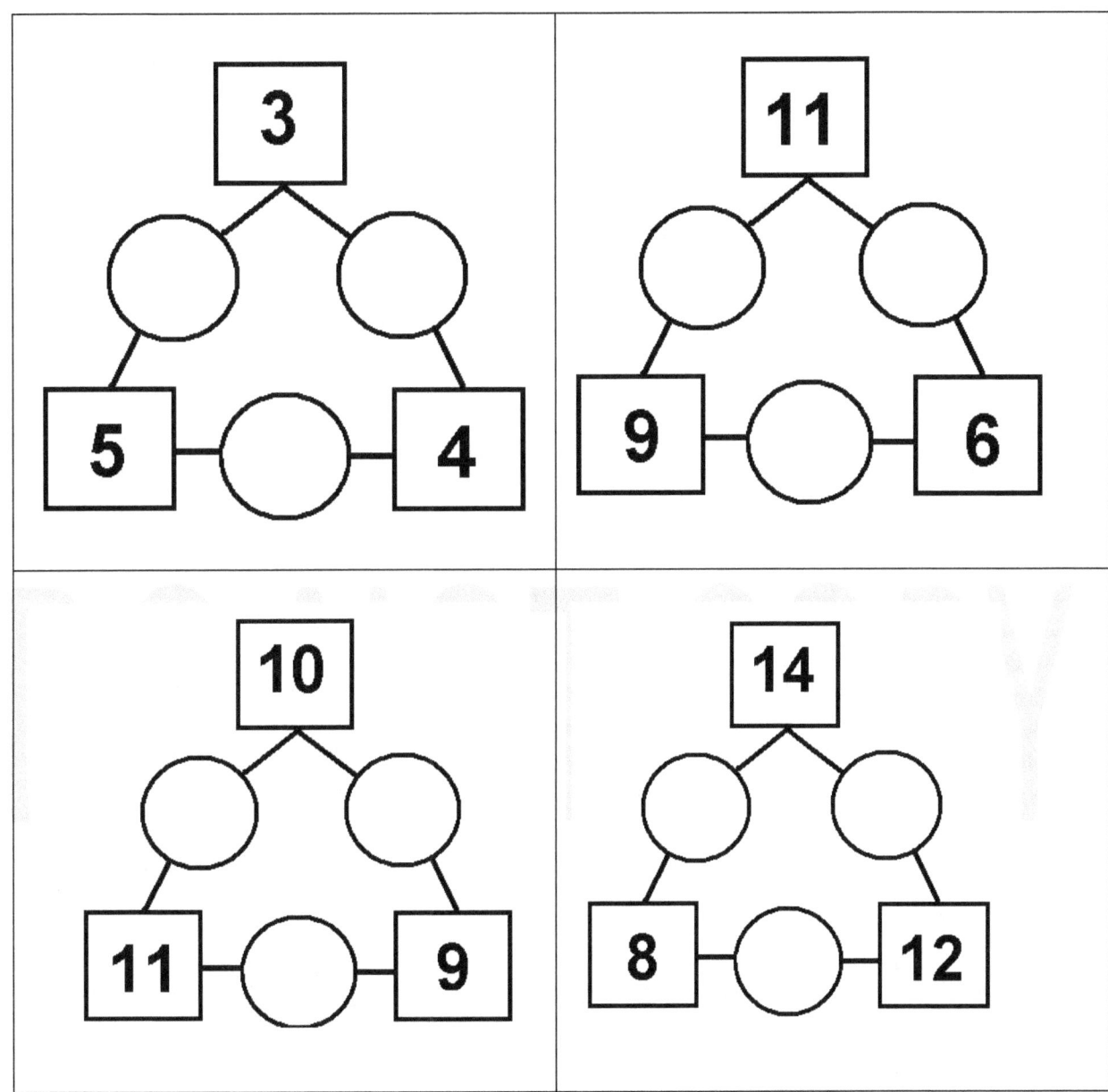

213, 742, 645, 593

Mom! I Learn Division Using Math-Chess-Puzzles Connection

Ho Math Chess 何数棋谜 妈!我会棋谜式除法啦!

Frank Ho, Amanda Ho © 2004 – 2017, all rights reserved.

Student's Name _____ Date _____

Paired whole numbers

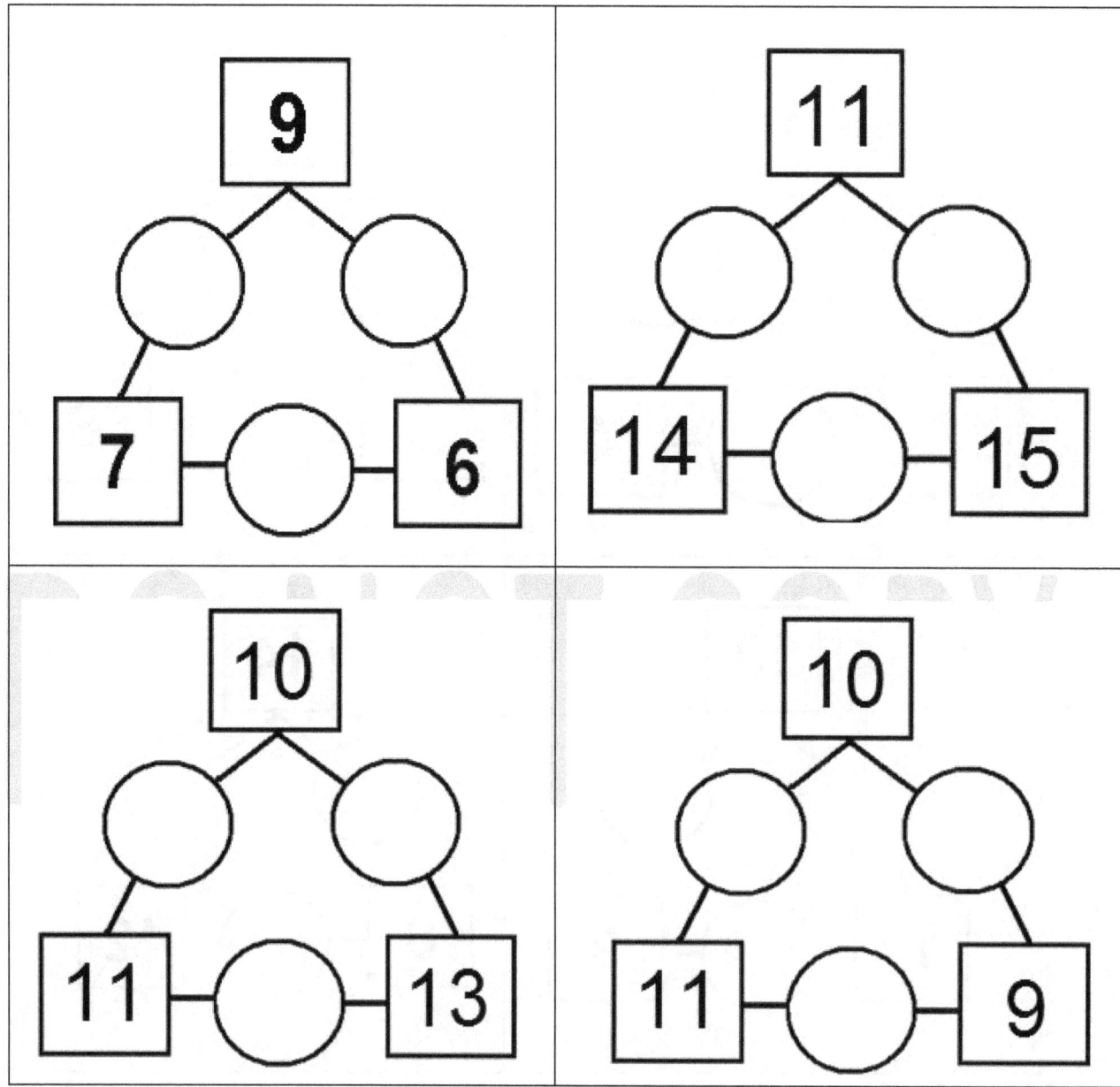

5 4 2
5 6 9
4 6 7
6 8 9

Mom! I Learn Division Using Math-Chess-Puzzles Connection

Ho Math Chess 何数棋谜 妈!我会棋谜式除法啦!

Frank Ho, Amanda Ho © 2004 – 2017, all rights reserved.

Student's Name _____ Date _____

Adding with convergent thinking

	a	b	c	d	e
5					
4					
3			6		
2					
1					

Answers may locate at different squares.

You are at c3 = ☐

Fill in each box with one number from 1 to 9 such that these 2 numbers adding in the direction of 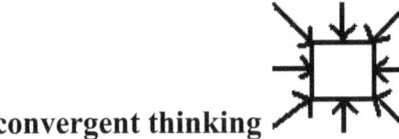 will have the sum of ☐. For example, 1 + 5 = 6.

0+6
6+0
1+5
5+1
2+4
4+2
3+3
3+3

Mom! I Learn Division Using Math-Chess-Puzzles Connection

Ho Math Chess 何数棋谜 妈!我会棋谜式除法啦!

Frank Ho, Amanda Ho © 2004 － 2017, all rights reserved.

Student's Name _____ Date _____

Adding with convergent thinking

	a	b	c	d	e
5					
4					
3			7		
2					
1					

Answers may locate at different squares.

You are at c3 = ☐

Fill in each box with one number from 1 to 9 such that these 2 numbers adding in the direction of ✦ will have the sum of ☐. For example, 1 + 6 = 7.

0+7=7
7+0=7
1+6=7
6+1=7
2+5=7
5+2=7
3+4=7
4+3=7

Mom! I Learn Division Using Math-Chess-Puzzles Connection

Ho Math Chess 何数棋谜 妈!我会棋谜式除法啦!

Frank Ho, Amanda Ho © 2004 − 2017, all rights reserved.

Student's Name _____ Date _____

Adding with convergent thinking

	a	b	c	d	e
5					
4					
3			8		
2					
1					

Answers may locate at different squares.

You are at c3 = ☐

Fill in each box with one number from 1 to 9 such that these 2 numbers adding in the direction of 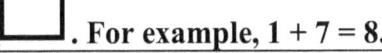 will have the sum of ☐. For example, 1 + 7 = 8.

0+8=8
8+0=8
1+7=8
7+1=8
2+6=8
6+2=8
3+5=8
5+3=8
4+4=8

Mom! I Learn Division Using Math-Chess-Puzzles Connection

Ho Math Chess 何数棋谜 妈!我会棋谜式除法啦!

Frank Ho, Amanda Ho © 2004 – 2017, all rights reserved.

Student's Name _____ Date _____

Adding with convergent thinking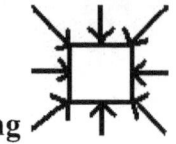

	a	b	c	d	e
5					
4					
3			9		
2					
1					

Answers may locate at different squares.

You are at c3 = ☐

Fill in each box with one number from 1 to 9 such that these 2 numbers adding in the direction of  will have the sum of ☐ . For example, 1 + 8 = 9.

0+9=9
9+0=9
1+8=9
8+1=9
2+7=9
7+2=9
3+6=9
6+3=9
4+5=9
5+4=9

Mom! I Learn Division Using Math-Chess-Puzzles Connection

 Math Chess   何数棋谜   妈!我会棋谜式除法啦!

Frank Ho, Amanda Ho © 2004 – 2017, all rights reserved.

Student's Name _____ Date _____

Intelligent math worksheet

5		7		0	
4	6	8	9	10	1
3		11	5, 6	12	
2	5	13	14	15	2
1		4		3	
	a	b	c	d	e

You are at c3 = ☐.

Pick a number = ____.

Use the picked number for all the following problems.

☐ + ↔ = ___ + ___ = ___

☐ + ↔ = ___ + ___ = ___

☐ + ↔ = ___ + ___ = ___

☐ + ↔ = ___ + ___ = ___

☐ + ✕ = ___ + ___ = ___

☐ + ✕ = ___ + ___ = ___

☐ + ✕ = ___ + ___ = ___

☐ + ✕ = ___ + ___ = ___

Picked 5, 17, 19, 16, 14, 21, 20, 18, 13
Picked 6, 18, 20, 17, 15, 22, 21, 19, 14

Mom! I Learn Division Using Math-Chess-Puzzles Connection

Ho Math Chess 何数棋谜 妈!我会棋谜式除法啦!

Frank Ho, Amanda Ho © 2004 − 2017, all rights reserved.

Student's Name _____ Date _____

5		7		0	
4	6	8	9	10	1
3		11	8, 9	12	
2	5	13	14	15	2
1		4		3	
	a	b	c	d	e

You are at c3 = ☐.

Pick a number = ___.

Use the picked number for all the following problems.

☐ + ✥ = ___ + ___ = ___

☐ + ✥ = ___ + ___ = ___

☐ + ✥ = ___ + ___ = ___

☐ + ✥ = ___ + ___ = ___

☐ + ✕ = ___ + ___ = ___

☐ + ✕ = ___ + ___ = ___

☐ + ✕ = ___ + ___ = ___

☐ + ✕ = ___ + ___ = ___

Picked 8, 20, 22, 19, 17, 18, 23, 21, 16

Mom! I Learn Division Using Math-Chess-Puzzles Connection

Ho Math Chess 何数棋谜 妈!我会棋谜式除法啦!

Frank Ho, Amanda Ho © 2004 − 2017, all rights reserved.

Student's Name _____ Date _____

	a	b	c	d	e
5		7		0	
4	6	8	9	10	1
3		11	7, 8	12	
2	5	13	14	15	2
1		4		3	

You are at c3 = ☐.

Pick a number = ___.

☐ + ✥ = ___ + ___ = ___

☐ + ✥ = ___ + ___ = ___

☐ + ✥ = ___ + ___ = ___

☐ + ✥ = ___ + ___ = ___

☐ + ✕ = ___ + ___ = ___

☐ + ✕ = ___ + ___ = ___

☐ + ✕ = ___ + ___ = ___

☐ + ✕ = ___ + ___ = ___

Picked 7, 19, 21, 18, 16, 17, 22, 20 15

Mom! I Learn Division Using Math-Chess-Puzzles Connection

Ho Math Chess 何数棋谜 妈!我会棋谜式除法啦!

Frank Ho, Amanda Ho © 2004 – 2017, all rights reserved.

Student's Name _____ Date _____

5		7		0	
4	6	8	9	10	1
3		11	9, 10	12	
2	5	13	14	15	2
1		4		3	
	a	b	c	d	e

You are at c3 = ☐.

Pick a number = ___.

☐ + ✢ = __ + __ = __

☐ + ↔ = __ + __ = __

☐ + ↔ = __ + __ = __

☐ + ↔ = __ + __ = __

☐ + ✕ = __ + __ = __

☐ + ✕ = __ + __ = __

☐ + ✕ = __ + __ = __

☐ + ✕ = __ + __ = __

Picked 9, 21, 23, 20, 18, 19, 24, 22, 17

Mom! I Learn Division Using Math-Chess-Puzzles Connection

Ho Math Chess   何数棋谜   妈!我会棋谜式除法啦!

Frank Ho, Amanda Ho © 2004 − 2017, all rights reserved.

Student's Name _____ Date _____

5		7		0	
4	6	8	9	10	1
3		11	11,12	12	
2	5	13	14	15	2
1		4		3	
	a	b	C	d	e

You are at c3 = ☐.

Pick a number = ___.

☐ + ↔↕ = __ + __ = __

☐ + ↔↕ = __ + __ = __

☐ + ↔↕ = __ + __ = __

☐ + ↔↕ = __ + __ = __

☐ + ✕ = __ + __ = __

☐ + ✕ = __ + __ = __

☐ + ✕ = __ + __ = __

☐ + ✕ = __ + __ = __

Picked 11, 23, 25, 22, 21. 26, 24, 19

Mom! I Learn Division Using Math-Chess-Puzzles Connection

Ho Math Chess 何数棋谜 妈!我会棋谜式除法啦!

Frank Ho, Amanda Ho © 2004 – 2017, all rights reserved.

Student's Name _____ Date _____

5		7		0	
4	6	8	9	10	1
3		11	16, 17	12	
2	5	13	14	15	2
1			4		3
	A	b	c	d	e

You are at c3 = ☐.

Pick a number = ___.

☐ + ↔ = ___ + ___ = ___

☐ + ↔ = ___ + ___ = ___

☐ + ↔ = ___ + ___ = ___

☐ + ↔ = ___ + ___ = ___

☐ + ✕ = ___ + ___ = ___

☐ + ✕ = ___ + ___ = ___

☐ + ✕ = ___ + ___ = ___

☐ + ✕ = ___ + ___ = ___

Picked 16, 28, 30, 27, 25, 26, 31, 20, 24

Mom! I Learn Division Using Math-Chess-Puzzles Connection

Ho Math Chess 何数棋谜 妈!我会棋谜式除法啦!

Frank Ho, Amanda Ho © 2004 − 2017, all rights reserved.

Student's Name _____ Date _____

5	2	3	4	5	6
4	6	8	9	10	11
3	12	13		14	15
2	16	17	18	19	20
1	21	22	23	24	25
	a	b	c	d	e

You are at c3 = ☐.

$a5 \times b4 + \square = d2 \times e1$ __ × __ + __ = __ × __

$2 \times 8 + \square_{(443)} = 19 \times 25 = 459$

$a3 \times b3 + \square = d3 \times e3$ __ × __ + __ = __ × __

$d4 \times e5 + \square = a1 \times b2$ __ × __ + __ = __ × __

$c4 \times c5 + \square = c1 \times c2$ __ × __ + __ = __ × __

$a5 \times b4 + \square = a1 \times b2$ __ × __ + __ = __ × __

$a3 \times b3 + \square = d2 \times e1$ __ × __ + __ = __ × __

$c4 \times c5 + \square = d4 \times e5$ __ × __ + __ = __ × __

$d4 \times e5 + \square = c1 \times c2$ __ × __ + __ = __ × __

459
54
297
368
341
319
36
354

No part of this publication can be copied, duplicated, or reproduced.

Mom! I Learn Division Using Math-Chess-Puzzles Connection

Ho Math Chess 何数棋谜 妈!我会棋谜式除法啦!

Frank Ho, Amanda Ho © 2004 − 2017, all rights reserved.

Student's Name _____ Date _____

Spatial relation and subtraction operation

7	8	3
6	11	5
2	9	4

7	2	4
6	11	5
9	8	3

4	9	5
8	12	11
7	3	6

11	4	7
5	12	9
3	8	6

$11 - 8 = 3$ $2 + 9 = 11$ $12 - 9 = 3$ $4 + 8 = 12$

$11 - 3 = 8$ $7 + 4 = 11$ $12 - 5 = 7$ $11 + 1 = 12$

$11 - 5 = 6$ $5 + 6 = 11$ $12 - 11 = 1$ $9 + 3 = 12$

$11 - 4 = 7$ $9 + 2 = 11$ $12 - 6 = 6$ $3 + 9 = 12$

$11 - 9 = 2$ $8 + 3 = 11$ $12 - 3 = 9$ $8 + 4 = 12$

$11 - 2 = 9$ $3 + 8 = 11$ $12 - 7 = 5$ $6 + 6 = 12$

$11 - 6 = 5$ $6 + 5 = 11$ $12 - 8 = 4$ $5 + 7 = 12$

$11 - 7 = 4$ $4 + 7 = 11$ $12 - 4 = 8$ $7 + 5 = 12$

Mom! I Learn Division Using Math-Chess-Puzzles Connection

Ho Math Chess 何数棋谜 妈!我会棋谜式除法啦!

Frank Ho, Amanda Ho © 2004 – 2017, all rights reserved.

Student's Name _____ Date _____

Spatial relation and subtraction operation

7	8	11
6	13	5
12	9	4

7	12	4
6	13	5
9	8	11

13	9	5
8	14	12
7	11	6

11	6	7
5	14	9
12	8	13

$13 - 8 = 5$ $12 + 1 = 13$ $14 - 9 = 5$ $6 + 8 = 14$

$13 - 11 = 2$ $7 + 6 = 13$ $14 - 9 = 9$ $11 + 3 = 14$

$13 - 5 = 8$ $5 + 8 = 13$ $14 - 12 = 2$ $9 + 5 = 14$

$13 - 4 = 9$ $9 + 4 = 13$ $14 - 6 = 8$ $12 + 2 = 14$

$13 - 9 = 4$ $8 + 5 = 13$ $14 - 11 = 3$ $8 + 6 = 14$

$13 - 12 = 1$ $11 + 2 = 13$ $14 - 7 = 7$ $13 + 1 = 14$

$13 - 6 = 7$ $6 + 7 = 13$ $14 - 8 = 6$ $5 + 9 = 14$

$13 - 7 = 6$ $4 + 9 = 13$ $14 - 13 = 1$ $7 + 7 = 14$

Mom! I Learn Division Using Math-Chess-Puzzles Connection

Ho Math Chess 何数棋谜 妈!我会棋谜式除法啦!

Frank Ho, Amanda Ho © 2004 − 2017, all rights reserved.

Student's Name_____ Date_____

Spatial relation and subtraction operation

8	7	13
9	15	6
14	11	12

7	9	14
6	15	13
12	8	11

13	8	15
9	16	7
14	11	12

11	7	15
14	16	13
12	8	9

$\underline{15} - \underline{7} = \underline{8}$

$\underline{9} + \underline{6} = \underline{15}$

$\underline{16} - \underline{8} = \underline{8}$

$\underline{7} + \underline{9} = \underline{16}$

___ − ___ = ___   15−13=2

___ + ___ = ___   15−7=8

___ − ___ = ___   16−15=1

___ + ___ = ___   11+5=16

___ − ___ = ___   15−6=7

___ + ___ = ___   15−13=2

___ − ___ = ___   16−7=9

___ + ___ = ___   13+3=16

___ − ___ = ___   15−12=3

___ + ___ = ___   15−12=3

___ − ___ = ___   16−12=4

___ + ___ = ___   12+4=16

___ − ___ = ___   15−11=4

___ + ___ = ___   15−8=7

___ − ___ = ___   16−11=5

___ + ___ = ___   8+8=16

___ − ___ = ___   15−14=1

___ + ___ = ___   15−11=4

___ − ___ = ___   16−14=2

___ + ___ = ___   9+7=16

___ − ___ = ___   15−9=6

___ + ___ = ___   15−6=9

___ − ___ = ___   16−9=5

___ + ___ = ___   14+2=16

___ − ___ = ___   15−8=7

___ + ___ = ___   15−14=1

___ − ___ = ___   16−13=3

___ + ___ = ___   15+1=16

Mom! I Learn Division Using Math-Chess-Puzzles Connection

Ho Math Chess 何数棋谜 妈!我会棋谜式除法啦!

Frank Ho, Amanda Ho © 2004 − 2017, all rights reserved.

Student's Name _____ Date _____

Spatial relation and subtraction operation

1

13	8	9
15	17	16
14	11	12

11	9	14
16	17	13
12	8	15

13	9	15
11	18	16
14	12	17

13	17	15
16	18	14
12	9	11

$\underline{17} - \underline{8} = \underline{9}$ $\quad \underline{9} + \underline{8} = \underline{17}$ $\quad \underline{18} - \underline{9} = 9$ $\quad \underline{17} + \underline{1} = \underline{18}$

17-9=8   11+6=17   18-15=31   13+5=18
17-16=1   13+4=17   18-16=2   14+4=18
17-12=5   12+5=17   18-17=1   12+6=18
6,   8+9=17,   6,   9 + 9 = 18
3,   15+2=17,   4,   11+7=18
2,   16+1=17,   7,   16+2=18
4,   14+3=17,   5,   15+3=18

Page 77

Mom! I Learn Division Using Math-Chess-Puzzles Connection

Ho Math Chess   何数棋谜   妈!我会棋谜式除法啦!

Frank Ho, Amanda Ho © 2004 – 2017, all rights reserved.

Student's Name _____ Date _____

Spatial relation and subtraction operation

1

8	7	13
5	19	6
14	16	12

7	9	14
6	19	13
12	8	11

13	8	15
9	21	7
14	16	12

11	7	15
14	21	13
12	8	9

19 − 7 = 12   9 + 10 = 19   21 − 8 = 13   7 + 14 = 21

6	7+12=19	6	11+10=21
13	13+6=19	14	13+8=21
7	12+7=19	9	12+9=21
3	8+11=19	5	8+13=21
5	11+8=19	7	9+12=21
14	6+13=19	12	14+77=21
11	14+5=19	8	15+6=21

No part of this publication can be copied, duplicated, or reproduced.   Page 78

Mom! I Learn Division Using Math-Chess-Puzzles Connection

Ho Math Chess　何数棋谜　妈!我会棋谜式除法啦!

Frank Ho, Amanda Ho © 2004 – 2017, all rights reserved.

Student's Name _____ Date _____

Spatial relation and multiplication operation

1

6	3	2
4	2	5
7	9	8

7	9	4
6	3	3
2	8	5

3	8	5
9	4	7
6	4	2

6	7	5
4	5	3
2	8	9

2 × 3 = 6

3 × 9 = 27

6	27	32	35
4	21	20	30
10	9	28	15
16	6	8	10
18	24	16	40
14	15	24	45
8	18	36	20
12	12	12	25

No part of this publication can be copied, duplicated, or reproduced.

Mom! I Learn Division Using Math-Chess-Puzzles Connection

Ho Math Chess 何数棋谜 妈!我会棋谜式除法啦!

Frank Ho, Amanda Ho © 2004 – 2017, all rights reserved.

Student's Name _____ Date _____

Spatial relation and multiplication operation

6	3	2
4	6	5
7	9	8

7	9	4
6	7	3
2	8	5

3	8	5
9	8	7
6	4	2

6	7	5
4	9	3
2	8	9

6 × 3 = 18

7 × 9 = 63

```
12    49    64    63
30    21    40    54
48    14    56    27
54    56    16    18
42    35    32    72
24    42    48    81
36    28    72    36
            24    45
```

Page 80

Mom! I Learn Division Using Math-Chess-Puzzles Connection

Ho Math Chess 何数棋谜 妈!我会棋谜式除法啦!

Frank Ho, Amanda Ho © 2004 — 2017, all rights reserved.

Student's Name _____ Date _____

Spatial relation and multiplication operation

16	13	12
14	2	15
17	19	18

17	19	14
16	3	3
12	18	15

13	18	15
19	4	17
16	14	12

16	17	15
14	5	13
12	18	19

2 × 13 = 26   3 × 19 = 57   __ × __ = __   __ × __ = __

26	57	72	85
24	51	60	70
30	9	68	65
36	36	48	60
38	54	56	90
34	45	64	95
28	48	76	70
32	42	52	75

Mom! I Learn Division Using Math-Chess-Puzzles Connection

Ho Math Chess 何数棋谜 妈!我会棋谜式除法啦!

Frank Ho, Amanda Ho © 2004 − 2017, all rights reserved.

Student's Name _____ Date _____

Spatial relation and multiplication operation

16	13	12
14	6	15
17	19	18

17	19	14
16	7	3
12	18	15

13	18	15
19	8	17
16	14	12

16	17	15
14	9	13
12	18	19

2 × 13 = 26

3 × 19 = 57

72	144	153	144
90	119	120	117
108	21	136	108
114	84	96	146
102	126	72	171
84	105	128	126
96	112	172	135
	98	104	

Page 82

Mom! I Learn Division Using Math-Chess-Puzzles Connection

Ho Math Chess 何数棋谜 妈!我会棋谜式除法啦!

Frank Ho, Amanda Ho © 2004 − 2017, all rights reserved.

Student's Name _____ Date _____

Intelligent worksheets of division and remainder

Division and remainder

3	10	30	15
2	20	40	25
1	5	45	45
	a	b	c

You are at b2 = ☐ .

3	1	2	3
2	4	5	6
1	7	8	9
	d	e	f

You are at e2 = ☐ .

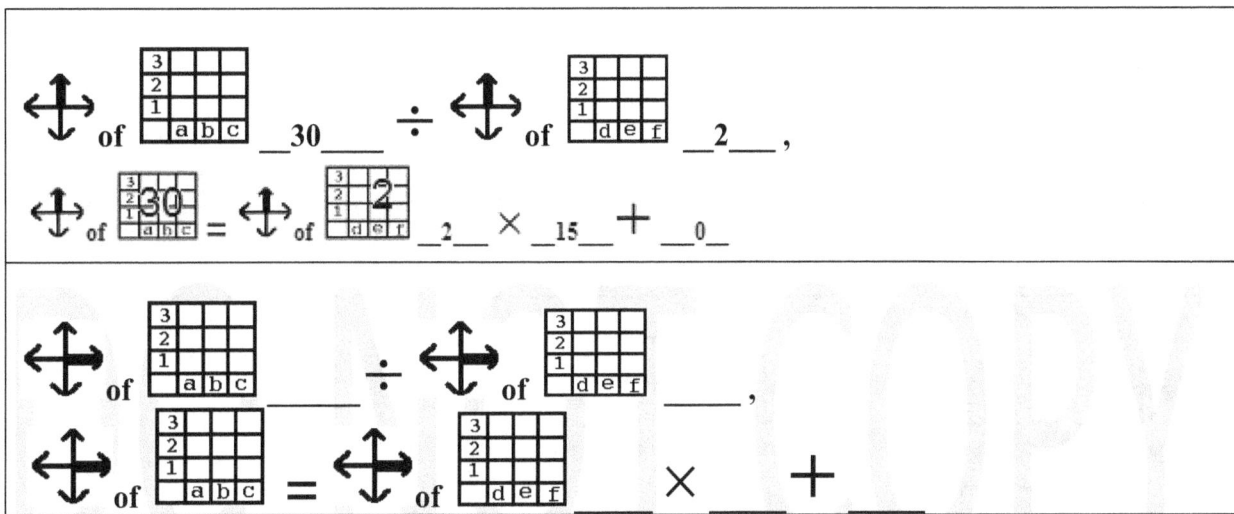

25 = 6 × 4 + 1

Mom! I Learn Division Using Math-Chess-Puzzles Connection

Ho Math Chess 何数棋谜 妈!我会棋谜式除法啦!

Frank Ho, Amanda Ho © 2004 – 2017, all rights reserved.

Student's Name _____ Date _____

Division and remainder

3	10	30	15
2	20	40	25
1	5	45	45
	a	b	c

You are at b2 = ☐.

3	1	2	3
2	4	5	6
1	7	8	9
	d	e	f

You are at e2 = ☐.

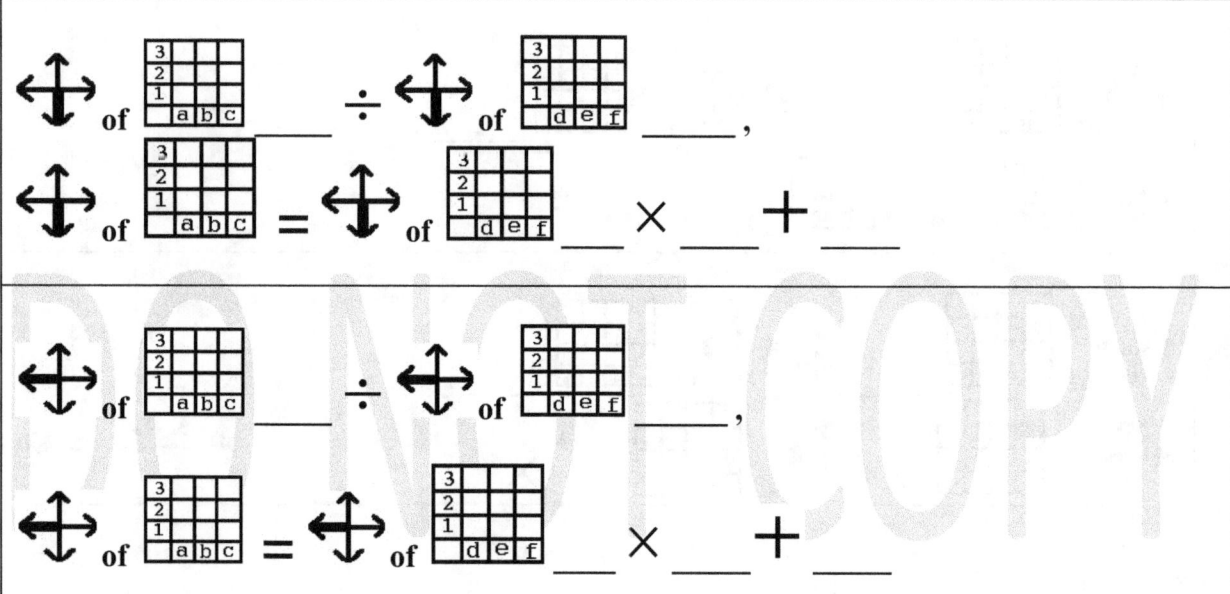

$45 = 8 \times 5 + 5$

$20 = 4 \times 5 + 0$

Mom! I Learn Division Using Math-Chess-Puzzles Connection

Ho Math Chess　何数棋谜　妈!我会棋谜式除法啦!

Frank Ho, Amanda Ho © 2004 − 2017, all rights reserved.

Student's Name _____ Date _____

Division and remainder

3	10	30	15
2	20	40	25
1	5	45	45
	a	b	c

You are at b2 = ☐ .

3	1	2	3
2	4	5	6
1	7	8	9
	d	e	f

You are at e2 = ☐ .

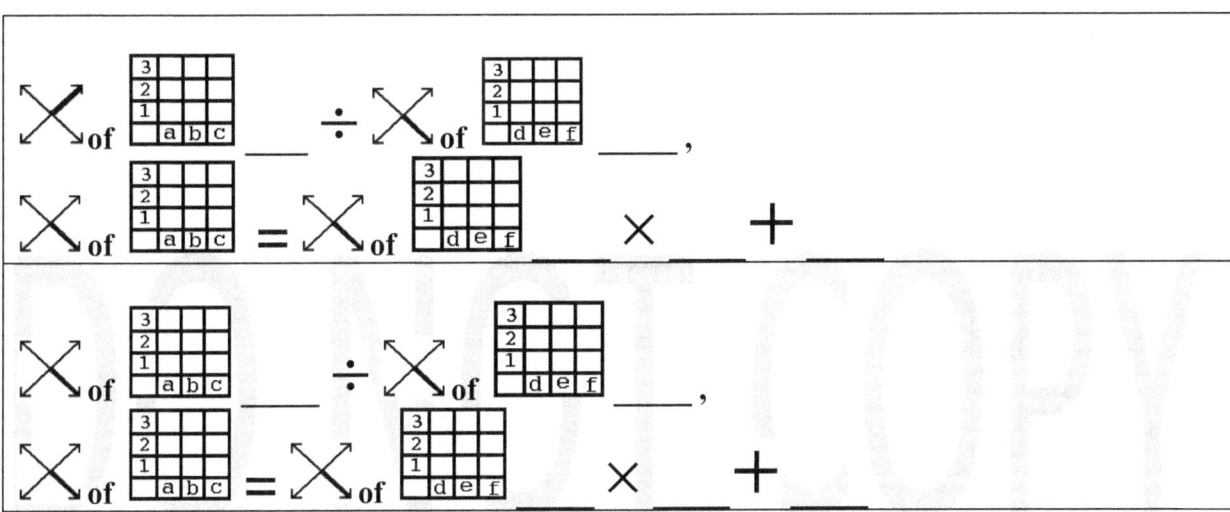

15 = 9 × 1+6
45 = 9 × 5+0

Mom! I Learn Division Using Math-Chess-Puzzles Connection

Ho Math Chess 何数棋谜 妈!我会棋谜式除法啦!

Frank Ho, Amanda Ho © 2004 − 2017, all rights reserved.

Student's Name_____ Date_____

Division and remainder

3	10	30	15
2	20	40	25
1	5	45	45
	a	b	c

You are at b2 = ☐ .

3	1	2	3
2	4	5	6
1	7	8	9
	d	e	f

You are at e2 = ☐ .

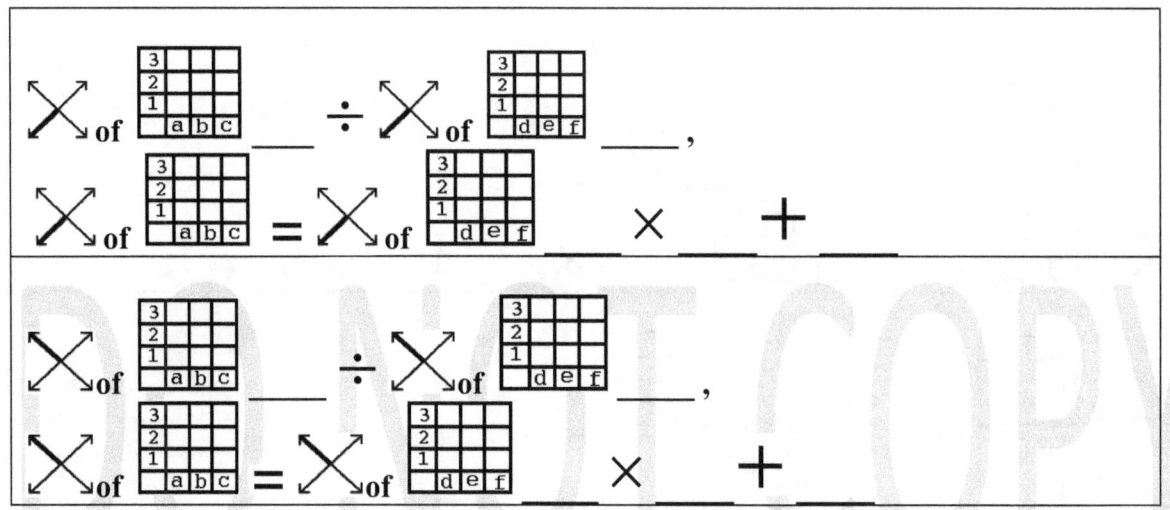

5 = 7 × 0 + 5

10 = 1 × 10 + 0

Mom! I Learn Division Using Math-Chess-Puzzles Connection

Ho Math Chess 何数棋谜 妈!我会棋谜式除法啦!

Frank Ho, Amanda Ho © 2004 − 2017, all rights reserved.

Student's Name _____ Date _____

Division and remainder

3	12	54	24
2	48	6	36
1	18	30	42
	a	b	c

You are at b2 = ☐.

3	5	2	3
2	4	6	6
1	7	8	9
	d	e	f

You are at e2 = ☐.

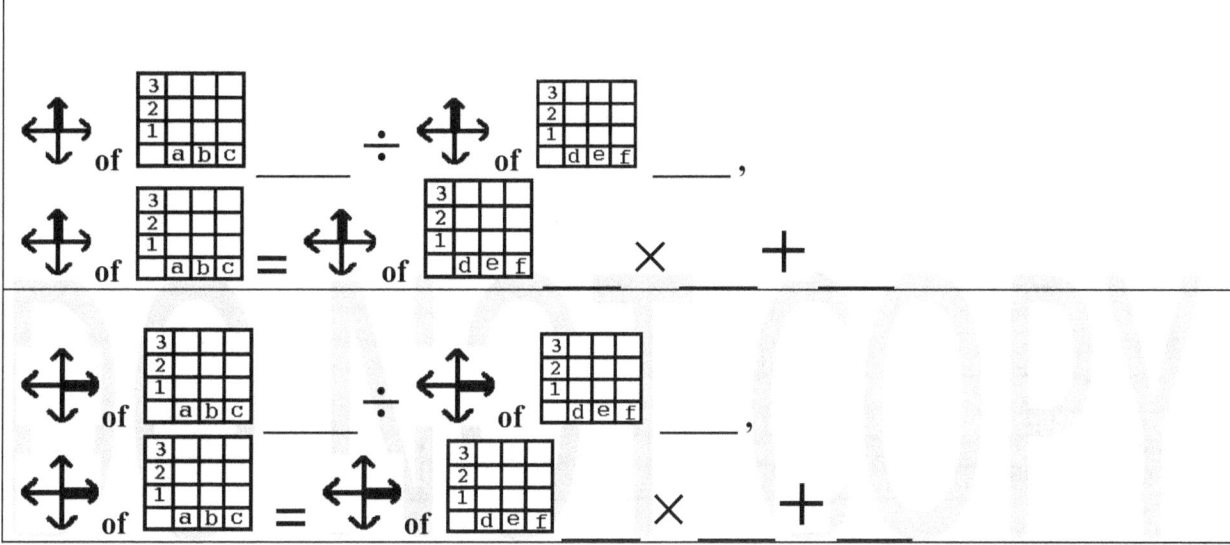

54 = 2 × 27+0

36 = 6 × 6+0

Mom! I Learn Division Using Math-Chess-Puzzles Connection

Ho Math Chess 何数棋谜 妈!我会棋谜式除法啦!

Frank Ho, Amanda Ho © 2004 – 2017, all rights reserved.

Student's Name _____ Date _____

Division and remainder

3	12	54	24
2	48	6	36
1	18	30	42
	a	b	c

You are at b2 = ☐.

3	5	2	3
2	4	6	6
1	7	8	9
	d	e	f

You are at e2 = ☐.

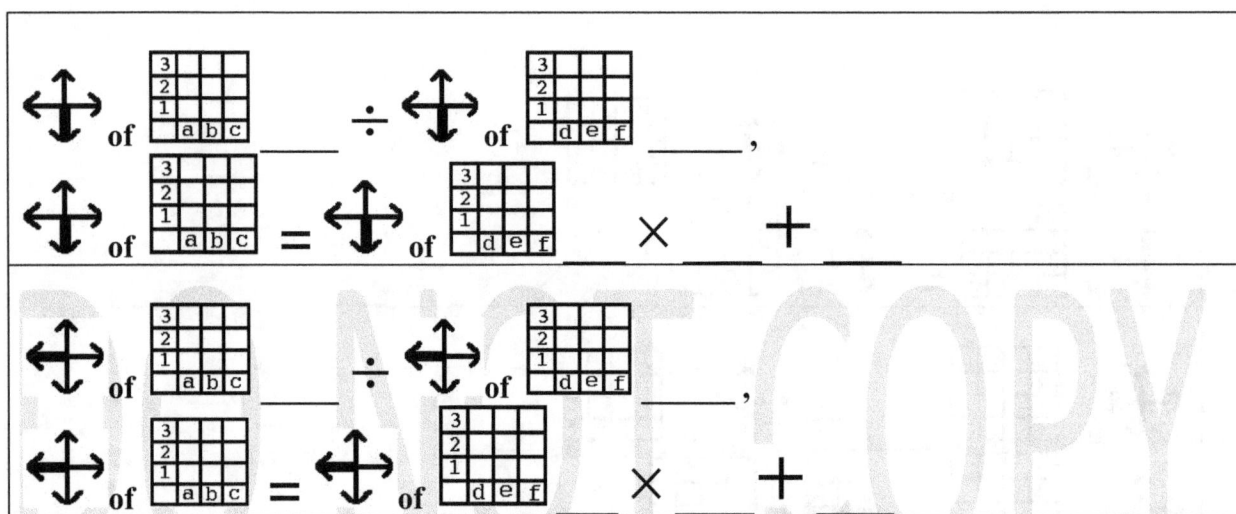

30 = 8 × 3 + 6

48 = 4 × 12 + 0

Mom! I Learn Division Using Math-Chess-Puzzles Connection

Ho Math Chess 何数棋谜 妈!我会棋谜式除法啦!

Frank Ho, Amanda Ho © 2004 − 2017, all rights reserved.

Student's Name _____ Date _____

Division and remainder

3	12	54	24
2	48	6	36
1	18	30	42
	a	b	c

You are at b2 = ☐.

3	5	2	3
2	4	6	6
1	7	8	9
	d	e	f

You are at e2 = ☐.

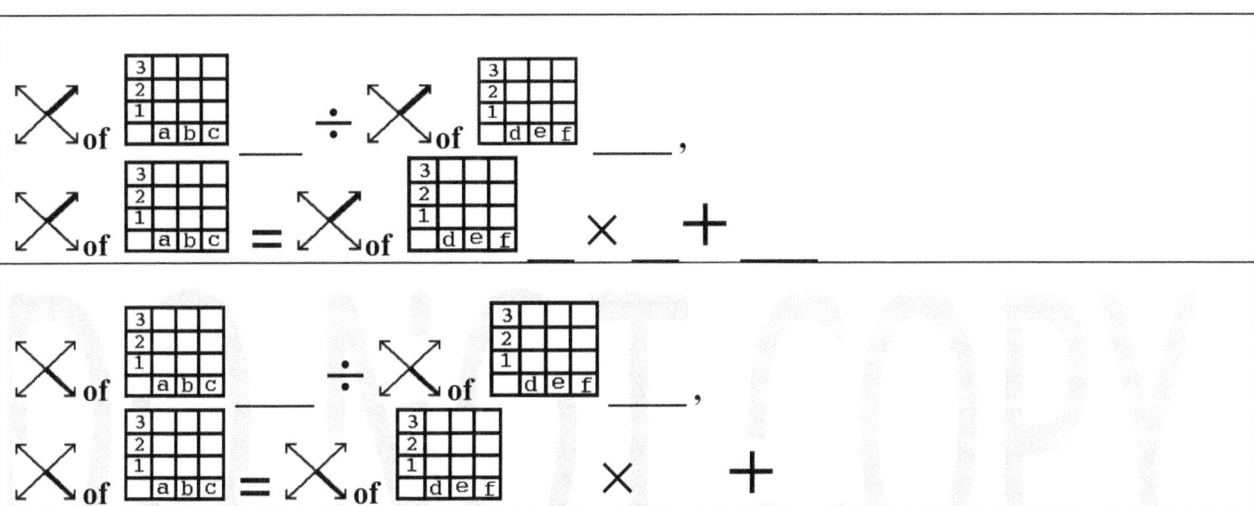

24 = 3 × 8 + 0

42 = 9 × 4 + 6

Mom! I Learn Division Using Math-Chess-Puzzles Connection

Ho Math Chess 何数棋谜 妈!我会棋谜式除法啦!

Frank Ho, Amanda Ho © 2004 – 2017, all rights reserved.

Student's Name _____ Date _____

Division and remainder

3	12	54	24
2	48	6	36
1	18	30	42
	a	b	c

You are at b2 = ☐.

3	5	2	3
2	4	6	6
1	7	8	9
	d	e	f

You are at e2 = ☐.

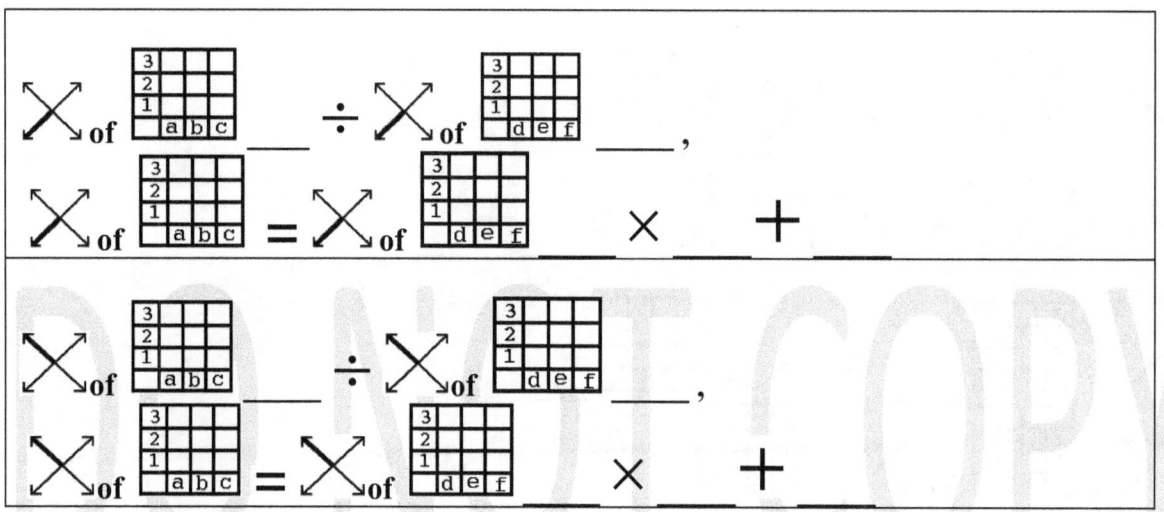

48 = 7 × 6 + 6

12 = 5 × 2 + 2

Mom! I Learn Division Using Math-Chess-Puzzles Connection

Ho Math Chess 何数棋谜 妈!我会棋谜式除法啦!

Frank Ho, Amanda Ho © 2004 − 2017, all rights reserved.

Student's Name _____ Date _____

Division and remainder

3	14	35	7
2	28	40	21
1	56	49	42
	a	b	c

You are at b2 = ☐.

3	1	2	3
2	4	7	6
1	5	8	9
	d	e	f

You are at e2 = ☐.

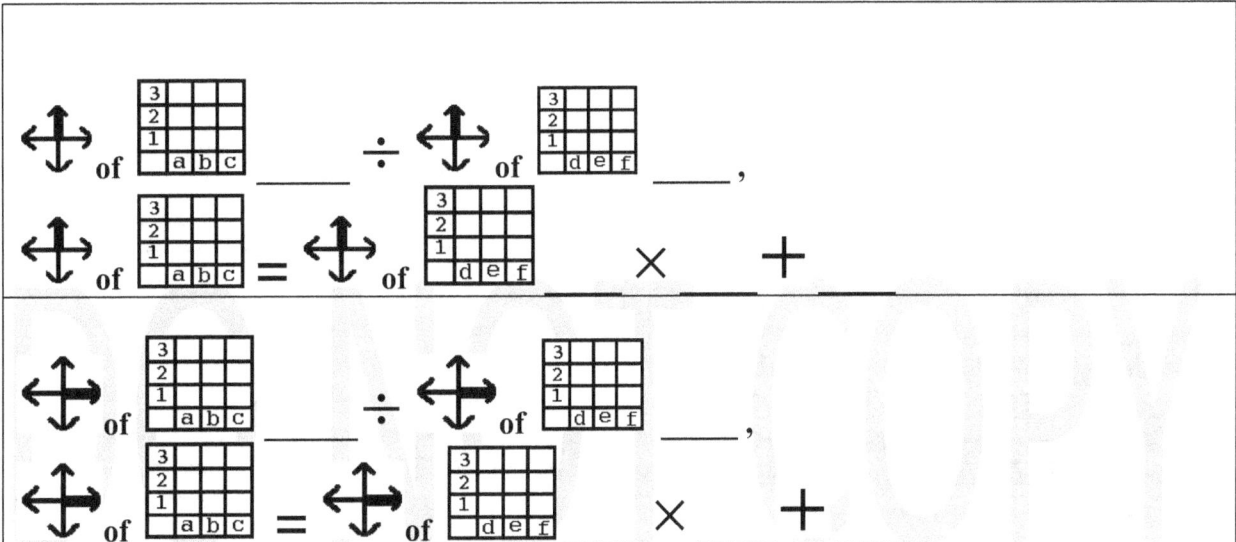

$35 = 2 \times 17 + 1$

$21 = 6 \times 3 + 3$

Page 91

Mom! I Learn Division Using Math-Chess-Puzzles Connection

Ho Math Chess 何数棋谜 妈!我会棋谜式除法啦!

Frank Ho, Amanda Ho © 2004 – 2017, all rights reserved.

Student's Name _____ Date _____

Division and remainder

3	14	35	7
2	28	40	21
1	56	49	42
	a	b	c

You are at b2 = ☐.

3	1	2	3
2	4	7	6
1	5	8	9
	d	e	f

You are at e2 = ☐.

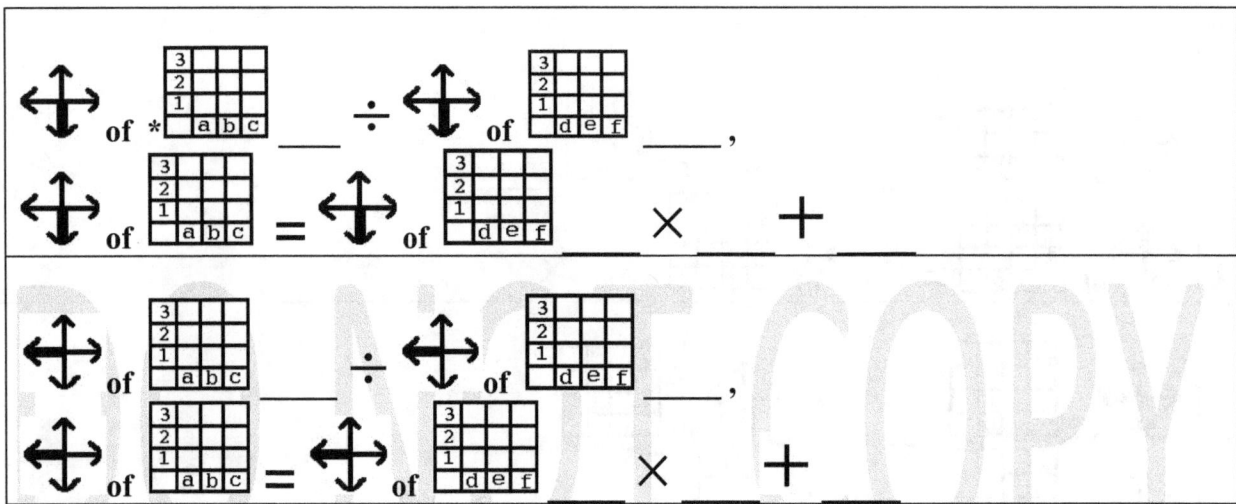

49 = 8 × 6 + 1

28 = 4 × 7 + 0

Mom! I Learn Division Using Math-Chess-Puzzles Connection

Ho Math Chess 何数棋谜 妈!我会棋谜式除法啦!

Frank Ho, Amanda Ho © 2004 − 2017, all rights reserved.

Student's Name _____ Date _____

Division and remainder

3	14	35	7
2	28	40	21
1	56	49	42
	a	b	c

You are at b2 = ☐.

3	1	2	3
2	4	7	6
1	5	8	9
	d	e	f

You are at e2 = ☐.

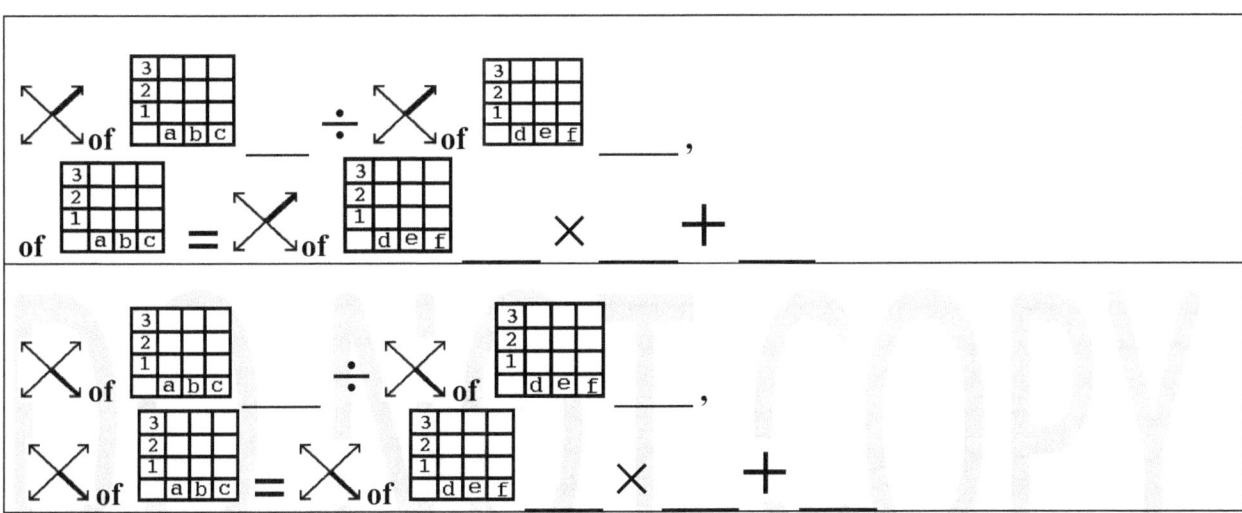

7 = 3 × 2+1

42 = 9 × 4+6

Mom! I Learn Division Using Math-Chess-Puzzles Connection

Ho Math Chess　何数棋谜　妈!我会棋谜式除法啦!

Frank Ho, Amanda Ho © 2004 – 2017, all rights reserved.

Student's Name_____ Date_____

Division and remainder

3	14	35	7
2	28	40	21
1	56	49	42
	a	b	c

You are at b2 = ☐.

3	1	2	3
2	4	7	6
1	5	8	9
	d	e	f

You are at e2 = ☐.

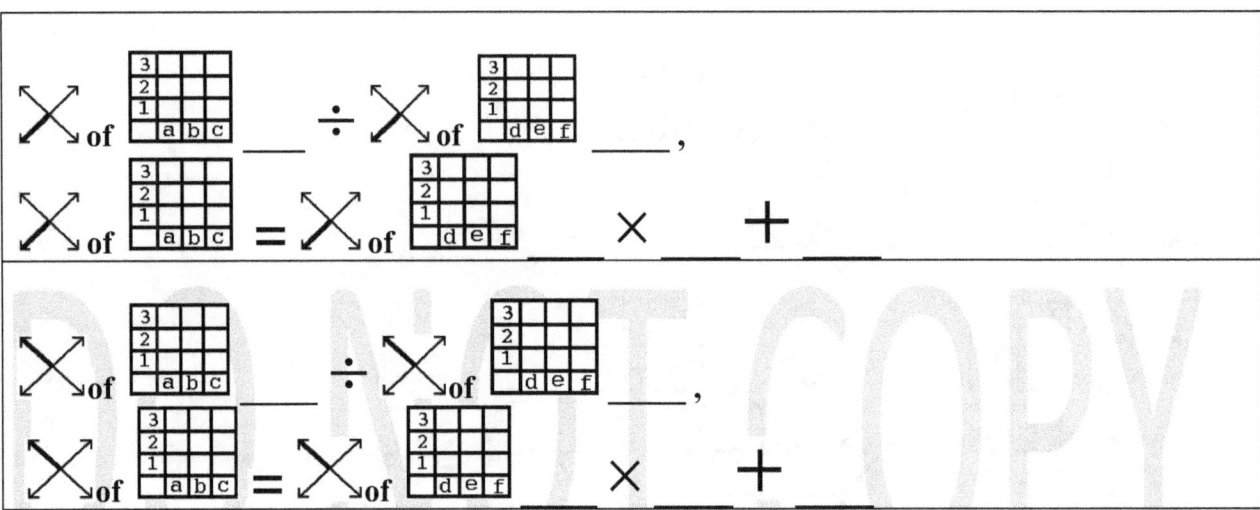

56 = 5 × 11 + 1

14 = 1 × 14 + 0

Mom! I Learn Division Using Math-Chess-Puzzles Connection

Ho Math Chess 何数棋谜 妈!我会棋谜式除法啦!

Frank Ho, Amanda Ho © 2004 − 2017, all rights reserved.

Student's Name _____ Date _____

Division and remainder

3	24	32	56
2	16	40	64
1	8	72	48
	a	b	c

You are at b2 = ☐.

3	1	2	3
2	4	8	6
1	7	5	9
	d	e	f

You are at e2 = ☐.

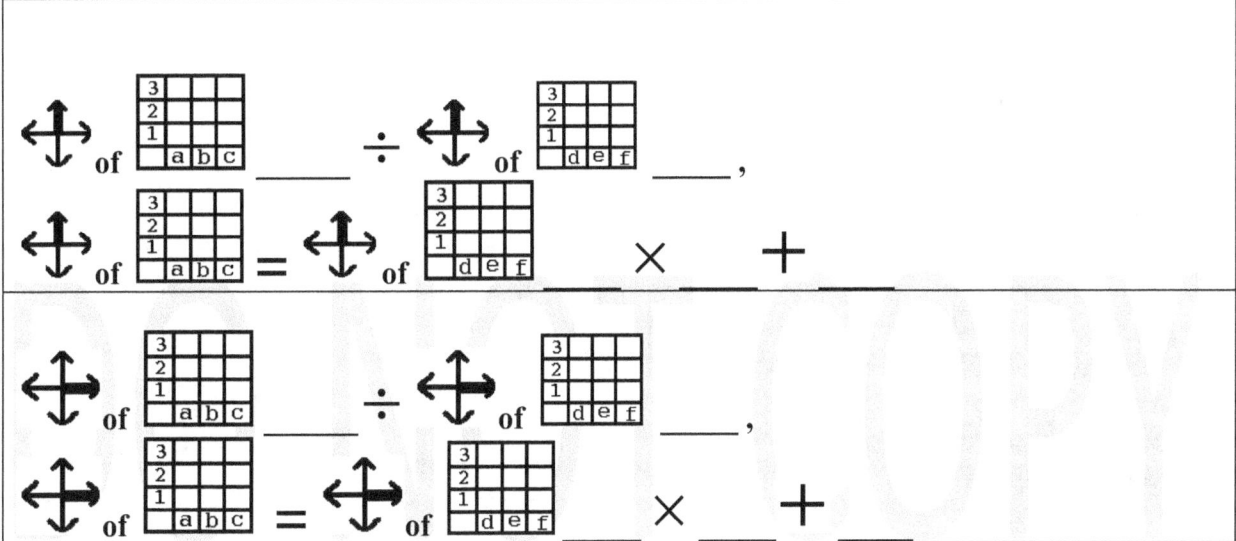

$32 = 2 \times 16 + 0$

$64 = 6 \times 10 + 4$

Page 95

Mom! I Learn Division Using Math-Chess-Puzzles Connection

Ho Math Chess 何数棋谜 妈!我会棋谜式除法啦!

Frank Ho, Amanda Ho © 2004 – 2017, all rights reserved.

Student's Name _____ Date _____

Division and remainder

3	24	32	56
2	16	40	64
1	8	72	48
	a	b	c

You are at b2 = ☐.

3	1	2	3
2	4	8	6
1	7	5	9
	d	e	f

You are at e2 = ☐.

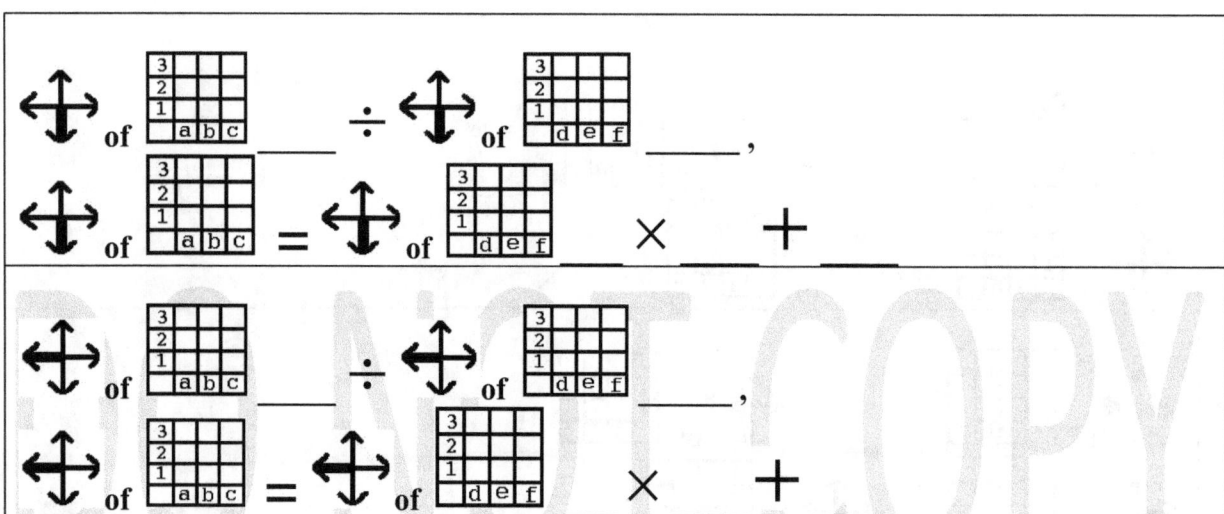

72 = 5 × 14 + 2

16 = 4 × 4 + 0

Mom! I Learn Division Using Math-Chess-Puzzles Connection

Ho Math Chess　何数棋谜　妈!我会棋谜式除法啦!

Frank Ho, Amanda Ho © 2004 − 2017, all rights reserved.

Student's Name _____ Date _____

Division and remainder

3	24	32	56
2	16	40	64
1	8	72	48
	a	b	c

You are at b2 = ☐.

3	1	2	3
2	4	8	6
1	7	5	9
	d	e	f

You are at e2 = ☐.

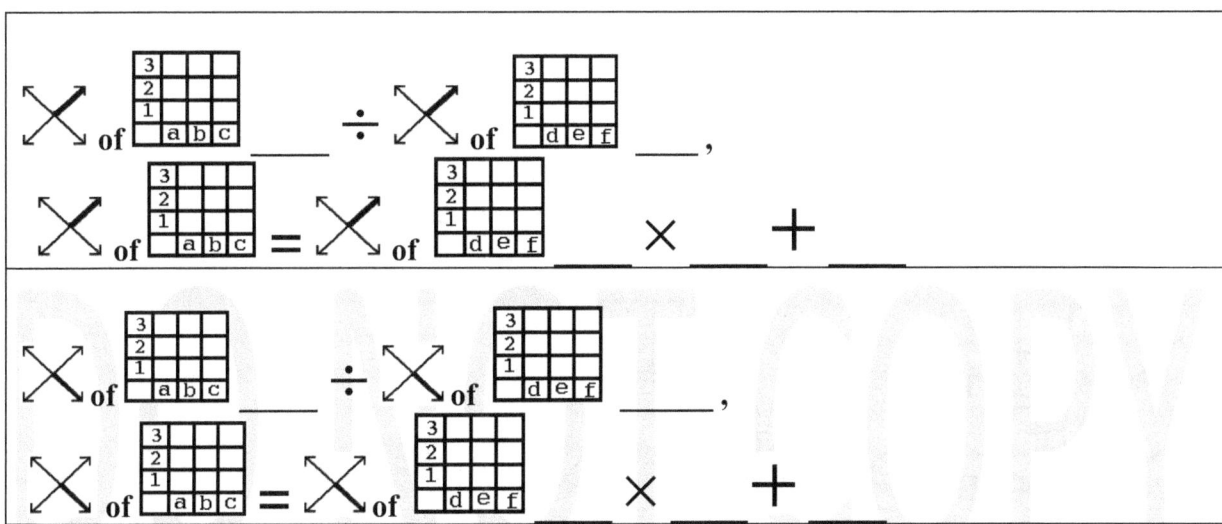

$56 = 3 \times 18 + 2$

$48 = 9 \times 5 + 3$

Mom! I Learn Division Using Math-Chess-Puzzles Connection

Ho Math Chess 何数棋谜 妈!我会棋谜式除法啦!

Frank Ho, Amanda Ho © 2004 – 2017, all rights reserved.

Student's Name _____ Date _____

Division and remainder

3	24	32	56
2	16	40	64
1	8	72	48
	a	b	c

You are at b2 = ☐.

3	1	2	3
2	4	8	6
1	7	5	9
	d	e	f

You are at e2 = ☐.

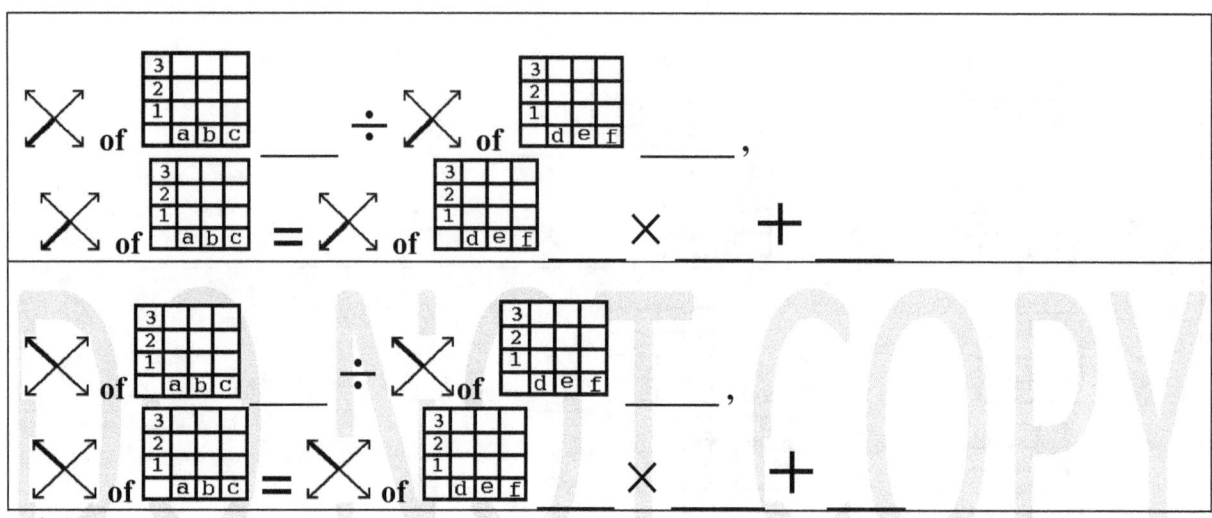

8 = 7 × 1 + 1

24 = 1 × 24 + 0

Mom! I Learn Division Using Math-Chess-Puzzles Connection

Ho Math Chess   何数棋谜   妈!我会棋谜式除法啦!

Frank Ho, Amanda Ho © 2004 – 2017, all rights reserved.

Student's Name _____   Date _____

Division and remainder

3	9	72	18
2	54	81	27
1	36	45	63
	a	b	c

You are at b2 = ☐.

3	1	2	3
2	4	9	6
1	7	8	5
	d	e	f

You are at e2 = ☐.

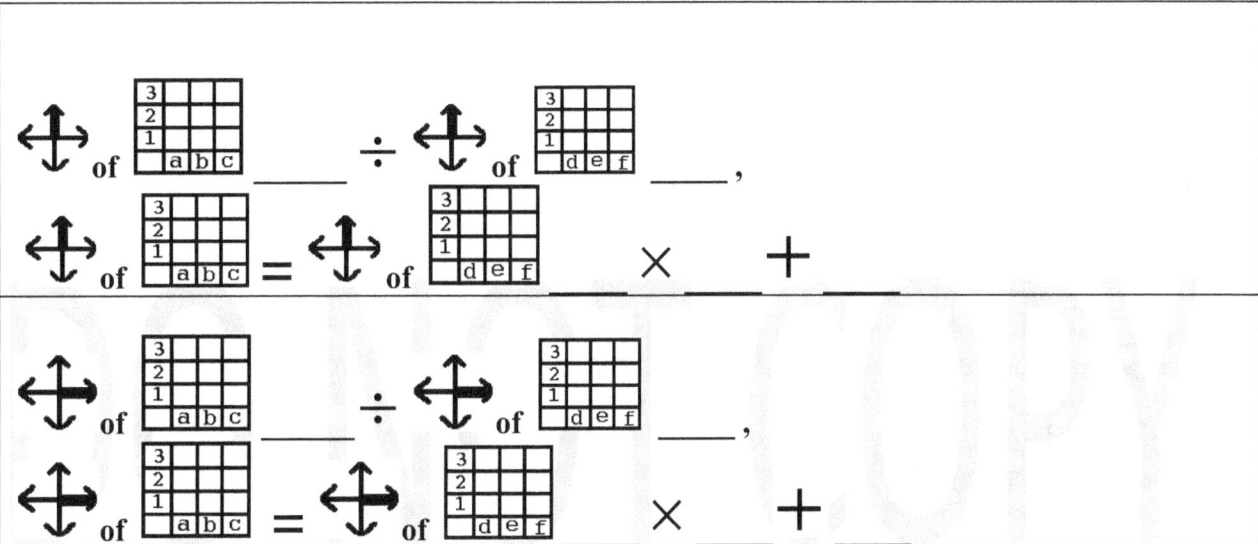

72 = 36 × 2 + 0

27 = 6 × 4 + 3

Page 99

Mom! I Learn Division Using Math-Chess-Puzzles Connection

Ho Math Chess 何数棋谜 妈!我会棋谜式除法啦!

Frank Ho, Amanda Ho © 2004 – 2017, all rights reserved.

Student's Name _____ Date _____

Division and remainder

3	9	72	18
2	54	81	27
1	36	45	63
	a	b	c

You are at b2 = ☐.

3	1	2	3
2	4	9	6
1	7	8	5
	d	e	f

You are at e2 = ☐.

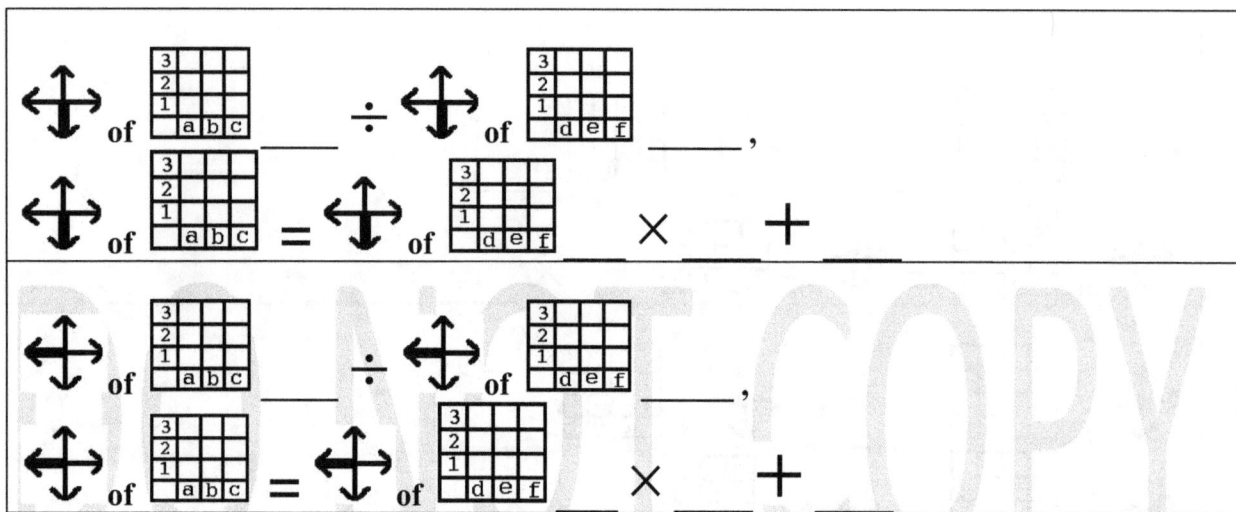

45 = 8 × 5 + 5

54 = 4 × 13 + 2

Mom! I Learn Division Using Math-Chess-Puzzles Connection

Ho Math Chess 何数棋谜 妈!我会棋谜式除法啦!

Frank Ho, Amanda Ho © 2004 − 2017, all rights reserved.

Student's Name _____ Date _____

Division and remainder

3	9	72	18
2	54	81	27
1	36	45	63
	a	b	c

You are at b2 = ☐.

3	1	2	3
2	4	9	6
1	7	8	5
	d	e	f

You are at e2 = ☐.

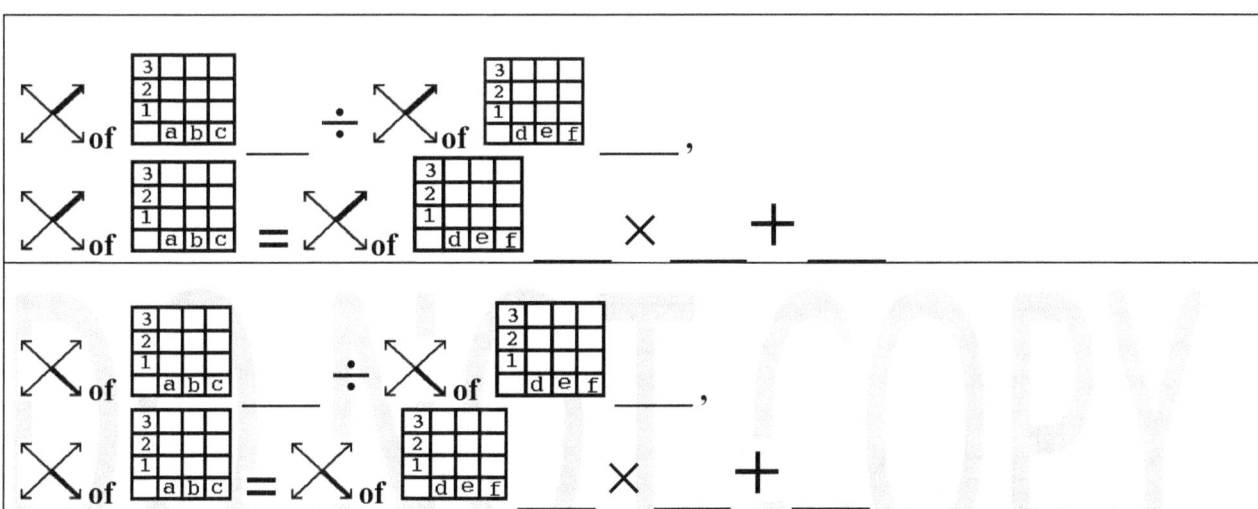

$18 = 3 \times 6 + 0$

$63 = 5 \times 12 + 3$

Mom! I Learn Division Using Math-Chess-Puzzles Connection

Ho Math Chess 何数棋谜 妈!我会棋谜式除法啦!

Frank Ho, Amanda Ho © 2004 – 2017, all rights reserved.

Student's Name _____ Date _____

Division and remainder

3	9	72	18
2	54	81	27
1	36	45	63
	a	b	c

You are at b2 = ☐.

3	1	2	3
2	4	9	6
1	7	8	5
	d	e	f

You are at e2 = ☐.

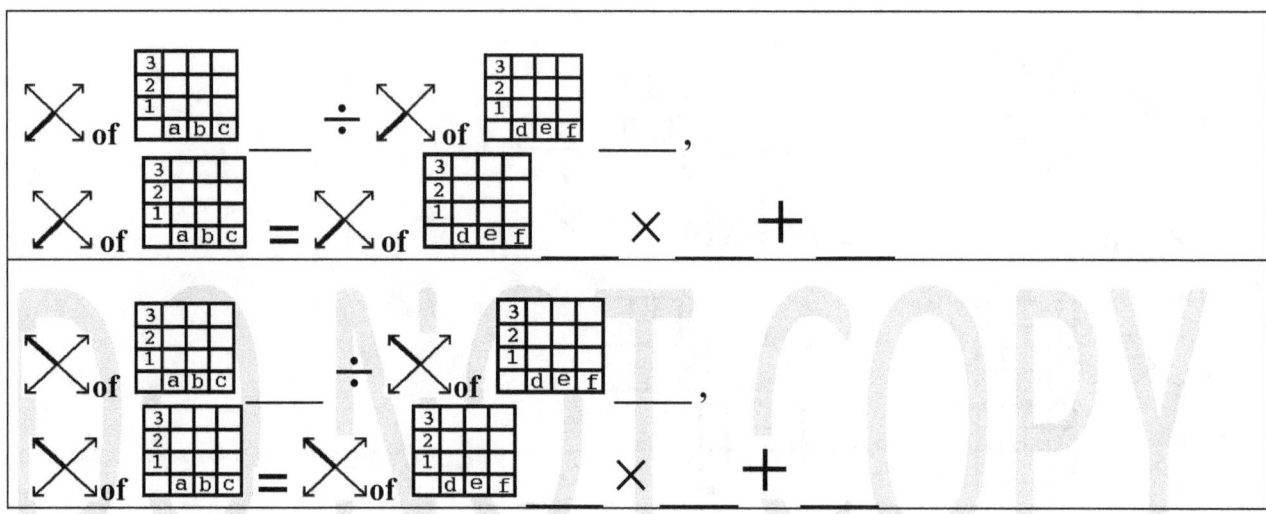

36 = 7 × 5 + 1

9 = 1 × 9 + 0

Mom! I Learn Division Using Math-Chess-Puzzles Connection

Ho Math Chess 何数棋谜 妈!我会棋谜式除法啦!

Frank Ho, Amanda Ho © 2004 − 2017, all rights reserved.

Student's Name _____   Date _____

Division and remainder

3	8	32	16
2	20	4	24
1	12	28	36
	a	b	c

You are at b2 = ☐.

3	1	2	3
2	5	4	6
1	7	8	9
	d	e	f

You are at e2 = ☐.

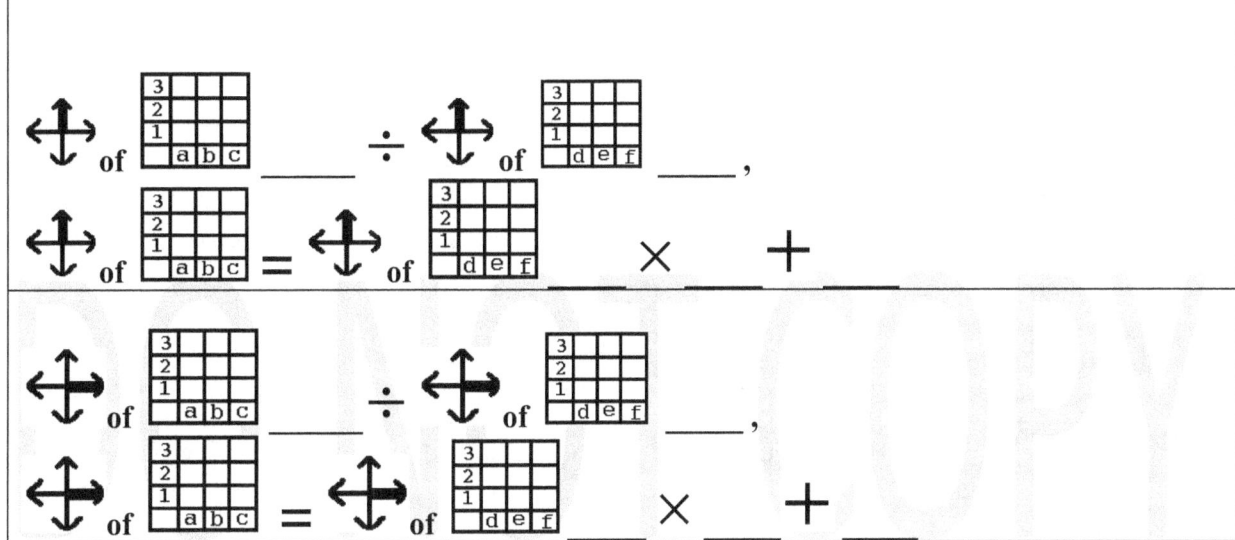

$32 = 2 \times 16 + 0$

$24 = 6 \times 4 + 0$

Mom! I Learn Division Using Math-Chess-Puzzles Connection

Ho Math Chess　何数棋谜　妈!我会棋谜式除法啦!

Frank Ho, Amanda Ho © 2004 – 2017, all rights reserved.

Student's Name _____　　Date _____

Division and remainder

3	8	32	16
2	20	4	24
1	12	28	36
	a	b	c

You are at b2 = ☐.

3	1	2	3
2	5	4	6
1	7	8	9
	d	e	f

You are at e2 = ☐.

↔ of [abc] ___ ÷ ↔ of [def] ___ ,

↕ of [abc] ___ = ↕ of [def] ___ × ___ + ___

↔ of [abc] ___ ÷ ↔ of [def] ___ ,

↕ of [abc] ___ = ↕ of [def] ___ × ___ + ___

28 = 8 × 3 + 4

20 = 5 × 4 + 0

Mom! I Learn Division Using Math-Chess-Puzzles Connection

Ho Math Chess 何数棋谜 妈!我会棋谜式除法啦!

Frank Ho, Amanda Ho © 2004 – 2017, all rights reserved.

Student's Name _____ Date _____

Division and remainder

3	8	32	16
2	20	4	24
1	12	28	36
	a	b	c

You are at b2 = ☐.

3	1	2	3
2	5	4	6
1	7	8	9
	d	e	f

You are at e2 = ☐.

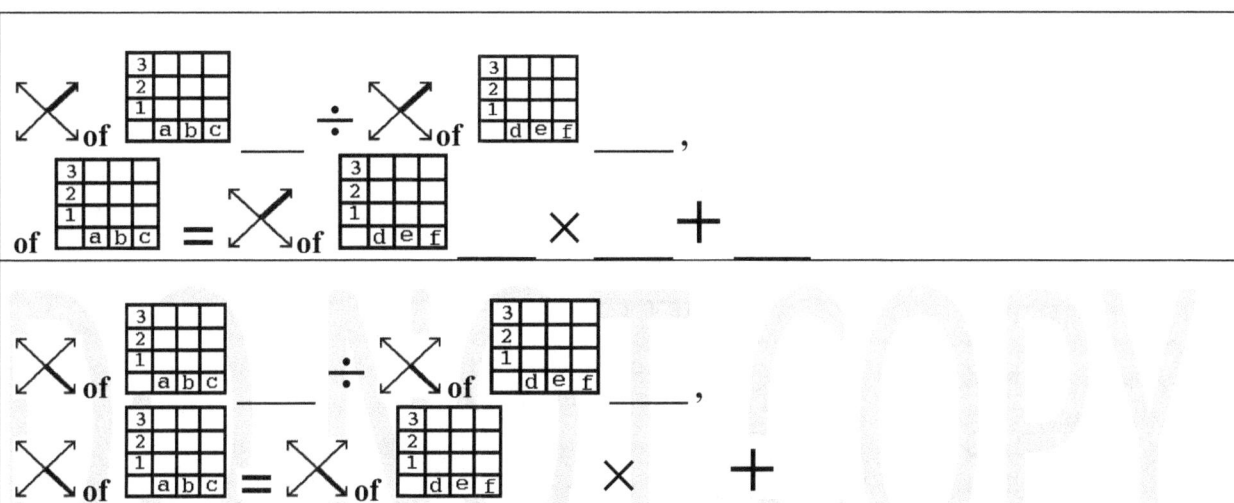

16 = 3 × 5 + 1
24 = 9 × 4 + 0

Mom! I Learn Division Using Math-Chess-Puzzles Connection

Ho Math Chess 何数棋谜 妈!我会棋谜式除法啦!

Frank Ho, Amanda Ho © 2004 – 2017, all rights reserved.

Student's Name _____ Date _____

Division and remainder

3	8	32	16
2	20	4	24
1	12	28	36
	a	b	c

You are at b2 = ☐ .

3	1	2	3
2	5	4	6
1	7	8	9
	d	e	f

You are at e2 = ☐ .

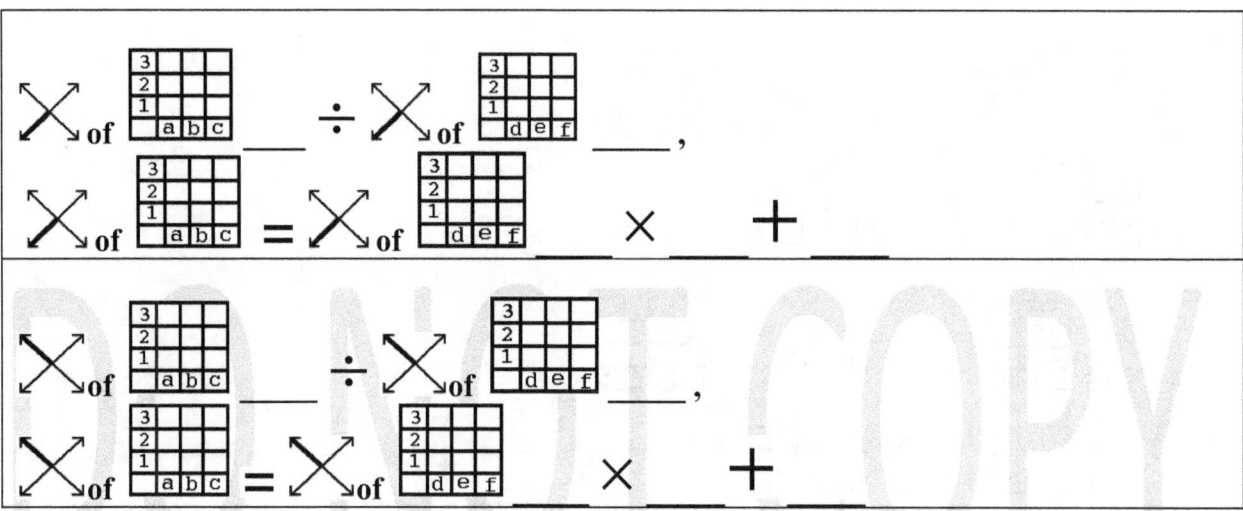

12 = 7 × 1 + 5

8 = 1 × 8 + 0

Mom! I Learn Division Using Math-Chess-Puzzles Connection

Ho Math Chess 何数棋谜 妈!我会棋谜式除法啦!

Frank Ho, Amanda Ho © 2004 – 2017, all rights reserved.

Student's Name _____ Date _____

Division and remainder

3	6	12	15
2	18	3	21
1	27	24	9
	a	b	c

You are at b2 = ☐.

3	1	2	5
2	4	3	6
1	7	8	9
	d	e	f

You are at e2 = ☐.

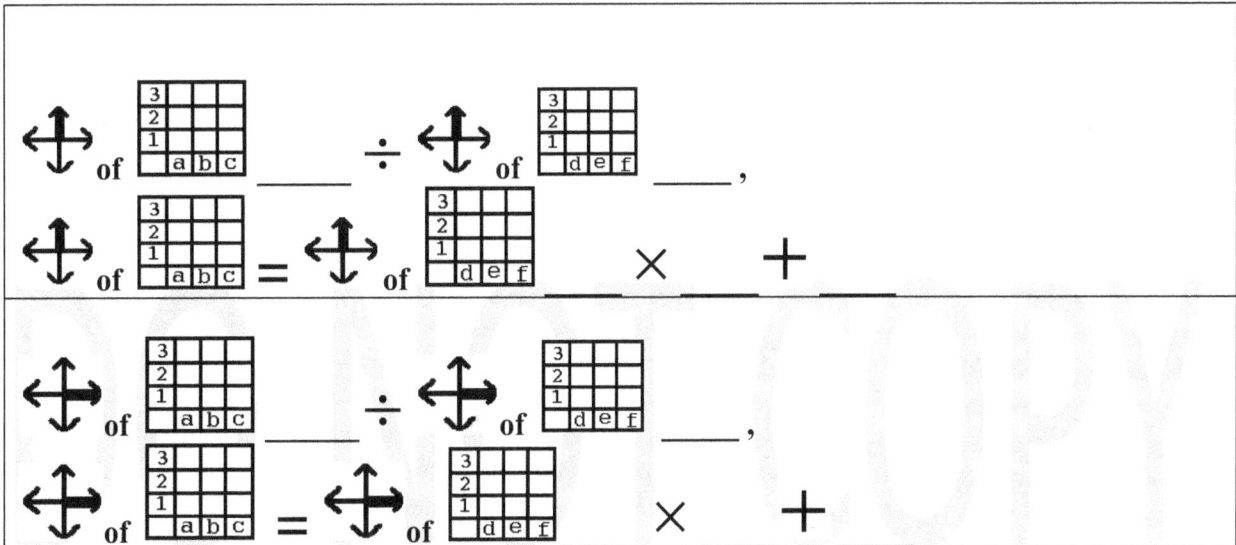

$12 = 2 \times 6 + 0$

$21 = 6 \times 3 + 3$

Mom! I Learn Division Using Math-Chess-Puzzles Connection

Ho Math Chess 何数棋谜 妈!我会棋谜式除法啦!

Frank Ho, Amanda Ho © 2004 – 2017, all rights reserved.

Student's Name _____ Date _____

Division and remainder

3	6	12	15
2	18	3	21
1	27	24	9
	a	b	c

You are at b2 = ☐.

3	1	2	5
2	4	3	6
1	7	8	9
	d	e	f

You are at e2 = ☐.

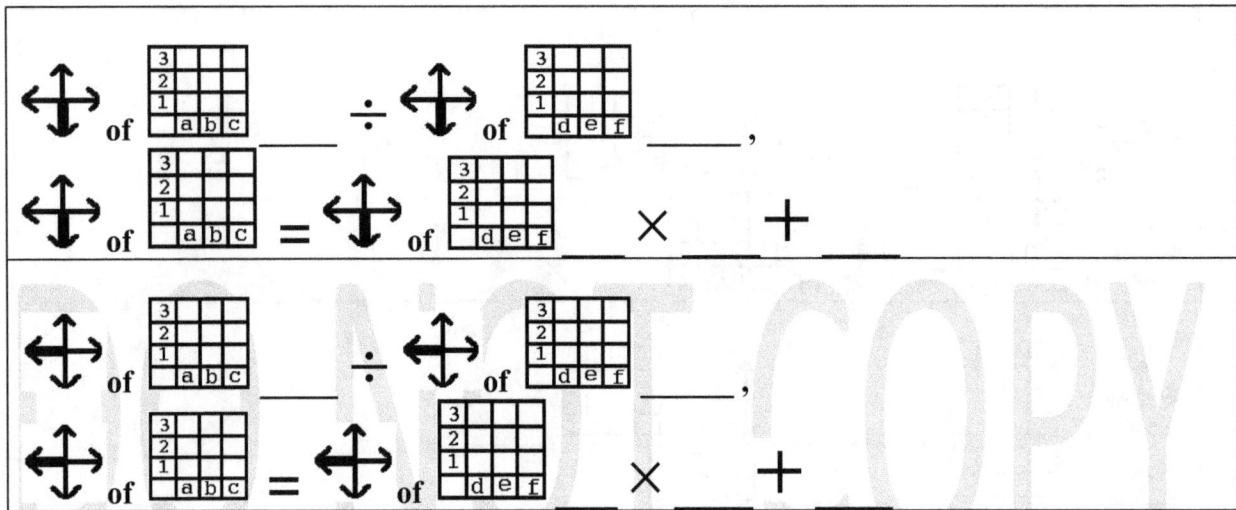

24 = 8 × 3 + 0

18 = 4 × 4 + 2

Mom! I Learn Division Using Math-Chess-Puzzles Connection

Ho Math Chess 何数棋谜 妈!我会棋谜式除法啦!

Frank Ho, Amanda Ho © 2004 − 2017, all rights reserved.

Student's Name _____ Date _____

Division and remainder

3	6	12	15
2	18	3	21
1	27	24	9
	a	b	c

You are at b2 = ☐.

3	1	2	5
2	4	3	6
1	7	8	9
	d	e	f

You are at e2 = ☐.

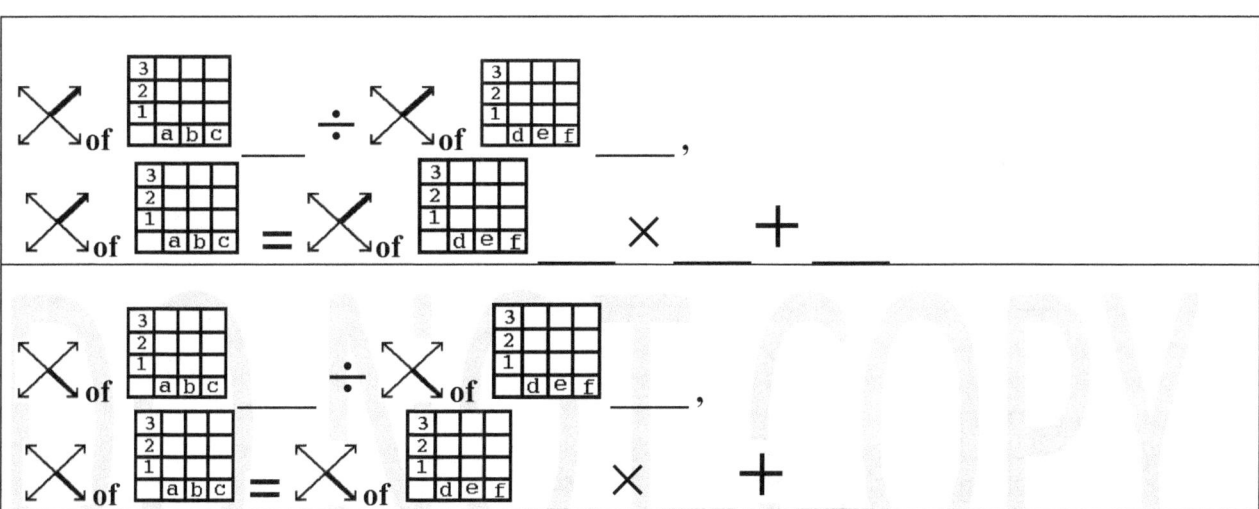

$15 = 5 \times 3 + 0$

$9 = 9 \times 1 + 0$

Mom! I Learn Division Using Math-Chess-Puzzles Connection

Division and remainder

3	6	12	15
2	18	3	21
1	27	24	9
	a	b	c

You are at b2 = ☐.

3	1	2	5
2	4	3	6
1	7	8	9
	d	e	f

You are at e2 = ☐.

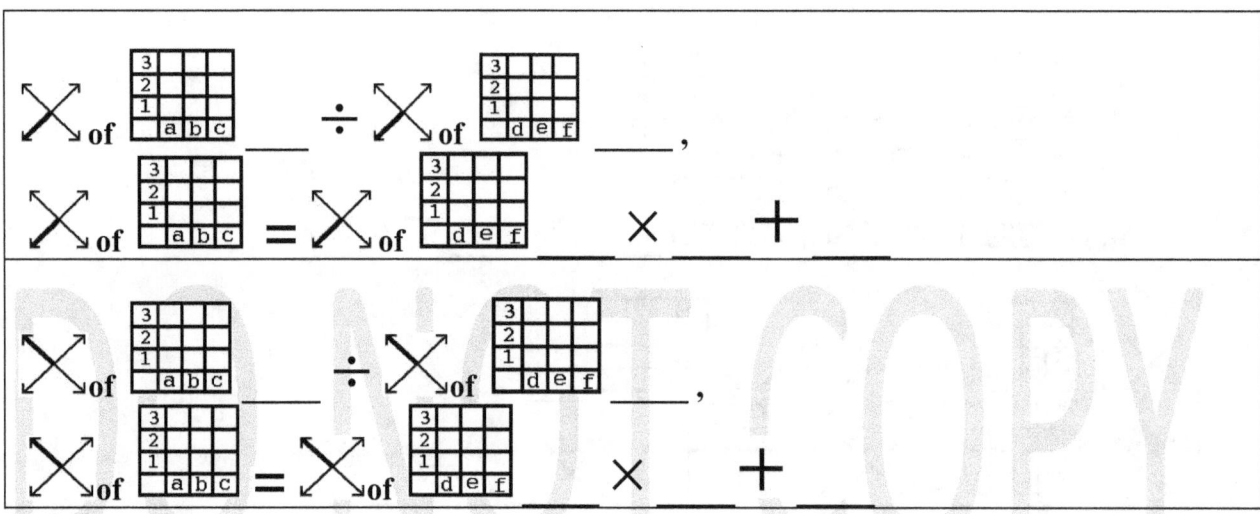

$27 = 7 \times 3 + 6$

$6 = 1 \times 6 + 0$

Mom! I Learn Division Using Math-Chess-Puzzles Connection

Ho Math Chess 何数棋谜 妈!我会棋谜式除法啦!

Frank Ho, Amanda Ho © 2004 − 2017, all rights reserved.

Student's Name_____ Date_____

Division with minimum quotient and no remainder

3	1	2	3
2	4	5	6
1	7	8	9
	a	b	c

3	19	15	13
2	12	11	18
1	14	16	12
	d	e	f

$d3 \div a3 = \underline{19} \div \underline{3}\ (\underline{19} - \underline{1}) \div \underline{3} = \underline{18} \div \underline{3} = \underline{6}$ with no remainder.

$e3 \div b3 = \underline{\ \ } \div \underline{\ \ }\ (\underline{\ \ } - \underline{\ \ }) \div \underline{\ \ } = \underline{\ \ } \div \underline{\ \ } = \underline{\ \ }$ with no remainder.

$f3 \div c3 = \underline{\ \ } \div \underline{\ \ }\ (\underline{\ \ } - \underline{\ \ }) \div \underline{\ \ } = \underline{\ \ } \div \underline{\ \ } = \underline{\ \ }$ with no remainder.

$d2 \div a2 = \underline{\ \ } \div \underline{\ \ }\ (\underline{\ \ } - \underline{\ \ }) \div \underline{\ \ } = \underline{\ \ } \div \underline{\ \ } = \underline{\ \ }$ with no remainder.

$d2 \div a2 = \underline{\ \ } \div \underline{\ \ }\ (\underline{\ \ } - \underline{\ \ }) \div \underline{\ \ } = \underline{\ \ } \div \underline{\ \ } = \underline{\ \ }$ with no remainder.

$e2 \div b2 = \underline{\ \ } \div \underline{\ \ }\ (\underline{\ \ } - \underline{\ \ }) \div \underline{\ \ } = \underline{\ \ } \div \underline{\ \ } = \underline{\ \ }$ with no remainder.

$f2 \div c2 = \underline{\ \ } \div \underline{\ \ }\ (\underline{\ \ } - \underline{\ \ }) \div \underline{\ \ } = \underline{\ \ } \div \underline{\ \ } = \underline{\ \ }$ with no remainder.

$d1 \div a1 = \underline{\ \ } \div \underline{\ \ }\ (\underline{\ \ } - \underline{\ \ }) \div \underline{\ \ } = \underline{\ \ } \div \underline{\ \ } = \underline{\ \ }$ with no remainder.

$e1 \div b1 = \underline{\ \ } \div \underline{\ \ }\ (\underline{\ \ } - \underline{\ \ }) \div \underline{\ \ } = \underline{\ \ } \div \underline{\ \ } = \underline{\ \ }$ with no remainder.

$f1 \div c1 = \underline{\ \ } \div \underline{\ \ }\ (\underline{\ \ } - \underline{\ \ }) \div \underline{\ \ } = \underline{\ \ } \div \underline{\ \ } = \underline{\ \ }$ with no remainder.

$14 \div 2 = 7$

$12 \div 3 = 4$

$12 \div 4 = 3$

$10 \div 5 = 2$

$18 \div 6 = 3$

$14 \div 7 = 2$

$16 \div 8 = 2$

$9 \div 9 = 1$

Mom! I Learn Division Using Math-Chess-Puzzles Connection

Ho Math Chess 何数棋谜 妈!我会棋谜式除法啦!

Frank Ho, Amanda Ho © 2004 – 2017, all rights reserved.

Student's Name_____ Date_____

Division with minimum quotient and no remainder

3	1	2	3
2	4	5	6
1	7	8	9
	a	B	c

3	14	19	17
2	15	11	13
1	18	12	16
	d	e	f

$d3 \div a3 =$ ___ $\div$ ___ (___ $-$ ___) $\div$ ___ $=$ ___ $\div$ ___ $=$ ___ with no remainder.

$e3 \div b3 =$ ___ $\div$ ___ (___ $-$ ___) $\div$ ___ $=$ ___ $\div$ ___ $=$ ___ with no remainder.

$f3 \div c3 =$ ___ $\div$ ___ (___ $-$ ___) $\div$ ___ $=$ ___ $\div$ ___ $=$ ___ with no remainder.

$14 \div 1 = 14$
$18 \div 2 = 9$
$15 \div 3 = 5$

Mom! I Learn Division Using Math-Chess-Puzzles Connection

Ho Math Chess 何数棋谜 妈!我会棋谜式除法啦!

Frank Ho, Amanda Ho © 2004 − 2017, all rights reserved.

Student's Name _____ Date _____

Division and remainder

Reduce the following fractions.

1. $\dfrac{\cancel{2}^{1}}{\cancel{4}_{2}} = \dfrac{1}{2}$	2. $\dfrac{8}{10} = $ ___ $\dfrac{4}{5}$	3. $\dfrac{2}{6} = $ ___ $\dfrac{1}{3}$
4. $\dfrac{4}{14} = $ ___ $\dfrac{2}{7}$	5. $\dfrac{6}{16} = $ ___ $\dfrac{3}{8}$	6. $\dfrac{8}{18} = $ ___ $\dfrac{4}{9}$
7. $\dfrac{12}{14} = $ ___ $\dfrac{6}{7}$	8. $\dfrac{14}{16} = $ ___ $\dfrac{7}{8}$	9. $\dfrac{16}{18} = $ ___ $\dfrac{8}{9}$
10. $\dfrac{22}{24} = $ ___ $\dfrac{11}{12}$	11. $\dfrac{18}{20} = $ ___ $\dfrac{9}{10}$	12. $\dfrac{8}{22} = $ ___ $\dfrac{4}{11}$
13. $\dfrac{24}{34} = $ ___ $\dfrac{12}{17}$	14. $\dfrac{26}{36} = $ ___ $\dfrac{13}{18}$	15. $\dfrac{28}{38} = $ ___ $\dfrac{14}{19}$
16. $\dfrac{16}{46} = $ ___ $\dfrac{8}{23}$	17. $\dfrac{14}{44} = $ ___ $\dfrac{7}{22}$	18. $\dfrac{24}{46} = $ ___ $\dfrac{12}{23}$
19. $\dfrac{10}{52} = $ ___ $\dfrac{5}{26}$	20. $\dfrac{16}{82} = $ ___ $\dfrac{8}{41}$	21. $\dfrac{18}{76} = $ ___ $\dfrac{9}{38}$

Mom! I Learn Division Using Math-Chess-Puzzles Connection

Ho Math Chess 何数棋谜 妈!我会棋谜式除法啦!

Frank Ho, Amanda Ho © 2004 – 2017, all rights reserved.

Student's Name _____ Date _____

Reduce the following fractions.

1.	$\dfrac{3}{9}=$ ___	$\dfrac{1}{3}$	2.	$\dfrac{12}{15}=$ ___	$\dfrac{4}{5}$	3.	$\dfrac{9}{12}=$ ___	$\dfrac{3}{4}$
4.	$\dfrac{6}{15}=$ ___	$\dfrac{2}{5}$	5.	$\dfrac{12}{21}=$ ___	$\dfrac{4}{7}$	6.	$\dfrac{15}{24}=$ ___	$\dfrac{5}{8}$
7.	$\dfrac{18}{33}=$ ___	$\dfrac{6}{11}$	8.	$\dfrac{15}{36}=$ ___	$\dfrac{5}{12}$	9.	$\dfrac{15}{42}=$ ___	$\dfrac{5}{14}$
10.	$\dfrac{27}{30}=$ ___	$\dfrac{9}{10}$	11.	$\dfrac{18}{57}=$ ___	$\dfrac{6}{19}$	12.	$\dfrac{21}{63}=$ ___	$\dfrac{7}{21}$
13.	$\dfrac{36}{63}=$ ___	$\dfrac{11}{21}$	14.	$\dfrac{24}{51}=$ ___	$\dfrac{8}{17}$	15.	$\dfrac{24}{45}=$ ___	$\dfrac{8}{15}$
16.	$\dfrac{27}{57}=$ ___	$\dfrac{9}{19}$	17.	$\dfrac{39}{81}=$ ___	$\dfrac{13}{27}$	18.	$\dfrac{63}{78}=$ ___	$\dfrac{21}{26}$

Mom! I Learn Division Using Math-Chess-Puzzles Connection

Ho Math Chess 何数棋谜 妈!我会棋谜式除法啦!

Frank Ho, Amanda Ho © 2004 − 2017, all rights reserved.

Student's Name _____ Date _____

Reduce the following fractions.

1. $\dfrac{5}{25} = $ _____ $\dfrac{1}{5}$ 2. $\dfrac{10}{35} = $ _____ $\dfrac{2}{10}$ 3. $\dfrac{15}{25} = $ _____ $\dfrac{3}{5}$

4. $\dfrac{15}{40} = $ _____ $\dfrac{3}{8}$ 5. $\dfrac{25}{55} = $ _____ $\dfrac{5}{11}$ 6. $\dfrac{10}{25} = $ _____ $\dfrac{2}{5}$

7. $\dfrac{25}{60} = $ _____ $\dfrac{5}{12}$ 8. $\dfrac{30}{65} = $ _____ $\dfrac{6}{13}$ 9. $\dfrac{30}{35} = $ _____ $\dfrac{6}{7}$

10. $\dfrac{15}{50} = $ _____ $\dfrac{3}{10}$ 11. $\dfrac{20}{45} = $ _____ $\dfrac{4}{9}$ 12. $\dfrac{35}{100} = $ _____ $\dfrac{7}{20}$

13. $\dfrac{30}{85} = $ _____ $\dfrac{6}{17}$ 14. $\dfrac{35}{75} = $ _____ $\dfrac{7}{15}$ 15. $\dfrac{50}{95} = $ _____ $\dfrac{10}{19}$

16. $\dfrac{40}{85} = $ _____ $\dfrac{8}{17}$ 17. $\dfrac{55}{75} = $ _____ $\dfrac{11}{15}$ 18. $\dfrac{60}{85} = $ _____ $\dfrac{12}{17}$

Mom! I Learn Division Using Math-Chess-Puzzles Connection

Ho Math Chess 何数棋谜 妈!我会棋谜式除法啦!

Frank Ho, Amanda Ho © 2004 – 2017, all rights reserved.

Student's Name _____ Date _____

Reduce the following fractions.

1. $\dfrac{7}{77} = \dfrac{1}{11}$ 2. $\dfrac{21}{35} = \dfrac{3}{5}$ 3. $\dfrac{21}{49} = \dfrac{3}{7}$

4. $\dfrac{14}{63} = \dfrac{2}{9}$ 5. $\dfrac{14}{77} = \dfrac{2}{11}$ 6. $\dfrac{28}{49} = \dfrac{4}{7}$

7. $\dfrac{56}{77} = \dfrac{8}{11}$ 8. $\dfrac{35}{63} = \dfrac{5}{9}$ 9. $\dfrac{28}{77} = \dfrac{4}{11}$

10. $\dfrac{42}{91} = \dfrac{6}{13}$ 11. $\dfrac{49}{84} = \dfrac{7}{12}$ 12. $\dfrac{77}{84} = \dfrac{11}{12}$

13. $\dfrac{35}{98} = \dfrac{5}{14}$ 14. $\dfrac{42}{91} = \dfrac{6}{13}$ 15. $\dfrac{35}{84} = \dfrac{5}{12}$

16. $\dfrac{63}{77} = \dfrac{9}{11}$ 17. $\dfrac{63}{98} = \dfrac{9}{14}$ 18. $\dfrac{49}{84} = \dfrac{7}{12}$

Mom! I Learn Division Using Math-Chess-Puzzles Connection

Ho Math Chess 何数棋谜 妈!我会棋谜式除法啦!

Frank Ho, Amanda Ho © 2004 − 2017, all rights reserved.

Student's Name _____ Date _____

Reduce the following fractions.

1. $\dfrac{10}{100} = \dfrac{1}{10}$ 2. $\dfrac{20}{50} = \dfrac{2}{5}$ 3. $\dfrac{30}{40} = \dfrac{3}{4}$

4. $\dfrac{70}{200} = \dfrac{7}{20}$ 5. $\dfrac{40}{150} = \dfrac{4}{15}$ 6. $\dfrac{50}{160} = \dfrac{5}{16}$

7. $\dfrac{20}{230} = \dfrac{2}{23}$ 8. $\dfrac{120}{350} = \dfrac{12}{35}$ 9. $\dfrac{100}{1000} = \dfrac{1}{10}$

10. $\dfrac{80}{130} = \dfrac{8}{13}$ 11. $\dfrac{60}{700} = \dfrac{6}{70}$ 12. $\dfrac{160}{900} = \dfrac{16}{90}$

13. $\dfrac{200}{900} = \dfrac{2}{9}$ 14. $\dfrac{300}{800} = \dfrac{3}{8}$ 15. $\dfrac{400}{700} = \dfrac{4}{7}$

16. $\dfrac{600}{1100} = \dfrac{6}{11}$ 17. $\dfrac{700}{1000} = \dfrac{7}{10}$ 18. $\dfrac{400}{9000} = \dfrac{4}{90}$

Mom! I Learn Division Using Math-Chess-Puzzles Connection

Reduce the following fractions.

1. $\dfrac{6}{15} = \dfrac{3}{5}$ 2. $\dfrac{8}{14} = \dfrac{4}{7}$ 3. $\dfrac{12}{21} = \dfrac{4}{7}$

4. $\dfrac{16}{22} = \dfrac{8}{11}$ 5. $\dfrac{12}{22} = \dfrac{6}{11}$ 6. $\dfrac{8}{26} = \dfrac{4}{13}$

7. $\dfrac{6}{28} = \dfrac{3}{14}$ 8. $\dfrac{12}{15} = \dfrac{4}{5}$ 9. $\dfrac{4}{18} = \dfrac{2}{9}$

10. $\dfrac{12}{21} = \dfrac{4}{7}$ 11. $\dfrac{15}{24} = \dfrac{5}{8}$ 12. $\dfrac{8}{26} = \dfrac{4}{13}$

13. $\dfrac{18}{57} = \dfrac{6}{19}$ 14. $\dfrac{14}{36} = \dfrac{7}{18}$ 15. $\dfrac{1}{26} = \dfrac{8}{13}$

16. $\dfrac{18}{39} = \dfrac{9}{13}$ 17. $\dfrac{15}{36} = \dfrac{5}{12}$ 18. $\dfrac{24}{51} = \dfrac{8}{17}$

Mom! I Learn Division Using Math-Chess-Puzzles Connection

Ho Math Chess　何数棋谜　妈!我会棋谜式除法啦!

Frank Ho, Amanda Ho © 2004 − 2017, all rights reserved.

Student's Name _____　　Date _____

Reduce the following fractions.

1. $\dfrac{6}{9} = \underline{} \quad \dfrac{2}{3}$ 　　2. $\dfrac{10}{25} = \underline{} \quad \dfrac{2}{5}$ 　　3. $\dfrac{12}{45} = \underline{} \quad \dfrac{4}{15}$

4. $\dfrac{15}{25} = \underline{} \quad \dfrac{3}{5}$ 　　5. $\dfrac{12}{15} = \underline{} \quad \dfrac{4}{5}$ 　　6. $\dfrac{15}{25} = \underline{} \quad \dfrac{3}{5}$

7. $\dfrac{10}{15} = \underline{} \quad \dfrac{2}{3}$ 　　8. $\dfrac{15}{35} = \underline{} \quad \dfrac{3}{7}$ 　　9. $\dfrac{15}{36} = \underline{} \quad \dfrac{5}{12}$

10. $\dfrac{30}{39} = \underline{} \quad \dfrac{10}{13}$ 　　11. $\dfrac{30}{55} = \underline{} \quad \dfrac{6}{11}$ 　　12. $\dfrac{9}{15} = \underline{} \quad \dfrac{3}{5}$

13. $\dfrac{20}{45} = \underline{} \quad \dfrac{4}{9}$ 　　14. $\dfrac{21}{45} = \underline{} \quad \dfrac{7}{15}$ 　　15. $\dfrac{42}{45} = \underline{} \quad \dfrac{14}{15}$

16. $\dfrac{45}{50} = \underline{} \quad \dfrac{9}{10}$ 　　17. $\dfrac{45}{66} = \underline{} \quad \dfrac{15}{22}$ 　　18. $\dfrac{25}{30} = \underline{} \quad \dfrac{5}{6}$

Mom! I Learn Division Using Math-Chess-Puzzles Connection

Ho Math Chess　何数棋谜　妈!我会棋谜式除法啦!

Frank Ho, Amanda Ho © 2004 – 2017, all rights reserved.

Student's Name _____ Date _____

Reduce the following fractions.

1. $\dfrac{35}{42} = \dfrac{5}{6}$ 　　 2. $\dfrac{49}{70} = \dfrac{7}{10}$ 　　 3. $\dfrac{25}{35} = \dfrac{5}{7}$

4. $\dfrac{15}{40} = \dfrac{3}{8}$ 　　 5. $\dfrac{28}{63} = \dfrac{4}{9}$ 　　 6. $\dfrac{35}{55} = \dfrac{7}{11}$

7. $\dfrac{70}{85} = \dfrac{14}{17}$ 　　 8. $\dfrac{56}{91} = \dfrac{8}{13}$ 　　 9. $\dfrac{30}{65} = \dfrac{6}{13}$

10. $\dfrac{35}{84} = \dfrac{5}{12}$ 　　 11. $\dfrac{30}{55} = \dfrac{6}{11}$ 　　 12. $\dfrac{45}{85} = \dfrac{9}{17}$

13. $\dfrac{40}{85} = \dfrac{8}{17}$ 　　 14. $\dfrac{65}{80} = \dfrac{13}{16}$ 　　 15. $\dfrac{84}{91} = \dfrac{12}{13}$

16. $\dfrac{63}{84} = \dfrac{9}{12}$ 　　 17. $\dfrac{63}{91} = \dfrac{9}{13}$ 　　 18. $\dfrac{70}{84} = \dfrac{10}{12}$

Mom! I Learn Division Using Math-Chess-Puzzles Connection

Ho Math Chess 何数棋谜 妈!我会棋谜式除法啦!

Frank Ho, Amanda Ho © 2004 − 2017, all rights reserved.

Student's Name _____ Date _____

Reduce the following fractions.

1. $\dfrac{15}{27} = $ _____ $\dfrac{5}{9}$ 2. $\dfrac{20}{30} = $ _____ $\dfrac{2}{3}$ 3. $\dfrac{24}{42} = $ _____ $\dfrac{8}{14}$

4. $\dfrac{20}{50} = $ _____ $\dfrac{2}{5}$ 5. $\dfrac{45}{84} = $ _____ $\dfrac{15}{28}$ 6. $\dfrac{10}{40} = $ _____ $\dfrac{1}{4}$

7. $\dfrac{36}{45} = $ _____ $\dfrac{12}{15}$ 8. $\dfrac{30}{70} = $ _____ $\dfrac{3}{7}$ 9. $\dfrac{39}{60} = $ _____ $\dfrac{13}{20}$

10. $\dfrac{50}{70} = $ _____ $\dfrac{5}{7}$ 11. $\dfrac{60}{93} = $ _____ $\dfrac{20}{31}$ 12. $\dfrac{40}{70} = $ _____ $\dfrac{4}{7}$

13. $\dfrac{48}{87} = $ _____ $\dfrac{12}{29}$ 14. $\dfrac{30}{40} = $ _____ $\dfrac{3}{4}$ 15. $\dfrac{20}{70} = $ _____ $\dfrac{2}{7}$

16. $\dfrac{27}{42} = $ _____ $\dfrac{9}{14}$ 17. $\dfrac{30}{50} = $ _____ $\dfrac{3}{5}$ 18. $\dfrac{30}{93} = $ _____ $\dfrac{10}{31}$

Mom! I Learn Division Using Math-Chess-Puzzles Connection

Ho Math Chess   何数棋谜   妈!我会棋谜式除法啦!

Frank Ho, Amanda Ho © 2004 – 2017, all rights reserved.

Student's Name _____   Date _____

dd divided by dd

3	17	19	14
2	18	23	12
1	13	15	11
	a	b	c

The original square is at b2.

	Long division	Dividend = ?	Division in fraction form
b2 ÷ ✗ = 23 ÷ 14	$14\overline{)23}$ remainder: $\frac{1}{}$, 14, 9	b2 (23) = ✗ (14) × 1 + 9	$\dfrac{b2}{✗} = \dfrac{23}{14} = 1\dfrac{9}{14}$
b2 ÷ ✗	$\overline{)}$	b2 (__) = ✗ (__) × __ + __	$\dfrac{b2}{✗} = \dfrac{○}{○} = ○\dfrac{○}{○}$

23 = 14 × 1 + 9
23 = 2 × 11 + 1

Page 122

Mom! I Learn Division Using Math-Chess-Puzzles Connection

Ho Math Chess 何数棋谜 妈!我会棋谜式除法啦!

Frank Ho, Amanda Ho © 2004 − 2017, all rights reserved.

Student's Name _____ Date _____

dd divided by dd

3	17	19	14
2	18	32	12
1	13	15	11
	a	b	c

The original square is at b2.

	Long division	Dividend = ?	Division in fractional form
b2 ÷ ⬌	⟌	b2 (__) = ⬌ (__) × __ + __	$\frac{b2}{↕} = \frac{○}{○} = ○\frac{○}{○}$
b2 ÷ ⬌	⟌	b2 (__) = ⬌ (__) × __ + __	$\frac{b2}{⬌} = \frac{○}{○} = ○\frac{○}{○}$

$32 = 1 \times 19 + 13$

$32 = 12 \times 2 + 8$

Mom! I Learn Division Using Math-Chess-Puzzles Connection

Ho Math Chess 何数棋谜 妈!我会棋谜式除法啦!

Frank Ho, Amanda Ho © 2004 − 2017, all rights reserved.

Student's Name _____ Date _____

dd divided by dd

3	17	19	14
2	18	32	12
1	13	15	11
	a	b	c

The original square is at b2.

b2 ÷ ✗	Long division	Dividend = ? b2 (__) = ✗ (__) ✗ __ + __	Division in fraction form $\frac{b2}{✗} = \frac{○}{○} = ○\frac{○}{○}$
b2 ÷ ✗		b2 (__) = ✗ (__) ✗ __ + __	$\frac{b2}{✗} = \frac{○}{○} = ○\frac{○}{○}$

32 = 14 × 2 + 4

32 = 11 × 2 + 10

Page 124

Mom! I Learn Division Using Math-Chess-Puzzles Connection

Ho Math Chess 何数棋谜 妈!我会棋谜式除法啦!

Frank Ho, Amanda Ho © 2004 – 2017, all rights reserved.

Student's Name _____ Date _____

dd divided by dd

3	17	19	14
2	18	47	12
1	13	15	11
	A	b	c

The original square is at b2.

	Long division	Dividend = ?	Division in fractional form
b2 ÷ ⇔	⌐	b2(__) = ⚓(__) × __ + __	$\frac{b2}{\leftrightarrow} = \frac{O}{O} = O\frac{O}{O}$
b2 ÷ ⇔	⌐	b2(__) = ⚓(__) × __ + __	$\frac{b2}{\leftrightarrow} = \frac{O}{O} = O\frac{O}{O}$

32 = 19 × 1 + 13
32 = 12 × 2 + 8

Mom! I Learn Division Using Math-Chess-Puzzles Connection

Ho Math Chess 何数棋谜 妈!我会棋谜式除法啦!

Frank Ho, Amanda Ho © 2004 − 2017, all rights reserved.

Student's Name _____ Date _____

dd divided by dd

3	17	19	14
2	18	47	12
1	13	15	11
	a	b	c

The original square is at b2.

	Long division	Dividend = ?	Division in fraction form
b2 ÷ ✗	⟌	b2 (__) = ✗ (__) ✗ __ + __	$\frac{b2}{✗} = \frac{○}{○} = ○\frac{○}{○}$
b2 ÷ ✗	⟌	b2 (__) = ✗ (__) ✗ __ + __	$\frac{b2}{✗} = \frac{○}{○} = ○\frac{○}{○}$

47 = 12 ✗ 3 + 11

47 = 11 ✗ 4 + 3

Mom! I Learn Division Using Math-Chess-Puzzles Connection

Ho Math Chess 何数棋谜 妈!我会棋谜式除法啦!

Frank Ho, Amanda Ho © 2004 − 2017, all rights reserved.

Student's Name _____ Date _____

dd divided by dd

3	17	19	14
2	18	45	12
1	13	15	11
	a	b	c

The original square is at b2.

	Long division	Dividend = ?	Division in fractional form
b2 ÷ ✥	⟌	b2 (_) = ✥ (_) × _ + _	$\frac{b2}{✥} = \frac{○}{○} = ○\frac{○}{○}$
b2 ÷ ✥	⟌	b2 (_) = ✥ (_) × _ + _	$\frac{b2}{✥} = \frac{○}{○} = ○\frac{○}{○}$

45 = 19 × 2 + 7

45 = 12 × 3 + 9

Mom! I Learn Division Using Math-Chess-Puzzles Connection

Ho Math Chess   何数棋谜   妈!我会棋谜式除法啦!

Frank Ho, Amanda Ho © 2004 – 2017, all rights reserved.

Student's Name _____ Date _____

dd divided by dd

3	17	19	14
2	18	45	12
1	13	15	11
	a	b	C

The original square is at b2.

	Long division	Dividend = ?	Division in fraction form
b2 ÷ ✗	⟌ _____	b2 (__) = ✗ (__) ✗ __ + __	$\frac{b2}{✗} = \frac{○}{○} = ○\frac{○}{○}$
b2 ÷ ✗	⟌ _____	b2 (__) = ✗ (__) ✗ __ + __	$\frac{b2}{✗} = \frac{○}{○} = ○\frac{○}{○}$

45 = 14 × 3 + 3
45 = 11 × 4 + 1

Mom! I Learn Division Using Math-Chess-Puzzles Connection

Ho Math Chess 何数棋谜 妈!我会棋谜式除法啦!

Frank Ho, Amanda Ho © 2004 – 2017, all rights reserved.

Student's Name _____ Date _____

dd divided by dd

3	17	19	14
2	18	51	12
1	13	15	11
	A	b	C

The original square is at b2.

51 = 19 × 2 + 13

51 = 12 × 4 + 3

Mom! I Learn Division Using Math-Chess-Puzzles Connection

Ho Math Chess 何数棋谜　妈!我会棋谜式除法啦!

Frank Ho, Amanda Ho © 2004 – 2017, all rights reserved.

Student's Name _____ Date _____

dd divided by dd

3	17	19	14
2	18	53	12
1	13	15	11
	a	B	C

The original square is at b2.

	Long division	Dividend = ?	Division in fraction form
b2 ÷ ✕	⟌	b2 (__) = ✕ (__) ✕ __ + __	$\dfrac{b2}{✕} = \dfrac{\bigcirc}{\bigcirc} = \bigcirc \dfrac{\bigcirc}{\bigcirc}$
b2 ÷ ✕	⟌	b2 (__) = ✕ (__) ✕ __ + __	$\dfrac{b2}{✕} = \dfrac{\bigcirc}{\bigcirc} = \bigcirc \dfrac{\bigcirc}{\bigcirc}$

53 = 14 ✕ 3 + 11

53 = 11 ✕ 4 + 9

Mom! I Learn Division Using Math-Chess-Puzzles Connection

Ho Math Chess 何数棋谜 妈!我会棋谜式除法啦!

Frank Ho, Amanda Ho © 2004 – 2017, all rights reserved.

Student's Name _____ Date _____

dd divided by dd

3	17	19	14
2	18	62	12
1	13	15	11
	a	b	c

The original square is at b2.

	Long division	Dividend = ?	Division in fractional form
b2 ÷ ⇔	⌐	b2 (_) = ⇕ (_) × _ + _	$\frac{b2}{⇕} = \frac{○}{○} = ○\frac{○}{○}$
b2 ÷ ⇕	⌐	b2 (_) = ⇕ (_) × _ + _	$\frac{b2}{⇕} = \frac{○}{○} = ○\frac{○}{○}$

62 = 19 × 3 + 5

62 = 12 × 5 + 2

Mom! I Learn Division Using Math-Chess-Puzzles Connection

Ho Math Chess 何数棋谜 妈!我会棋谜式除法啦!

Frank Ho, Amanda Ho © 2004 – 2017, all rights reserved.

Student's Name _____ Date _____

dd divided by dd

3	17	19	14
2	18	67	12
1	13	15	11
	a	b	C

The original square is at b2.

	Long division	Dividend = ?	Division in fraction form
b2 ÷ ✕		b2 (__) = ✕ (__) ✕ __ + __	$\frac{b2}{✕} = \frac{○}{○} = ○\frac{○}{○}$
b2 ÷ ✕		b2 (__) = ✕ (__) ✕ __ + __	$\frac{b2}{✕} = \frac{○}{○} = ○\frac{○}{○}$

67 = 14 ✕ 4 + 11

67 = 11 ✕ 6 + 1

Mom! I Learn Division Using Math-Chess-Puzzles Connection

Ho Math Chess　何数棋谜　妈!我会棋谜式除法啦!

Frank Ho, Amanda Ho © 2004 – 2017, all rights reserved.

Student's Name _____ Date _____

dd divided by dd

3	17	19	14
2	18	75	12
1	13	15	11
	A	b	c

The original square is at b2.

	Long division	Dividend = ?	Division in fractional form
b2 ÷ ↕		b2 (__) = ↕ (__) × __ + __	$\frac{b2}{↕} = \frac{○}{○} = ○\frac{○}{○}$
b2 ÷ ↔		b2 (__) = ↔ (__) × __ + __	$\frac{b2}{↔} = \frac{○}{○} = ○\frac{○}{○}$

75 = 19 × 4 + 2

75 = 12 × 6 + 3

Mom! I Learn Division Using Math-Chess-Puzzles Connection

Ho Math Chess 何数棋谜 妈!我会棋谜式除法啦!

Frank Ho, Amanda Ho © 2004 − 2017, all rights reserved.

Student's Name _____ Date _____

dd divided by dd

3	17	19	14
2	18	75	12
1	13	15	11
	a	B	c

The original square is at b2.

	Long division	Dividend = ?	Division in fraction form
b2 ÷ ✕		b2 (__) = ✕ (__) ✕ __ + __	$\frac{b2}{✕} = \frac{○}{○} = ○\frac{○}{○}$
b2 ÷ ✕		b2 (__) = ✕ (__) ✕ __ + __	$\frac{b2}{✕} = \frac{○}{○} = ○\frac{○}{○}$

75 = 14 ✕ 5 + 5
75 = 11 ✕ 6 + 9

Mom! I Learn Division Using Math-Chess-Puzzles Connection

Ho Math Chess 何数棋谜 妈!我会棋谜式除法啦!

Frank Ho, Amanda Ho © 2004 – 2017, all rights reserved.

Student's Name _____ Date _____

dd divided by dd

3	17	19	14
2	18	78	12
1	13	15	11
	A	B	c

The original square is at b2.

	Long division	Dividend = ?	Division in fractional form
b2 ÷ ⇔	⌐	b2 (__) = ⇔ (__) × __ + __	$\frac{b2}{⇔} = \frac{○}{○} = ○\frac{○}{○}$
b2 ÷ ⇕	⌐	b2 (__) = ⇕ (__) × __ + __	$\frac{b2}{⇕} = \frac{○}{○} = ○\frac{○}{○}$

78 = 19 × 3 + 21
78 = 12 × 6 + 6

Mom! I Learn Division Using Math-Chess-Puzzles Connection

Ho Math Chess 何数棋谜 妈!我会棋谜式除法啦!

Frank Ho, Amanda Ho © 2004 – 2017, all rights reserved.

Student's Name_____ Date_____

dd divided by dd

3	17	19	14
2	18	78	12
1	13	15	11
	a	b	c

The original square is at b2.

b2 ÷ ✗	Long division	Dividend = ? b2 (__) = ✗ (__) × __ + __	Division in fraction form $\frac{b2}{✗} = \frac{○}{○} = ○\frac{○}{○}$
b2 ÷ ✗		b2 (__) = ✗ (__) × __ + __	$\frac{b2}{✗} = \frac{○}{○} = ○\frac{○}{○}$

78 = 14 × 5 + 8
78 = 11 × 7 + 1

Mom! I Learn Division Using Math-Chess-Puzzles Connection

Ho Math Chess 何数棋谜 妈!我会棋谜式除法啦!

Frank Ho, Amanda Ho © 2004 – 2017, all rights reserved.

Student's Name _____ Date _____

dd divided by dd

3	17	19	14
2	18	86	12
1	13	15	11
	a	b	c

The original square is at b2.

	Long division	Dividend = ?	Division in fractional form
b2 ÷ ⇔	⌐	b2 (__) = ⚓ (__) × __ + __	$\frac{b2}{⇔} = \frac{O}{O} = O\frac{O}{O}$
b2 ÷ ⇔	⌐	b2 (__) = ⚓ (__) × __ + __	$\frac{b2}{⇔} = \frac{O}{O} = O\frac{O}{O}$

$86 = 19 \times 40 + 10$

$86 = 12 \times 7 + 2$

Page 137

Mom! I Learn Division Using Math-Chess-Puzzles Connection

Ho Math Chess　何数棋谜　妈!我会棋谜式除法啦!

Frank Ho, Amanda Ho © 2004 – 2017, all rights reserved.

Student's Name _____　Date _____

dd divided by dd

3	17	19	14
2	18	89	12
1	13	15	11
	a	b	c

The original square is at b2.

	Long division	Dividend = ?	Division in fraction form
b2 ÷ ✗	⌐	b2 (__) = ✗ (__) ✗ __ + __	$\dfrac{b2}{✗} = \dfrac{○}{○} = ○\dfrac{○}{○}$
b2 ÷ ✗	⌐	b2 (__) = ✗ (__) ✗ __ + __	$\dfrac{b2}{✗} = \dfrac{○}{○} = ○\dfrac{○}{○}$

89 = 14 ✗ 6 + 5

89 = 11 ✗ 8 + 1

Mom! I Learn Division Using Math-Chess-Puzzles Connection

Ho Math Chess 何数棋谜 妈!我会棋谜式除法啦!

Frank Ho, Amanda Ho © 2004 – 2017, all rights reserved.

Student's Name _____ Date _____

dd divided by dd

3	17	19	14
2	18	93	12
1	13	15	11
	a	b	c

The original square is at b2.

	Long division	Dividend = ?	Division in fractional form
b2 ÷ ↔	⌐	b2 (_) = ↕ (_) × _ + _	$\frac{b2}{↕} = \frac{\bigcirc}{\bigcirc} = \bigcirc \frac{\bigcirc}{\bigcirc}$
b2 ÷ ↕	⌐	b2 (_) = ↕ (_) × _ + _	$\frac{b2}{↕} = \frac{\bigcirc}{\bigcirc} = \bigcirc \frac{\bigcirc}{\bigcirc}$

93 = 19 × 4 + 17
93 = 12 × 7 + 9

Mom! I Learn Division Using Math-Chess-Puzzles Connection

Ho Math Chess 何数棋谜 妈!我会棋谜式除法啦!

Frank Ho, Amanda Ho © 2004 − 2017, all rights reserved.

Student's Name _____ Date _____

dd divided by dd

3	17	19	14
2	18	97	12
1	13	15	11
	a	b	c

The original square is at b2.

	Long division	Dividend = ?	Division in fraction form
b2 ÷ ✕	) _____	b2 (__) = ✕ (__) ✕ __ + __	$\frac{b2}{✕} = \frac{○}{○} = ○\frac{○}{○}$
b2 ÷ ✕	) _____	b2 (__) = ✕ (__) ✕ __ + __	$\frac{b2}{✕} = \frac{○}{○} = ○\frac{○}{○}$

97 = 14 ✕ 6 + 13

97 = 11 ✕ 8 + 9

Mom! I Learn Division Using Math-Chess-Puzzles Connection

Ho Math Chess 何数棋谜 妈!我会棋谜式除法啦!

Frank Ho, Amanda Ho © 2004 − 2017, all rights reserved.

Student's Name _____ Date _____

ddd divided by dd

3	17	19	14
2	18	123	12
1	13	15	11
	a	b	c

The original square is at b2.

$123 = 19 \times 6 + 9$

$123 = 12 \times 10 + 3$

Mom! I Learn Division Using Math-Chess-Puzzles Connection

Ho Math Chess 何数棋谜 妈!我会棋谜式除法啦!

Frank Ho, Amanda Ho © 2004 − 2017, all rights reserved.

Student's Name _____ Date _____

ddd divided by dd

3	17	19	14
2	18	123	12
1	13	15	11
	a	b	c

The original square is at b2.

	Long division	Dividend = ?	Division in fraction form
b2 ÷ ✕	）⎯⎯	b2 (__) = ✕ (__) ✕ __ + __	$\dfrac{b2}{✕} = \dfrac{○}{○} = ○\dfrac{○}{○}$
b2 ÷ ✕	）⎯⎯	b2 (__) = ✕ (__) ✕ __ + __	$\dfrac{b2}{✕} = \dfrac{○}{○} = ○\dfrac{○}{○}$

123 = 14 ✕ 8 + 11

123 = 11 ✕ 11 + 2

Mom! I Learn Division Using Math-Chess-Puzzles Connection

Ho Math Chess 何数棋谜 妈!我会棋谜式除法啦!

Frank Ho, Amanda Ho © 2004 – 2017, all rights reserved.

Student's Name _____ Date _____

ddd divided by dd

3	17	19	14
2	18	223	12
1	13	15	11
	a	b	c

The original square is at b2.

	Long division	Dividend = ?	Division in fractional form
b2 ÷ ⬌	⌐	b2(_) = ⬌(_) × _ + _	$\frac{b2}{⬌} = \frac{○}{○} = ○\frac{○}{○}$
b2 ÷ ⬍	⌐	b2(_) = ⬍(_) × _ + _	$\frac{b2}{⬍} = \frac{○}{○} = ○\frac{○}{○}$

$223 = 19 \times 11 + 14$

$223 = 12 \times 18 + 7$

Mom! I Learn Division Using Math-Chess-Puzzles Connection

Ho Math Chess 何数棋谜 妈!我会棋谜式除法啦!

Frank Ho, Amanda Ho © 2004 – 2017, all rights reserved.

Student's Name_____ Date_____

ddd divided by dd

3	17	19	14
2	18	475	12
1	13	15	11
	a	b	c

The original square is at b2.

	Long division	Dividend = ?	Division in fractional form
b2 ÷ ✥	⌐	b2 (__) = ✥ (__) × __ + __	$\frac{b2}{✥} = \frac{○}{○} = ○\frac{○}{○}$
b2 ÷ ✥	⌐	b2 (__) = ✥ (__) × __ + __	$\frac{b2}{✥} = \frac{○}{○} = ○\frac{○}{○}$

475 = 14 × 33 + 13

475 = 11 × 43 + 2

Page 144

Mom! I Learn Division Using Math-Chess-Puzzles Connection

***** **Part 2 Multiplication Review** *****

Many students only mastered the 1 digit multiplying 1 digit times table and have difficulties in doing 2-digit multiplying 2-digit or 3-digit multiplying 2-digit multiplication, so when they learn division they equally have problems doing a number divided by 2-digit. Because of this reason, this section has a specially designed multiplication format to train students to get familiar with the multi-digit multiplication procedures.

Mom! I Learn Division Using Math-Chess-Puzzles Connection

Ho Math Chess 何数棋谜 妈!我会棋谜式除法啦!

Frank Ho, Amanda Ho © 2004 − 2017, all rights reserved.

Student's Name _____ Date _____

dd × dd multiplication concepts

Horizontal multiplication

$23 \times 24 = 23 \times (4 + 20) = 23 \times 4 + 23 \times 20 = 92 + 460 = 552$

Vertical multiplication

It is extremely important for the teacher to explain the concepts of why and how multiplication is done. Repeated drills without explanations only add prolong learning curve which could have been reduced if concepts such as the following had been explained.

1. Why line up ones multiplication at the rightmost position? Because it is ones place.
2. Why a 0 is placed in the ones place when doing tens place multiplication? Because tens place multiplication always has a 0 at ones place such as 20 in the example, the ones place value is 0.
3. How is the horizontal multiplication related to the vertical multiplication? The vertical multiplication is using the concept of distributive law to do the work but written in a vertical way. The following is an example.

```
      27
  ×   36
  ─────
      42
     120
      21
  +  600
  ─────
     972
```

Mom! I Learn Division Using Math-Chess-Puzzles Connection

Ho Math Chess 何数棋谜 妈!我会棋谜式除法啦!

Frank Ho, Amanda Ho © 2004 – 2017, all rights reserved.

Student's Name _____ Date _____

Step 1	Step 2
2 3 X 4 9 2	2 3 X 2 0 4 6 0

Step 3: The answer is 92 + 460 = 552

$25 \times 24 = 25 \times (4 + 20) = 25 \times 4 + 25 \times 20 =$

$24 \times 25 = 24 \times (5 + 20) = 24 \times 5 + 24 \times 20 =$

$25 \times 36 = 25 \times (6 + 30) = 25 \times 6 + 25 \times 30 =$

$36 \times 25 = 36 \times (5 + 20) = 36 \times 5 + 36 \times 20 =$

$27 \times 28 = 27 \times (8 + 20) = 27 \times 8 + 27 \times 20 =$

$28 \times 27 = 28 \times (7 + 20) = 28 \times 7 + 28 \times 20 =$

600, 600, 900, 900, 756, 756

Mom! I Learn Division Using Math-Chess-Puzzles Connection

Ho Math Chess 何数棋谜 妈!我会棋谜式除法啦!

Frank Ho, Amanda Ho © 2004 – 2017, all rights reserved.

Student's Name _____ Date _____

dd × dd with carrying

```
      2
    1 3          1 4          1 5          1 6
   x 8 8        x 8 8        x 8 8        x 8 8
   1 0 4        ☐☐☐         ☐☐☐          ☐☐☐
 + 1 0 4      + ☐☐☐        + ☐☐☐         + ☐☐☐
   ─────        ─────        ─────         ─────
   ☐☐☐☐        ☐☐☐☐         ☐☐☐☐          ☐☐☐☐
```

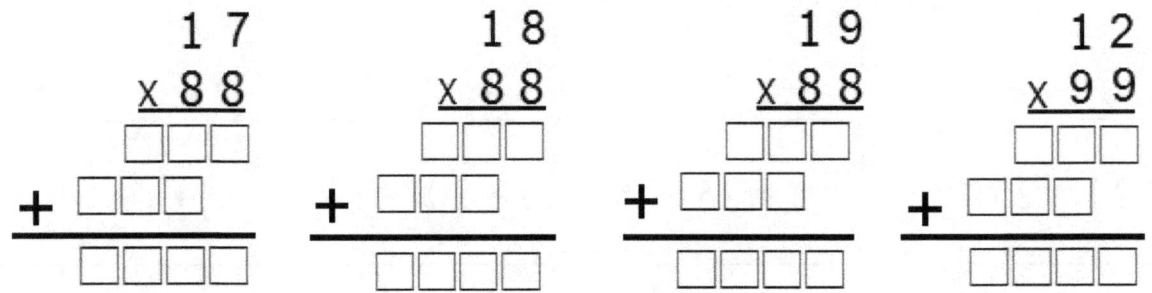

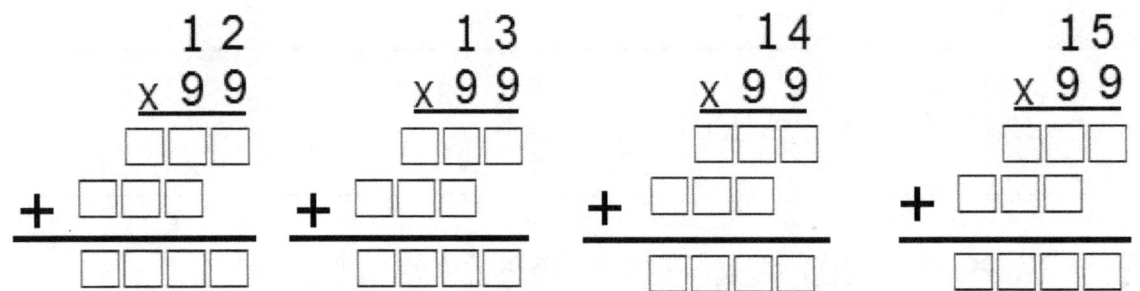

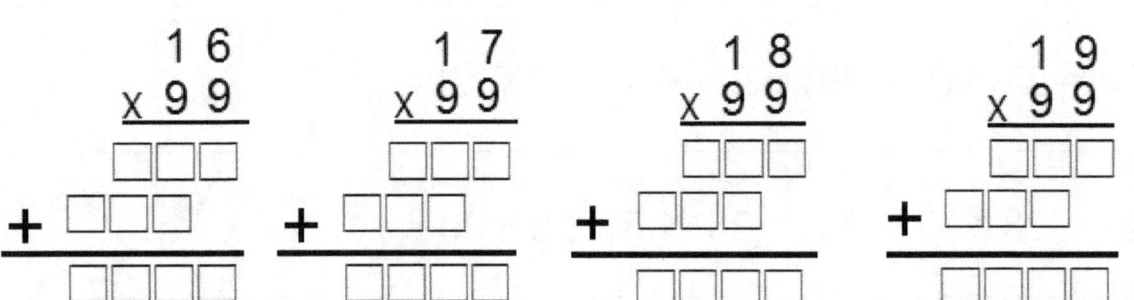

1144, 1232, 1320, 1408,
1496, 1584, 1672, 1188,
1188, 1287, 1386, 1485,
1584, 1683, 1782, 1881

dd × dd with carrying

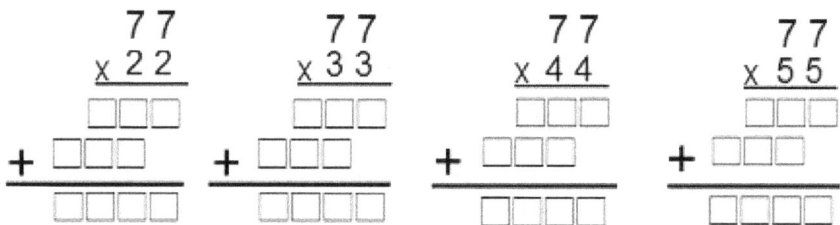

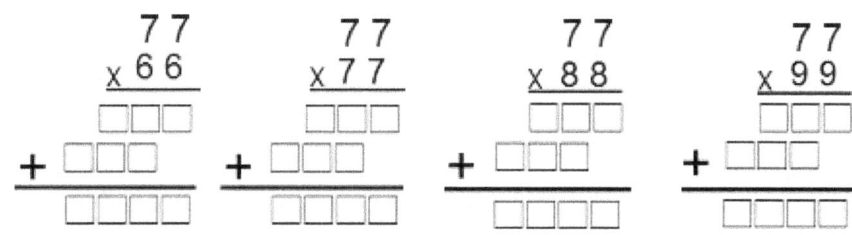

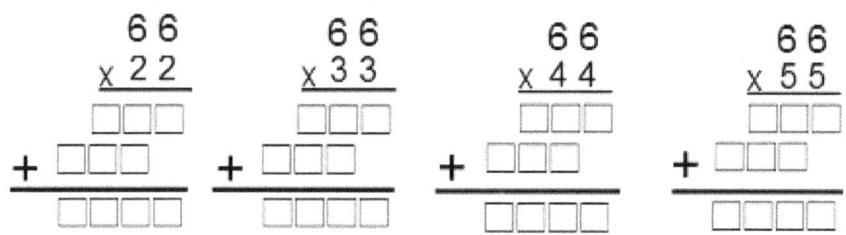

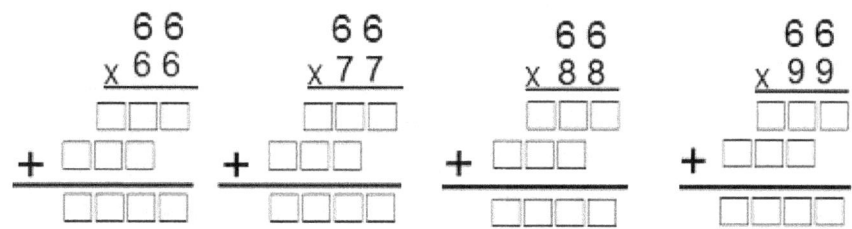

1694, 2541, 3388, 4235
5082, 5929, 6776, 7623
1452, 2178, 2904, 3630
4356, 5082, 5808, 6534

dd × dd without carrying

```
   47        32        23        38
 × 11      × 22      × 33      × 11
  517       704       759       418


   42        32        29        37
 × 22      × 22      × 11      × 11
  924       704       319       407


   27        33        37        14
 × 11      × 22      × 11      × 22
  297       726       407       308
```

Mom! I Learn Division Using Math-Chess-Puzzles Connection

dd × dd with carrying

```
   45        36        27        38
 x 25      x 46      x 57      x 48
 ☐☐☐      ☐☐☐      ☐☐☐      ☐☐☐
☐☐☐      ☐☐☐      ☐☐☐      ☐☐☐


   33        22        24        44
 x 22      x 33      x 22      x 22
```

1125, 1656, 1539, 1824
726, 726, 528, 968

dd × dd with carrying

```
   27        36        37        18
 × 27      × 56      × 67      × 78
 □□□      □□□      □□□      □□□
  □□□      □□□      □□□      □□□


   59        26        27        88
 × 29      × 46      × 37      × 68
 □□□□     □□□□     □□□□     □□□□
   □□        □□        □□        □□


   17        26        25        48
 × 21      × 42      × 56      × 36
```

729, 2016,
2479, 1404
1711, 1196, 999,
5894, 357, 1092,
1400, 1728

Mom! I Learn Division Using Math-Chess-Puzzles Connection

Ho Math Chess 何数棋谜 妈!我会棋谜式除法啦!

Frank Ho, Amanda Ho © 2004 – 2017, all rights reserved.

Student's Name _____ Date _____

dd × dd with carrying

```
   45        12        29        37
  x19       x47       x55       x23


   27        11        57        14
  x11       x56       x26       x52


   32        23        24        24
  x21       x42       x32       x13
```

855, 564, 1595, 851
297, 616, 1482, 728
672, 966, 768, 312

Mom! I Learn Division Using Math-Chess-Puzzles Connection

Ho Math Chess 何数棋谜 妈!我会棋谜式除法啦!

Frank Ho, Amanda Ho © 2004 – 2017, all rights reserved.

Student's Name _____ Date _____

dd × dd with carrying

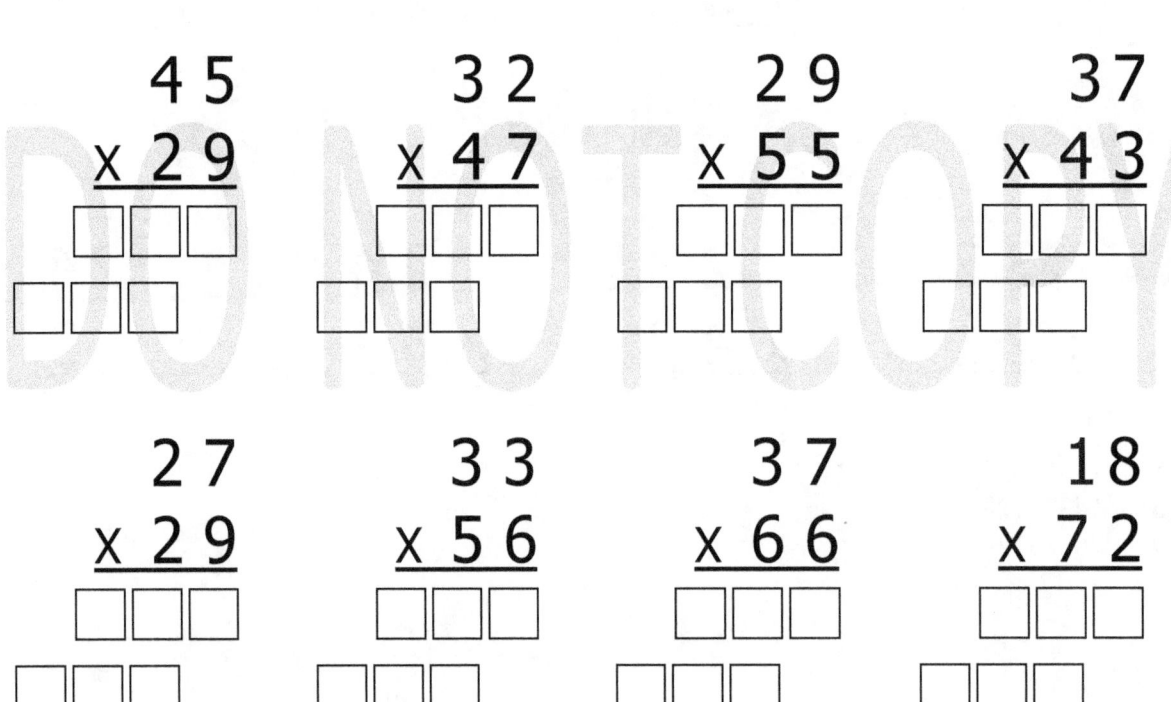

1316, 1656, 1512, 1748
1305, 1504, 1595, 1491
783, 1848, 2442, 1296

Mom! I Learn Division Using Math-Chess-Puzzles Connection

Ho Math Chess 何数棋谜 妈!我会棋谜式除法啦!

Frank Ho, Amanda Ho © 2004 − 2017, all rights reserved.

Student's Name _____ Date _____

dd × dd with carrying

```
  57        26        27        88
x 29      x 46      x 36      x 66
```

```
  51        36        29        68
x 28      x 42      x 31      x 62
```

```
  63        78        84        74
x 84      x 46      x 25      x 68
```

1653, 1196,
972, 5808
1428, 1512
899, 4216
5292, 3588,
2100, 5032

Mom! I Learn Division Using Math-Chess-Puzzles Connection

Ho Math Chess 何数棋谜 妈!我会棋谜式除法啦!

Frank Ho, Amanda Ho © 2004 – 2017, all rights reserved.

Student's Name _____ Date _____

dd × dd with carrying

```
   47        36        27        38
 x 28      x 46      x 56      x 46
 ☐☐☐      ☐☐☐      ☐☐☐      ☐☐☐
 ☐☐☐      ☐☐☐      ☐☐☐      ☐☐☐


   45        32        29        37
 x 29      x 47      x 55      x 43


   27        33        37        18
 x 29      x 56      x 66      x 72
```

1316, 1656, 1512, 1824
1305, 1504, 1595, 1591
783, 1848, 2492, 1296

Page 156

Mom! I Learn Division Using Math-Chess-Puzzles Connection

dd × dd with carrying

12 X 28 = 336   32 X 27 = 864   52 X 35 = 1820

33 X 45 = 1485   52 X 25 = 1300   63 X 21 = 1323

32 X 27 = 864   54 X 18 = 972   17 X 48 = 816

27 X 83 = 2241   62 X 24 = 1488   72 X 32 = 2304

Mom! I Learn Division Using Math-Chess-Puzzles Connection

Ho Math Chess 何数棋谜 妈!我会棋谜式除法啦!

Frank Ho, Amanda Ho © 2004 – 2017, all rights reserved.

Student's Name _____ Date _____

dd × dd with carrying

42 X 38 = 1596   35 X 25 = 875   52 X 25 = 1300

38 X 45 = 1710   48 X 25 = 1200   69 X 21 = 1449

76 X 27 = 2052   36 X 41 = 1476   95 X 28 = 2660

62 X 73 = 4528   53 X 26 = 1378   74 X 36 = 2664

Mom! I Learn Division Using Math-Chess-Puzzles Connection

Ho Math Chess 何数棋谜 妈!我会棋谜式除法啦!

Frank Ho, Amanda Ho © 2004 – 2017, all rights reserved.

Student's Name_____ Date_____

dd × dd with carrying

54 X 23 = 1242   62 X 23 = 1426   71 X 85 = 6035

53 X 45 = 2385   82 X 75 = 6150   63 X 48 = 3024

81 X 37 = 2997   76 X 52 = 3952   49 X 68 = 3332

77 X 84 = 648   93 X 54 = 5022   82 X 39 = 3198

Mom! I Learn Division Using Math-Chess-Puzzles Connection

ddd × dd with carrying

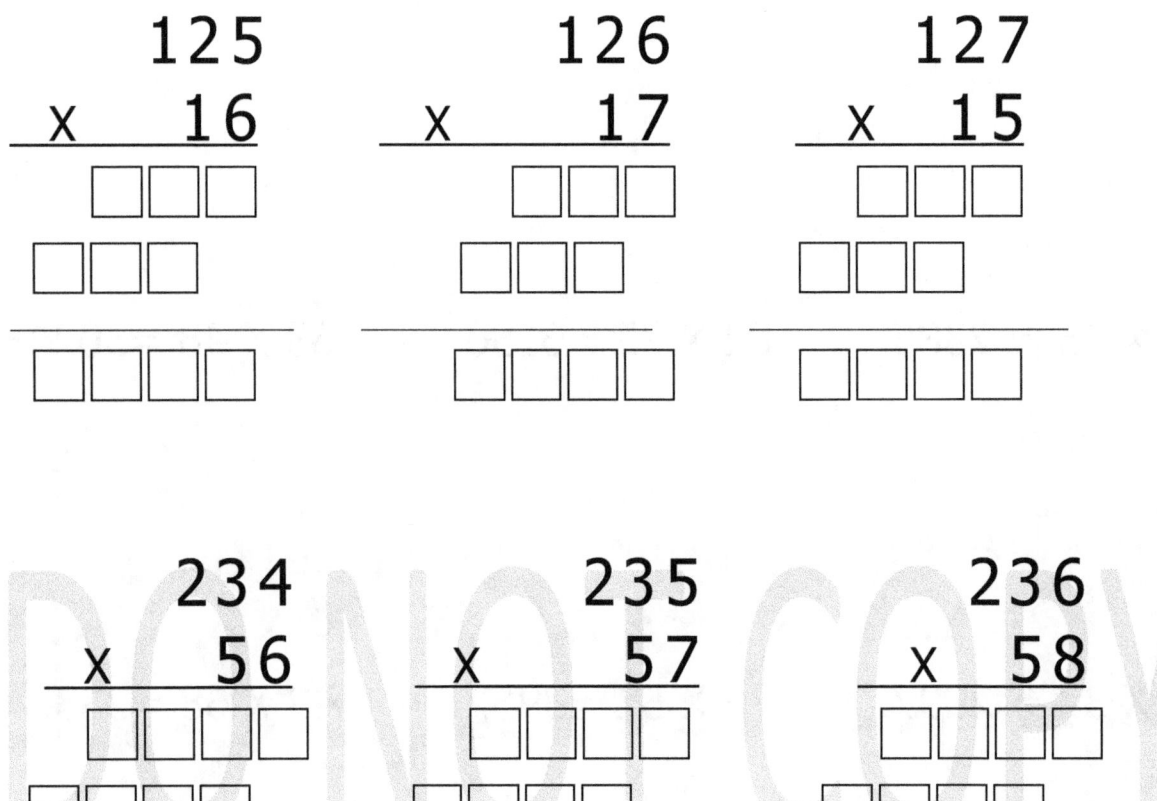

2000, 2142, 1905
13104, 13395, 13688

Mom! I Learn Division Using Math-Chess-Puzzles Connection

Ho Math Chess 何数棋谜 妈!我会棋谜式除法啦!

Frank Ho, Amanda Ho © 2004 – 2017, all rights reserved.

Student's Name _____ Date _____

ddd × dd with carrying

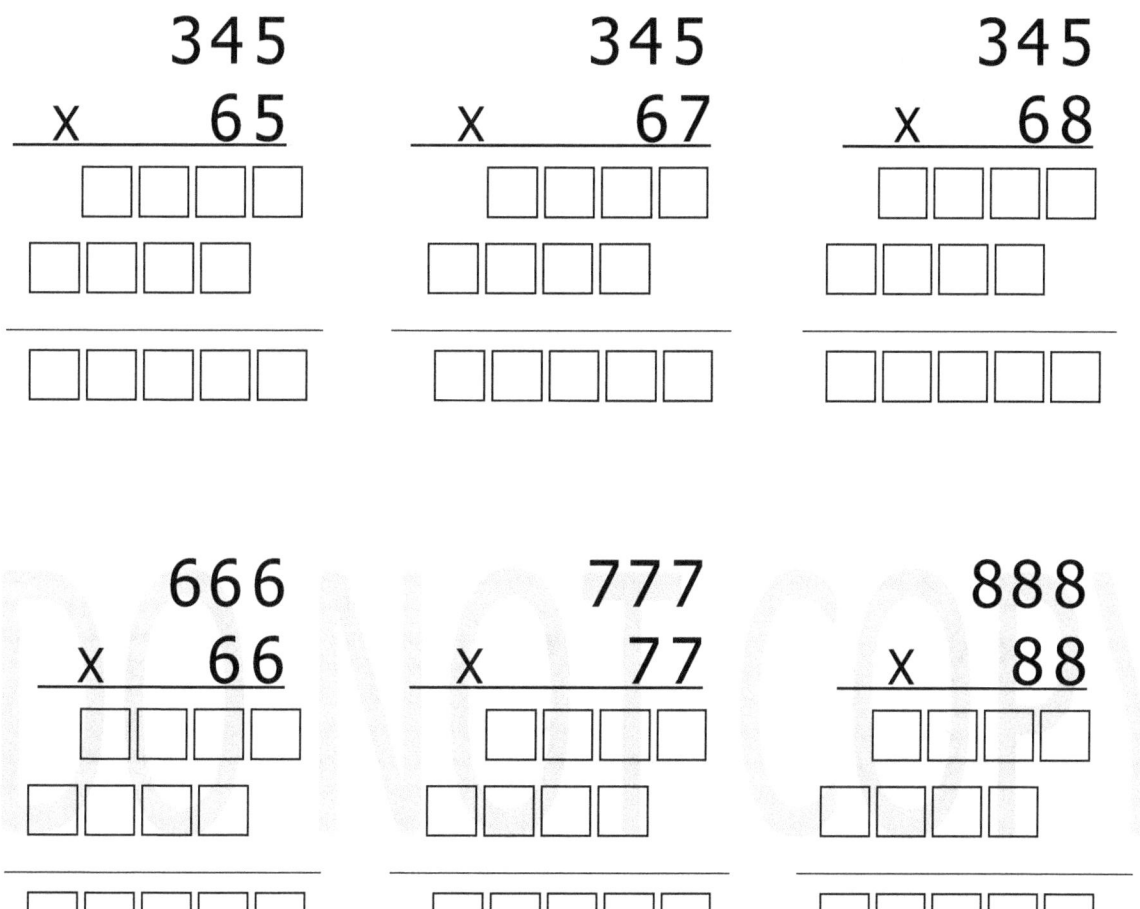

22425, 23115, 23460
43956, 59829, 78144

Mom! I Learn Division Using Math-Chess-Puzzles Connection

Ho Math Chess 何数棋谜 妈!我会棋谜式除法啦!

Frank Ho, Amanda Ho © 2004 – 2017, all rights reserved.

Student's Name _____ Date _____

ddd × dd with carrying

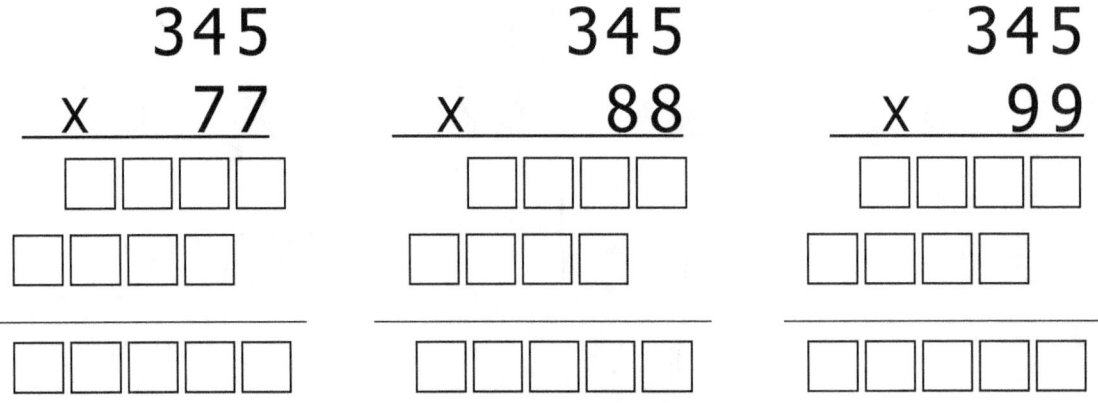

26565, 30360, 34155
76923, 87912, 98901

Mom! I Learn Division Using Math-Chess-Puzzles Connection

Ho Math Chess 何数棋谜 妈!我会棋谜式除法啦!

Frank Ho, Amanda Ho © 2004 – 2017, all rights reserved.

Student's Name _____ Date _____

ddd × dd with carrying

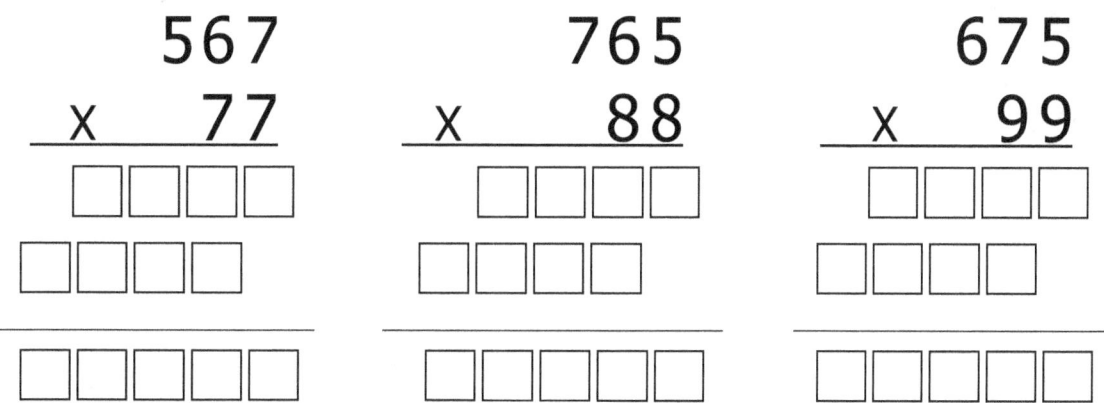

```
    567            765            675
 ×   77         ×   88         ×   99
  ☐☐☐☐          ☐☐☐☐           ☐☐☐☐
 ☐☐☐☐           ☐☐☐☐           ☐☐☐☐
 ─────          ─────           ─────
 ☐☐☐☐☐          ☐☐☐☐☐           ☐☐☐☐☐


    678            876            786
 ×   77         ×   88         ×   99
  ☐☐☐☐          ☐☐☐☐           ☐☐☐☐
 ☐☐☐☐           ☐☐☐☐           ☐☐☐☐
 ─────          ─────           ─────
 ☐☐☐☐☐          ☐☐☐☐☐           ☐☐☐☐☐
```

43659, 67320, 66825
52206, 77088, 77814

Mom! I Learn Division Using Math-Chess-Puzzles Connection

Ho Math Chess 何数棋谜 妈!我会棋谜式除法啦!

Frank Ho, Amanda Ho © 2004 – 2017, all rights reserved.

Student's Name _____ Date _____

ddd × dd without carrying

```
  472        425        432        384
x  11      x  22      x  33      x  11

  323        421        224        352
x  22      x  22      x  11      x  11

  286        412        374        243
x  11      x  22      x  11      x  22
```

5192, 9350, 14256, 4224
7106, 7262, 2464, 3872
3146, 9064, 4114, 5346

Mom! I Learn Division Using Math-Chess-Puzzles Connection

Ho Math Chess 何数棋谜 妈!我会棋谜式除法啦!

Frank Ho, Amanda Ho © 2004 – 2017, all rights reserved.

Student's Name _____ Date _____

ddd × dd with carrying

```
   474        316        237        589
 x  15      x  36      x  28      x  31


   457        628        275        874
 x  52      x  27      x  61      x  39


   577        368        779        147
 x  61      x  42      x  43      x  29
```

7110, 11376, 6636, 18259
23764, 16956, 16775, 34086
35197, 15456, 33497, 4263

Mom! I Learn Division Using Math-Chess-Puzzles Connection

ddd × dd with carrying

159 X 64 = 10176   357 X 24 = 8568   684 X 86 = 58824

268 X 57 = 15276   842 X 17 = 14314   368 X 43 = 15824

251 X 74 = 18574   961 X 19 = 18259   254 X 24 = 6096

741 X 27 = 20007   217 X 14 = 3038   364 X 43 = 15652

Mom! I Learn Division Using Math-Chess-Puzzles Connection

Ho Math Chess 何数棋谜 妈!我会棋谜式除法啦!

Frank Ho, Amanda Ho © 2004 – 2017, all rights reserved.

Student's Name _____ Date _____

ddd × dd with carrying

148 X 24 = 3552   572 X 47 = 26884   351 X 34 = 11934

381 X 56 = 21336   729 X 72 = 52488   349 X 764 = 266636

941 X 48 = 45168   149 X 24 = 3576   324 X 27 = 8748

327 X 34 = 11118   243 X 63 = 15309   751 X 82 = 61582

Mom! I Learn Division Using Math-Chess-Puzzles Connection

Ho Math Chess 何数棋谜 妈!我会棋谜式除法啦!

Frank Ho, Amanda Ho © 2004 – 2017, all rights reserved.

Student's Name _____ Date _____

d0d × dd

305 X 47 = 14335   507 X 55 = 27885   805 X 51 = 41055

609 X 34 = 20706   709 X 78 = 55302   501 X 39 = 19539

207 X 49 = 10143   608 X 56 = 34048   901 X 27 = 24327

206 X 91 = 18746   604 X 28 = 16912   908 X 62 = 56296

Mom! I Learn Division Using Math-Chess-Puzzles Connection

Ho Math Chess   何数棋谜   妈!我会棋谜式除法啦!

Frank Ho, Amanda Ho © 2004 – 2017, all rights reserved.

Student's Name _____ Date _____

dd X d0d

The 0s in the middle of a factor do not change the sum, so no product needs to be done.

Long form

```
    1 2 3
x   1 0 1
   □ □ □
  □ □ □
 □ □ □
 ─────────
 □ □ □ □ □
```

Short form

```
    1 2 3
x   1 0 1
   □ □ □
(Do not multiply 0)
 □ □ □
 ─────────
 □ □ □ □ □
```

```
    2 1           2 1           1 9           1 9
x 2 0 1       x 3 0 1       x 4 0 1       x 5 0 1
   □ □           □ □           □ □           □ □
  □ □           □ □           □ □           □ □
 ───────       ───────       ───────       ───────
 □ □ □ □       □ □ □ □       □ □ □ □       □ □ □ □
```

12423, 12423, 4221, 6321, 7619, 9519

Page 169

Mom! I Learn Division Using Math-Chess-Puzzles Connection

Ho Math Chess 何数棋谜 妈!我会棋谜式除法啦!

Frank Ho, Amanda Ho © 2004 – 2017, all rights reserved.

Student's Name _____ Date _____

***** Part 3 Traditional worksheets *****

This part contains more of traditional worksheets.

Mom! I Learn Division Using Math-Chess-Puzzles Connection

Ho Math Chess 何数棋谜 妈!我会棋谜式除法啦!

Frank Ho, Amanda Ho © 2004 − 2017, all rights reserved.

Student's Name_____ Date_____

Less than or equal $\leq$

The whole numbers $\leq$ 5 are 0, 1, 2, 3, 4, 5.
Fill in ☐ with the greatest factor such that the inequality exists.

Greatest factor   Greatest factor

3☐ × 2 $\leq$ 6   3☐ × ♗ $\leq$ 9

3☐ × 2 $\leq$ 7   3☐ × 3 $\leq$ 10

4☐ × 2 $\leq$ 8   3☐ × ♗ $\leq$ 11

4☐ × 2 $\leq$ ♕   4☐ × 3 $\leq$ 12

5☐ × 2 $\leq$ 10   4☐ × 3 $\leq$ 13

5☐ × 2 $\leq$ 11   4☐ × ♘ $\leq$ 14

8☐ × 4 $\leq$ 33   9☐ × 4 $\leq$ 37

9☐ × 4 $\leq$ 37   9☐ × 4 $\leq$ 38

6☐ × 5 $\leq$ 31   3☐ × ♖ $\leq$ 17

3☐ × 6 $\leq$ 19   4☐ × 6 $\leq$ 26

1☐ × 7 $\leq$ 11   2☐ × 7 $\leq$ 15

2☐ × 7 $\leq$ 20   3☐ × 7 $\leq$ 25

3☐ × 8 $\leq$ 26   5☐ × 8 $\leq$ 41

3☐ × 9 $\leq$ 29   4☐ × ♕ $\leq$ 44

Page 171

Mom! I Learn Division Using Math-Chess-Puzzles Connection

Ho Math Chess 何数棋谜 妈!我会棋谜式除法啦!

Frank Ho, Amanda Ho © 2004 – 2017, all rights reserved.

Student's Name _____ Date _____

Division notations

Symbols	Verbal expressions	Comments	Concept
$8 \div 2$	8 divided by 2 is (equals) 4.	Dividend ÷ divisor = quotient	♟♟♟♟ ♟♟♟♟ There are 8 pawns. $8 = 2 \times 4$ 1. If eight pawns are divided evenly into two group, how many pawns does each group get? 2. How many groups of 4 pawns are there?
$8 / 2$	The quotient of 8 and 2 is (equals) 4.		
$\frac{8}{2}$	The quotient of 8 divided 2 is (is equal) 4.		
$2\overline{)8}$	2 divides 8 is 4.		
$2\underline{)8}$	2 goes into 8 is 4.		

Mom! I Learn Division Using Math-Chess-Puzzles Connection

Ho Math Chess 何数棋谜 妈!我会棋谜式除法啦!

Frank Ho, Amanda Ho © 2004 – 2017, all rights reserved.

Student's Name _____ Date _____

Divisible by 2

Circle those numbers which can be divided by 2 with no remainder.

Observe the results and write the observation _____

♗	2	♘	4	♖	6	7	8	♕	10
11	12	13	14	15	16	17	18	19	20
21	22	23	24	25	26	27	28	29	30
31	32	33	34	35	36	37	38	39	40
41	42	43	44	45	46	47	48	49	50
51	52	53	54	55	56	57	58	59	60
61	62	63	64	65	66	67	68	69	70
71	72	73	74	75	76	77	78	79	80
81	82	83	84	85	86	87	88	89	90
91	92	93	94	95	96	97	98	99	100

35

Mom! I Learn Division Using Math-Chess-Puzzles Connection

Ho Math Chess　何数棋谜　妈!我会棋谜式除法啦!

Frank Ho, Amanda Ho © 2004 – 2017, all rights reserved.

Student's Name _____ Date _____

Divisible by 3

Circle those numbers which can be divided by 3 with no remainder.

Observe the results and write the observation: **If the sum of the digits is divisible by 3, then the number is divisible by 3.**

♗	2	♘	4	♖	6	7	8	♕	10
11	12	13	14	15	16	17	18	19	20
21	22	23	24	25	26	27	28	29	30
31	32	33	34	35	36	37	38	39	40
41	42	43	44	45	46	47	48	49	50
51	52	53	54	55	56	57	58	59	60
61	62	63	64	65	66	67	68	69	70
71	72	73	74	75	76	77	78	79	80
81	82	83	84	85	86	87	88	89	90
91	92	93	94	95	96	97	98	99	100

Mom! I Learn Division Using Math-Chess-Puzzles Connection

Ho Math Chess　何数棋谜　妈!我会棋谜式除法啦!

Frank Ho, Amanda Ho © 2004 – 2017, all rights reserved.

Student's Name _____ Date _____

Divisible by 4

Circle those numbers which can be divided by 4 with no remainder.

Observe the results and write the observation: **the unit digit is 0, 2, 4, 6, or 8.**

♗	2	♘	4	♖	6	7	8	♕	10
11	12	13	14	15	16	17	18	19	20
21	22	23	24	25	26	27	28	29	30
31	32	33	34	35	36	37	38	39	40
41	42	43	44	45	46	47	48	49	50
51	52	53	54	55	56	57	58	59	60
61	62	63	64	65	66	67	68	69	70
71	72	73	74	75	76	77	78	79	80
81	82	83	84	85	86	87	88	89	90
91	92	93	94	95	96	97	98	99	100

No part of this publication can be copied, duplicated, or reproduced.

Mom! I Learn Division Using Math-Chess-Puzzles Connection

Ho Math Chess 何数棋谜 妈!我会棋谜式除法啦!

Frank Ho, Amanda Ho © 2004 – 2017, all rights reserved.

Student's Name _____ Date _____

Divisible by 5

Circle those numbers which can be divided by 5 with no remainder.

Observe the results and write the observation: **The last digit is 5 or 0.**

♗	2	♘	4	♖	6	7	8	♕	10
11	12	13	14	15	16	17	18	19	20
21	22	23	24	25	26	27	28	29	30
31	32	33	34	35	36	37	38	39	40
41	42	43	44	45	46	47	48	49	50
51	52	53	54	55	56	57	58	59	60
61	62	63	64	65	66	67	68	69	70
71	72	73	74	75	76	77	78	79	80
81	82	83	84	85	86	87	88	89	90
91	92	93	94	95	96	97	98	99	100

Mom! I Learn Division Using Math-Chess-Puzzles Connection

Ho Math Chess   何数棋谜   妈!我会棋谜式除法啦!

Frank Ho, Amanda Ho © 2004 – 2017, all rights reserved.

Student's Name _____ Date _____

Divisible by 6

Circle those numbers which can be divided by 6 with no remainder.

Observe the results and write the observation: **It has to be an even number and divisible by 3.**

♗	2	♘	4	♖	6	7	8	♕	10
11	12	13	14	15	16	17	18	19	20
21	22	23	24	25	26	27	28	29	30
31	32	33	34	35	36	37	38	39	40
41	42	43	44	45	46	47	48	49	50
51	52	53	54	55	56	57	58	59	60
61	62	63	64	65	66	67	68	69	70
71	72	73	74	75	76	77	78	79	80
81	82	83	84	85	86	87	88	89	90
91	92	93	94	95	96	97	98	99	100

Mom! I Learn Division Using Math-Chess-Puzzles Connection

Ho Math Chess   何数棋谜   妈!我会棋谜式除法啦!

Frank Ho, Amanda Ho © 2004 – 2017, all rights reserved.

Student's Name _____ Date _____

Divisible by 9

Circle those numbers which can be divided by 9 with no remainder.

Observe the results and write the observation: **The sum of the digits is divisible by 9.**

♗	2	♘	4	♖	6	7	8	♕	10
11	12	13	14	15	16	17	18	19	20
21	22	23	24	25	26	27	28	29	30
31	32	33	34	35	36	37	38	39	40
41	42	43	44	45	46	47	48	49	50
51	52	53	54	55	56	57	58	59	60
61	62	63	64	65	66	67	68	69	70
71	72	73	74	75	76	77	78	79	80
81	82	83	84	85	86	87	88	89	90
91	92	93	94	95	96	97	98	99	100

Mom! I Learn Division Using Math-Chess-Puzzles Connection

Ho Math Chess 何数棋谜   妈!我会棋谜式除法啦!

Frank Ho, Amanda Ho © 2004 – 2017, all rights reserved.

Student's Name _____ Date _____

Divisible by 10

Circle those numbers which can be divided by 10 with no remainder.

Observe the results and write the observation: **The last digit is 0.**

♙	2	♞	4	♜	6	7	8	♛	10
11	12	13	14	15	16	17	18	19	20
21	22	23	24	25	26	27	28	29	30
31	32	33	34	35	36	37	38	39	40
41	42	43	44	45	46	47	48	49	50
51	52	53	54	55	56	57	58	59	60
61	62	63	64	65	66	67	68	69	70
71	72	73	74	75	76	77	78	79	80
81	82	83	84	85	86	87	88	89	90
91	92	93	94	95	96	97	98	99	100

Mom! I Learn Division Using Math-Chess-Puzzles Connection

Ho Math Chess 何数棋谜 妈!我会棋谜式除法啦!

Frank Ho, Amanda Ho © 2004 – 2017, all rights reserved.

Student's Name _____ Date_____

Forward slash (/) those numbers that are divisible by 2 and backslash (\) those numbers that are divisible by 4.

Observe the results and write the observation _____

♙	2	♘	4	♖	6	7	8	♕	10
11	12	13	14	15	16	17	18	19	20
21	22	23	24	25	26	27	28	29	30
31	32	33	34	35	36	37	38	39	40
41	42	43	44	45	46	47	48	49	50
51	52	53	54	55	56	57	58	59	60
61	62	63	64	65	66	67	68	69	70
71	72	73	74	75	76	77	78	79	80
81	82	83	84	85	86	87	88	89	90
91	92	93	94	95	96	97	98	99	100

Mom! I Learn Division Using Math-Chess-Puzzles Connection

Ho Math Chess　何数棋谜　妈!我会棋谜式除法啦!

Frank Ho, Amanda Ho © 2004 − 2017, all rights reserved.

Student's Name _____ Date _____

Forward slash (/) those numbers that are divisible by 3 and backslash (\) those numbers that are divisible by 9.

Observe the results and write the observation _____

♙	2	♗	4	♖	6	7	8	♕	10
11	12	13	14	15	16	17	18	19	20
21	22	23	24	25	26	27	28	29	30
31	32	33	34	35	36	37	38	39	40
41	42	43	44	45	46	47	48	49	50
51	52	53	54	55	56	57	58	59	60
61	62	63	64	65	66	67	68	69	70
71	72	73	74	75	76	77	78	79	80
81	82	83	84	85	86	87	88	89	90
91	92	93	94	95	96	97	98	99	100

Mom! I Learn Division Using Math-Chess-Puzzles Connection

Ho Math Chess 何数棋谜 妈!我会棋谜式除法啦!

Frank Ho, Amanda Ho © 2004 − 2017, all rights reserved.

Student's Name _____ Date_____

Forward slash (/) those numbers that are divisible by 5 and backslash (\) those numbers that are divisible by 10.

Observe the results and write the observation _____

♙	2	♗	4	♖	6	7	8	♕	10
11	12	13	14	15	16	17	18	19	20
21	22	23	24	25	26	27	28	29	30
31	32	33	34	35	36	37	38	39	40
41	42	43	44	45	46	47	48	49	50
51	52	53	54	55	56	57	58	59	60
61	62	63	64	65	66	67	68	69	70
71	72	73	74	75	76	77	78	79	80
81	82	83	84	85	86	87	88	89	90
91	92	93	94	95	96	97	98	99	100

Mom! I Learn Division Using Math-Chess-Puzzles Connection

Ho Math Chess 何数棋谜 妈!我会棋谜式除法啦!

Frank Ho, Amanda Ho © 2004 − 2017, all rights reserved.

Student's Name _____ Date _____

Dividing by relating

⌐÷ 2 ÷¬ ♙ ÷ 2 2☐ ♙ ☐1 ÷ ♙ ☐2	⌐÷ 4 ÷¬ 2 ÷ 4 2☐ 2 ☐1 ÷ ♙ ☐2	⌐÷ 8 ÷¬ 4 ÷ 4 2☐ 8 ☐2 ÷ ♙ ☐1
⌐÷ 16 ÷¬ 4 ÷ 8 4☐ 4 ☐2 ÷ 1 ☐4	⌐÷ 30 ÷¬ ♖ ÷ 6 6☐ ♖ ☐5 ÷ 1 ☐6	⌐÷ 42 ÷¬ 6 ÷ 7 7☐ 6 ☐6 ÷ ♙ ☐7
⌐÷ 56 ÷¬ 7 ÷ 8 8☐ 7 ☐7 ÷ ♙ ☐8	⌐÷ 72 ÷¬ 8 ÷ ♛ 9☐ 8 ☐8 ÷ 1 ☐9	⌐÷ 28 ÷¬ 4 ÷ 7 7☐ 4 ☐4 ÷ ♙ ☐7

Mom! I Learn Division Using Math-Chess-Puzzles Connection

Multiplying by relating

↳÷ 24 ÷↲	↳÷ 60 ÷↲	↳÷ 12 ÷↲
♘ ÷ 4	♘ ÷ 5	♝ ÷ 4
8☐ ♘ ☐6	20☐ 4 ☐	4☐ ♝ ☐3
÷	12	÷
♙	÷	♙
☐8	♙	☐4
	☐15	

↳÷ 35 ÷↲	↳÷ 15 ÷↲	↳÷ 18 ÷↲
5 ÷ 7	♘ ÷ ♖	♘ ÷ ♘
7☐ ♖ ☐5	5☐ 3 ☐3	6☐ 6 ☐6
÷	÷	÷
1	1	♙
☐7	☐5	☐3

↳÷ 18 ÷↲	↳÷ 21 ÷↲	↳÷ 24 ÷↲
♘ ÷ ♘	♘ ÷ ♘	♘ ÷ ♘
6☐ 6 ☐6	7☐ 7 ☐7	8☐ 8 ☐8
÷	÷	÷
♙	1	♙
☐3	☐3	☐3

Mom! I Learn Division Using Math-Chess-Puzzles Connection

Ho Math Chess 何数棋谜 妈!我会棋谜式除法啦!

Frank Ho, Amanda Ho © 2004 − 2017, all rights reserved.

Student's Name _____ Date _____

From multiplication to division procedure

In this workbook, the division procedure is based on the reverse procedure of multiplication, For example, $\square \times 2 = 6$, the division procedure is to find out what is the greatest factor of $\square$ such that $\square \times 2 \leq 6$ with the following division notation

$$2\overline{)6}$$

There are a few restrictions to follow such as the divisor must be a whole number and the remainder must be less than the divisor and divide the dividends one digit at a time. The reason of dividing the dividend digit one at a time is it automatically takes care of the zeros at the beginning, in the middle, and at the end. The divisor must be the whole number would make the decimal division easier.

A simple problem could be used to demonstrate the above concept. For example, $25 is to be divided equally among 5 children. The divisor is 5 children so it must be the whole number, but the $ amount could be decimals. If we would write the division as $25 ÷ 5 = $\frac{\$25}{5}$ then

$$\frac{\$25}{5} = \frac{2\$10 + 1\$5}{5} = 2\$2 + \$1 = \$5$$

If we follow the above procedure for the division, it would be very tedious, so we convert 2 $10 to 20 of $1 and add $5 to be 5 of $1. So the division procedure will be

$$5\overline{)25}$$

. This is the reason that quotient 5 must be placed rightmost to show we actually divide 25 of 1$ by 5 children.

For decimal division, the division flowchart included in this workbook can also be used. Bring down 0 until the desired decimal places are found. If the dividend has a decimal point, line up a decimal point in the quotient and just carry out the division as it is whole number division. If the dividend is a whole number, place a decimal point at the place after the dividend digit has been all used and before 0 needs to be brought down.

Mom! I Learn Division Using Math-Chess-Puzzles Connection

Ho Math Chess 何数棋谜 妈!我会棋谜式除法啦!

Frank Ho, Amanda Ho © 2004 − 2017, all rights reserved.

Student's Name _____ Date _____

From multiplication to division (d ÷ d)

Multiplication	Division
factor × factor ≤ product	$\overset{quotinet}{divisor\sqrt{dividend}}$
3☐ × 2 ≤ 6	×☐3 ← Think what times 2 is ≤ 6. 2)6 − ☐ ← Do subtraction 0 ← Remainder (what is left) = 0
4☐ × 2 ≤ 8	×☐4 ← Think what times 2 is ≤ 8. 2)8 − ☐ ← Do subtraction 0 ← Remainder (what is left) = 0
3☐ × 3 ≤ ♛	×☐3 ← Think what times 2 is ≤ 9. 3)9 − ☐ ← Do subtraction 0 ← Remainder (what is left) = 0

Mom! I Learn Division Using Math-Chess-Puzzles Connection

Ho Math Chess 何数棋谜 妈!我会棋谜式除法啦!

Frank Ho, Amanda Ho © 2004 − 2017, all rights reserved.

Student's Name _____ Date _____

From multiplication to division (d ÷ d)

4☐ × 2 ≤ 8	8 = ☐4 × 2	$\begin{array}{r} \times\ \square 4 \\ 2\overline{)8} \\ -\ \underline{\square} \\ 0 \end{array}$ ← step 1: What times 2 is ≤ 8. ← step 2: 8 − 8 = 0 ← Remainder = 0
0☐ × 3 ≤ 0	0 = ☐0 × ♗	$\begin{array}{r} \times\ \square 0 \\ 3\overline{)0} \\ -\ \underline{\square} \\ 0 \end{array}$ ← step 1: What times 3 is ≤ 0. ← step 2: 0 − 0 = 0 ← Remainder = 0
1☐ × 6 ≤ 6	6 = ☐1 × 6	$\begin{array}{r} \times\ \square 1 \\ 6\overline{)6} \\ -\ \underline{\square} \\ 0 \end{array}$ ← step 1: What times 6 is ≤ 6. ← step 2: 6 − 6 = 0 ← Remainder = 0

Mom! I Learn Division Using Math-Chess-Puzzles Connection

dd ÷ d with 1-digit quotient and no remainder

7□ × 6 = 42	42 = □₆ × 7	**Step1:** Do □ × 6 ≤ 42 (4 is too small, use 42) **Place the quotient in the rightmost position** × □₇ ← step 2: 7 × 6 = 42 6)42 −□□ ← step 3: 42 − 42 = 0 **0** ← Remainder = 0
9□ × 2 = 18	18 = □₂ × ♕	**Step1:** Do □ × 2 ≤ 18 (1 is too small, use 18) **Place the quotient in the rightmost position** × □₉ ← step 2: 9 × 2 = 18 2)18 −□□ ← step 3: 18 − 18 = 0 **0** ← Remainder = 0
9□ × ♕ = 81	81 = □₉ × 9	**Step1:** Do □ × 9 ≤ 81 (8 is too small, use 81) **Place the quotient in the rightmost position** × □₉ ← step 2: 9 × 9 = 81 9)81 −□□ ← step 3: 81 − 81 = 0 **0** ← Remainder = 0

Mom! I Learn Division Using Math-Chess-Puzzles Connection

Ho Math Chess　何数棋谜　妈!我会棋谜式除法啦!

Frank Ho, Amanda Ho © 2004 − 2017, all rights reserved.

Student's Name _____ Date _____

dd ÷ d with 1-digit quotient and no remainder

Step 1: Do ☐ × 3 ≤ 15 (1 is too small, use 15)

×　☐5 ← step 2: Do multiplication, 5 × 3 =

15

3)15

− ☐☐ ← step 3: Do subtraction, 15 − 15 = 0

0 ← Remainder = 0

Step 1: Do ☐ × 3 ≤ 18 (3 is too small, use 18)

×　☐6 ← step 2: Do multiplication, 6 × 3 =

18

3)18

− ☐☐ ← step 3: Do subtraction, 18 − 18 = 0

0 ← Remainder = 0

Step 1: Do ☐ × 5 ≤ 25 (2 is too small, use 25)

×　☐5 ← step 2: Do multiplication

5)25

− ☐☐ ← step 3: Do subtraction

0 ← Remainder = 0

Step 1: Do ☐ × 4 ≤ 28 (2 is too small, use 28)

×　☐7 ← step 2: Do multiplication

4)28

− ☐☐ ← step 3: Do subtraction

0 ← Remainder = 0

Step 1: Do ☐ × 4 ≤ 32 (3 is too small, use 32)

×　☐8 ← step 2: Do multiplication

4)32

− ☐☐ ← step 3: Do subtraction

0 ← Remainder = 0

Step 1: Do ☐ × 2 ≤ 16 (1 is too small, use 16)

×　☐8 ← step 2: Do multiplication

2)16

− ☐☐ ← step 3: Do subtraction

0 ← Remainder = 0

Mom! I Learn Division Using Math-Chess-Puzzles Connection

Ho Math Chess 何数棋谜 妈!我会棋谜式除法啦!

Frank Ho, Amanda Ho © 2004 − 2017, all rights reserved.

Student's Name _____ Date _____

From multiplication to division

$6\Box \times 2 \leq 12$ $2\Box \times 6 \leq 12$	$6\overline{)12}$ with $\times \Box 2$ on top and $\Box\Box$ below	$2\overline{)12}$ with $\times \Box 6$ on top and $\Box\Box$ below	$12 \div 2 = \Box_6$ $12 \div 6 = \Box_2$
$6\Box \times 3 \leq 18$ $3\Box \times \leq 18$	$6\overline{)18}$ with $\times \Box 3$ on top and $\Box\Box$ below	$3\overline{)18}$ with $\times \Box 6$ on top and $\Box\Box$ below	$18 \div ♞ = \Box_6$ $18 \div 6 = \Box_3$
$3\Box \times 4 \leq 12$ $4\Box \times 3 \leq 12$	$4\overline{)12}$ with $\times \Box 3$ on top and $\Box\Box$ below	$3\overline{)12}$ with $\times \Box 4$ on top and $\Box\Box$ below	$12 \div 4 = \Box_3$ $12 \div ♗ = \Box_4$

Mom! I Learn Division Using Math-Chess-Puzzles Connection

Ho Math Chess 何数棋谜 妈!我会棋谜式除法啦!

Frank Ho, Amanda Ho © 2004 − 2017, all rights reserved.

Student's Name _____ Date _____

From multiplication to division

$_3\square \times 5 \leq 15$ $_5\square \times 3 \leq 15$	$5\overline{)15}$ with $\times \square 3$ on top, $\square\square$ below	$3\overline{)15}$ with $\times \square 5$ on top, $\square\square$ below	$15 \div ♝ = \square_5$ $15 \div ♖ = \square_3$
$_6\square \times ♖ \leq 30$ $_5\square \times 6 \leq 30$	$6\overline{)30}$ with $\times \square 5$ on top, $\square\square$ below	$5\overline{)30}$ with $\times \square 6$ on top, $\square\square$ below	$30 \div 5 = \square_6$ $30 \div 6 = \square_5$
$_8\square \times 5 \leq 40$ $_5\square \times 8 \leq 40$	$5\overline{)40}$ with $\times \square 8$ on top, $\square\square$ below	$8\overline{)40}$ with $\times \square 5$ on top, $\square\square$ below	$40 \div 5 = \square_8$ $40 \div 8 = \square_5$

Mom! I Learn Division Using Math-Chess-Puzzles Connection

Ho Math Chess 何数棋谜 妈!我会棋谜式除法啦!

Frank Ho, Amanda Ho © 2004 − 2017, all rights reserved.

Student's Name _____ Date _____

From multiplication to division

$_9\square \times 5 \leq 45$ $_5\square \times 9 \leq 45$	$5\overline{)45}$ with $\times \square 9$ on top and $\square\square$ below	$9\overline{)45}$ with $\times \square 5$ on top and $\square\square$ below	$45 \div 9 = \square_5$ $45 \div \text{♖} = \square_9$
$_9\square \times \text{♖} \leq 10$ $_5\square \times 2 \leq 10$	$2\overline{)10}$ with $\times \square 5$ on top and $\square\square$ below	$5\overline{)10}$ with $\times \square 2$ on top and $\square\square$ below	$10 \div 5 = \square_2$ $10 \div 2 = \square_5$
$_5\square \times 5 \leq 25$ $_5\square \times \text{♖} \leq 25$	$5\overline{)25}$ with $\times \square 5$ on top and $\square\square$ below	$5\overline{)25}$ with $\times \square 5$ on top and $\square\square$ below	$25 \div 5 = \square_5$ $25 \div 5 = \square_5$

Mom! I Learn Division Using Math-Chess-Puzzles Connection

Ho Math Chess 何数棋谜 妈!我会棋谜式除法啦!

Frank Ho, Amanda Ho © 2004 – 2017, all rights reserved.

Student's Name _____ Date _____

From multiplication to division

$5\square \times 4 \leq 20$ $4\square \times 5 \leq 20$	$5\overline{)20}$ with $\times \square 4$ on top, $\square\square$ below	$4\overline{)20}$ with $\times \square 5$ on top, $\square\square$ below	$20 \div 4 = \square_5$ $20 \div \unicode{x2656} = \square_4$
$7\square \times \unicode{x2656} \leq 35$ $5\square \times 7 \leq 35$	$7\overline{)35}$ with $\times \square 5$ on top, $\square\square$ below	$5\overline{)35}$ with $\times \square 7$ on top, $\square\square$ below	$35 \div 5 = \square_7$ $35 \div 7 = \square_5$
$5\square \times 8 \leq 40$ $8\square \times \unicode{x2656} \leq 40$	$5\overline{)40}$ with $\times \square 8$ on top, $\square\square$ below	$8\overline{)40}$ with $\times \square 5$ on top, $\square\square$ below	$40 \div \unicode{x2656} = \square_8$ $40 \div 8 = \square_5$

Mom! I Learn Division Using Math-Chess-Puzzles Connection

Ho Math Chess 何数棋谜 妈!我会棋谜式除法啦!

Frank Ho, Amanda Ho © 2004 − 2017, all rights reserved.

Student's Name _____ Date_____

From multiplication to division (d ÷ d)

6□ × 4 ≤ 24 4□ × 6 ≤ 24	×□6 4)24 □□	×□4 6)24 □□	24÷4= □6 24÷6= □4
7□ × 6 ≤ 42 6□ × 7 ≤ 42	×□6 7)42 □□	×□7 6)42 □□	42÷6= □7 42÷7= □6
6□ × 6 ≤ 36 6□ × 6 ≤ 36	×□6 6)36 □□	×□6 6)36 □□	36÷6= □6 36÷6= □6

Page 194

Mom! I Learn Division Using Math-Chess-Puzzles Connection

Ho Math Chess 何数棋谜 妈!我会棋谜式除法啦!

Frank Ho, Amanda Ho © 2004 − 2017, all rights reserved.

Student's Name _____ Date _____

dd ÷ d with 1-digit quotient and no remainder

$6\square \times 5 \leq 30$ $6\square \times ♜ \leq 30$	$\overset{\times \square 5}{6\overline{)30}}$ $\square\square$	$\overset{\times \square 6}{5\overline{)30}}$ $\square\square$	$30 \div 5 = \square_6$ $30 \div 6 = \square_5$
$4\square \times 6 \leq 24$ $6\square \times 4 \leq 24$	$\overset{\times \square 6}{4\overline{)24}}$ $\square\square$	$\overset{\times \square 4}{6\overline{)24}}$ $\square\square$	$24 \div 6 = \square_4$ $24 \div 4 = \square_6$
$6\square \times ♝ \leq 18$ $3\square \times 6 \leq 18$	$\overset{\times \square 3}{6\overline{)18}}$ $\square\square$	$\overset{\times \square 6}{3\overline{)18}}$ $\square\square$	$18 \div 6 = \square_3$ $18 \div ♝ = \square_6$

Mom! I Learn Division Using Math-Chess-Puzzles Connection

Ho Math Chess 何数棋谜 妈!我会棋谜式除法啦!

Frank Ho, Amanda Ho © 2004 − 2017, all rights reserved.

Student's Name _____ Date _____

dd ÷ d with 1-digit quotient and no remainder

$9\square \times 5 \leq 45$ $5\square \times ♛ \leq 45$	$\begin{array}{r} \times \square 9 \\ 5\overline{)45} \\ \square\square \end{array}$	$\begin{array}{r} \times \square 5 \\ 9\overline{)45} \\ \square\square \end{array}$	$45 \div 5 = \square_9$ $45 \div ♛ = \square_5$
$8\square \times ♖ \leq 40$ $5\square \times 8 \leq 40$	$\begin{array}{r} \times \square 8 \\ 5\overline{)40} \\ \square\square \end{array}$	$\begin{array}{r} \times \square 5 \\ 8\overline{)40} \\ \square\square \end{array}$	$40 \div 5 = \square_8$ $40 \div 8 = \square_5$
$5\square \times 6 \leq 30$ $6\square \times 5 \leq 30$	$\begin{array}{r} \times \square 5 \\ 6\overline{)30} \\ \square\square \end{array}$	$\begin{array}{r} \times \square 6 \\ 5\overline{)30} \\ \square\square \end{array}$	$30 \div 6 = \square_5$ $30 \div ♖ = \square_6$

Mom! I Learn Division Using Math-Chess-Puzzles Connection

Ho Math Chess   何数棋谜   妈!我会棋谜式除法啦!

Frank Ho, Amanda Ho © 2004 — 2017, all rights reserved.

Student's Name _____ Date _____

dd ÷ d with 1-digit quotient and no remainder

$7\square \times ♖ \leq 35$ $5\square \times 7 \leq 35$	$\begin{array}{r} \times \square 7 \\ 5\overline{)35} \\ \underline{\square\square} \end{array}$	$\begin{array}{r} \times \square 5 \\ 7\overline{)35} \\ \underline{\square\square} \end{array}$	$35 \div ♖ = \square 7$ $35 \div 7 = \square 5$
$6\square \times 5 \leq 30$ $5\square \times 6 \leq 30$	$\begin{array}{r} \times \square 6 \\ 5\overline{)30} \\ \underline{\square\square} \end{array}$	$\begin{array}{r} \times \square 5 \\ 6\overline{)30} \\ \underline{\square\square} \end{array}$	$30 \div ♖ = \square 6$ $30 \div 6 = \square 5$
$5\square \times 4 \leq 20$ $4\square \times ♖ \leq 20$	$\begin{array}{r} \times \square 4 \\ 5\overline{)20} \\ \underline{\square\square} \end{array}$	$\begin{array}{r} \times \square 5 \\ 4\overline{)20} \\ \underline{\square\square} \end{array}$	$20 \div 4 = \square 5$ $20 \div ♖ = \square 4$

Mom! I Learn Division Using Math-Chess-Puzzles Connection

dd ÷ d with remainder vs. no remainder

$35 \div 7 = \Box_5$	$5\overline{)35}$ with $\times \Box 7$ above	$5\overline{)36}$ with $\times \Box 7$ above
$20 \div ♖ = \Box_4$	$4\overline{)20}$ with $\times \Box 5$ above	$4\overline{)22}$ with $\times \Box 5$ above
$56 \div 8 = \Box_7$	$7\overline{)56}$ with $\times \Box 8$ above	$7\overline{)59}$ with $\times \Box 8$ above
$81 \div ♕ = \Box_9$	$9\overline{)81}$ with $\times \Box 9$ above	$9\overline{)85}$ with $\times \Box 9$ above

Mom! I Learn Division Using Math-Chess-Puzzles Connection

Ho Math Chess 何数棋谜 妈!我会棋谜式除法啦!

Frank Ho, Amanda Ho © 2004 − 2017, all rights reserved.

Student's Name _____ Date _____

dd ÷ d with remainder vs. no remainder

21 ÷ ♘ = ☐7	x ☐3 7)21 ☐☐	x ☐3 7)25 ☐☐ ☐4
42 ÷ 6 = ☐7	x ☐6 7)42 ☐☐	x ☐6 7)45 ☐☐ ☐3
32 ÷ 4 = ☐8	x ☐4 8)32 ☐☐	x ☐4 8)38 ☐☐ ☐6
30 ÷ 6 = ☐5	x ☐6 5)30 ☐☐	x ☐6 5)33 ☐☐ ☐3

Page 199

Mom! I Learn Division Using Math-Chess-Puzzles Connection

Ho Math Chess 何数棋谜　妈!我会棋谜式除法啦!

Frank Ho, Amanda Ho © 2004 – 2017, all rights reserved.

Student's Name _____ Date _____

dd ÷ d with remainder vs. no remainder

18 ÷ ♛ = ☐2	x☐9 2)18 ☐☐	x☐9 2)19 ☐☐ 　☐1
12 ÷ 6 = ☐2	x☐6 2)12 ☐☐	x☐6 2)13 ☐☐ 　☐1
14 ÷ 7 = ☐2	x☐7 2)14 ☐☐	x☐7 2)15 ☐☐ 　☐1
28 ÷ 4 = ☐7	x☐4 7)28 ☐☐	x☐4 7)33 ☐☐ 　☐5

Mom! I Learn Division Using Math-Chess-Puzzles Connection

Ho Math Chess 何数棋谜 妈!我会棋谜式除法啦!

Frank Ho, Amanda Ho © 2004 – 2017, all rights reserved.

Student's Name _____ Date _____

dd ÷ d with remainder vs. no remainder

15 ÷ ♖ = ☐ 3	3)15 x☐5 ☐☐	3)16 x☐5 ☐☐ ☐1
18 ÷ 6 = ☐ 3	3)18 x☐6 ☐☐	3)19 x☐6 ☐☐ ☐1
24 ÷ 8 = ☐ 3	3)24 x☐8 ☐☐	3)26 x☐8 ☐☐ ☐2
27 ÷ ♕ = ☐ 3	3)27 x☐9 ☐☐	3)29 x☐9 ☐☐ ☐2

Mom! I Learn Division Using Math-Chess-Puzzles Connection

Ho Math Chess 何数棋谜 妈!我会棋谜式除法啦!

Frank Ho, Amanda Ho © 2004 − 2017, all rights reserved.

Student's Name _____ Date _____

dd ÷ d with remainder vs. no remainder

12 ÷ ♗ = ☐4	4)12 x☐3 ☐☐	4)13 x☐3 ☐☐ ☐1
16 ÷ 4 = ☐4	4)16 x☐4 ☐☐	4)18 x☐4 ☐☐ ☐2
20 ÷ ♖ = ☐4	4)20 x☐5 ☐☐	4)23 x☐5 ☐☐ ☐3
24 ÷ 6 = ☐4	4)24 x☐6 ☐☐	4)27 x☐6 ☐☐ ☐3

Page 202

Mom! I Learn Division Using Math-Chess-Puzzles Connection

Ho Math Chess 何数棋谜 妈!我会棋谜式除法啦!

Frank Ho, Amanda Ho © 2004 − 2017, all rights reserved.

Student's Name _____ Date _____

dd ÷ d with remainder vs. no remainder

$10 \div 2 = \Box_5$	$\begin{array}{r}{}^{\times}\Box 2 \\ 5\overline{)10} \\ \Box\Box\end{array}$	$\begin{array}{r}{}^{\times}\Box 2 \\ 5\overline{)14} \\ \Box\Box \\ \Box 4\end{array}$
$20 \div 4 = \Box_5$	$\begin{array}{r}{}^{\times}\Box 4 \\ 5\overline{)20} \\ \Box\Box\end{array}$	$\begin{array}{r}{}^{\times}\Box 4 \\ 5\overline{)24} \\ \Box\Box \\ \Box 4\end{array}$
$25 \div ♖ = \Box_5$	$\begin{array}{r}{}^{\times}\Box 5 \\ 5\overline{)25} \\ \Box\Box\end{array}$	$\begin{array}{r}{}^{\times}\Box 4 \\ 5\overline{)24} \\ \Box\Box \\ \Box 4\end{array}$
$40 \div 8 = \Box_5$	$\begin{array}{r}{}^{\times}\Box 8 \\ 5\overline{)40} \\ \Box\Box\end{array}$	$\begin{array}{r}{}^{\times}\Box 8 \\ 5\overline{)44} \\ \Box\Box \\ \Box 4\end{array}$

Mom! I Learn Division Using Math-Chess-Puzzles Connection

Ho Math Chess   何数棋谜   妈!我会棋谜式除法啦!

Frank Ho, Amanda Ho © 2004 − 2017, all rights reserved.

Student's Name_____ Date_____

From multiplication to division

Fill in the following ☐ with a number.

2 × ♛ = 18☐ ÷ 9 = ☐2	9 × 2 = 18☐ ÷ 2 = ☐9
3 × ♛ = 27☐ ÷ ♛ = ☐3	♛ × 3 = 27☐ ÷ 3 = ☐9
4 × 9 = 36☐ ÷ ♛ = ☐4	9 × 4 = 36☐ ÷ 4 = ☐9
5 × ♛ = 45☐ ÷ 9 = ☐5	9 × 5 = 45☐ ÷ 5 = ☐9
6 × 9 = 54☐ ÷ ♛ = ☐6	♛ × 6 = 54☐ ÷ 6 = ☐9
7 × 9 = 63☐ ÷ 9 = ☐7	♛ × 7 = 63☐ ÷ 7 = ☐9

Mom! I Learn Division Using Math-Chess-Puzzles Connection

Ho Math Chess   何数棋谜   妈!我会棋谜式除法啦!

Frank Ho, Amanda Ho © 2004 − 2017, all rights reserved.

Student's Name _____ Date _____

From multiplication to division

Fill in the following ☐ with a number.

2 × 8 16☐ ÷ 2 = ☐8	6 × 2 12☐ ÷ 2 = ☐6
♘ × 7 21☐ ÷ 3 = ☐7	♖ × 3 15☐ ÷ 3 = ☐5
4 × 6 24☐ ÷ 6 = ☐4	4 × 4 16☐ ÷ 4 = ☐4
♖ × 5 25☐ ÷ 5 = ☐5	7 × 5 35☐ ÷ ♖ = ☐7
6 × 4 24☐ ÷ 4 = ☐6	8 × 6 48☐ ÷ 8 = ☐6
7 × 8 56☐ ÷ 7 = ☐8	6 × 7 42☐ ÷ 6 = ☐7

Mom! I Learn Division Using Math-Chess-Puzzles Connection

From multiplication to division

Fill in the following ☐ with a number.

2 × 8 16☐ ÷ 2 = ☐8	8 × 2 16☐ ÷ 8 = ☐2
4 × 9 36☐ ÷ ♛ = ☐4	4 × 3 12☐ ÷ ♞ = ☐4
4 × 6 24☐ ÷ 4 = ☐6	8 × 4 32☐ ÷ 4 = ☐8
5 × 7 35☐ ÷ 7 = ☐5	4 × 5 20☐ ÷ 4 = ☐5
6 × 8 48☐ ÷ 6 = ☐8	6 × 6 36☐ ÷ 6 = ☐6
7 × ♞ 21☐ ÷ 3 = ☐7	4 × 7 28☐ ÷ 7 = ☐4

Mom! I Learn Division Using Math-Chess-Puzzles Connection

Ho Math Chess　何数棋谜　妈!我会棋谜式除法啦!

Frank Ho, Amanda Ho © 2004 − 2017, all rights reserved.

Student's Name _____ Date _____

From multiplication to division

Fill in the following ☐ with a number.

☐27　☐27　 ―――　÷ 3 × 3　　9 ♛	☐30　☐30 ―――　÷ 5 × ♜　　6 6
☐45　☐45 ―――　÷ 5 × 5　　♛ 9	☐42　☐42 ―――　÷ 7 × 7　　6 6
☐35　☐35 ―――　÷ ♜ × 5　　7 7	☐72　☐72 ―――　÷ 8 × 8　　9 ♛

Mom! I Learn Division Using Math-Chess-Puzzles Connection

From multiplication to division

Fill in the following ☐ with a number.

☐45 ☐45 ÷ ♖♕ × 5 9	☐48 ☐48 ÷ 8 6 × 8 6
☐40 ☐40 ÷ 5 8 × ♖ 8	☐24 ☐24 ÷ 4 6 × 4 6
☐42 ☐42 ÷ 6 7 × 6 7	☐24 ☐24 ÷ 8 3 × 8 ♗

Mom! I Learn Division Using Math-Chess-Puzzles Connection

Ho Math Chess　何数棋谜　妈!我会棋谜式除法啦!

Frank Ho, Amanda Ho © 2004 − 2017, all rights reserved.

Student's Name _____　Date _____

From multiplication to division

Fill in the following ☐ with a number.

☐20　☐20 ――― ÷ ――― × ♖　　5 　4　　4	☐72　☐72 ――― ÷ ――― × 8　　8 　♕　　♕
☐40　☐40 ――― ÷ ――― × 5　　♖ 　8　　8	☐32　☐32 ――― ÷ ――― × 4　　4 　8　　8
☐49　☐49 ――― ÷ ――― × 7　　7 　7　　7	☐18　☐18 ――― ÷ ――― × 6　　6 　3　　♗

Mom! I Learn Division Using Math-Chess-Puzzles Connection

Ho Math Chess 何数棋谜 妈!我会棋谜式除法啦!

Frank Ho, Amanda Ho © 2004 − 2017, all rights reserved.

Student's Name_____ Date_____

From multiplication to division

Fill in the following ☐ with a number.

☐15 × ♖ = ___ ÷ 5 = 3	☐27 × 3 = ___ ÷ ♘ = 9
(×♖, ÷5/3)	(×3 ♕, ÷♘/9) ☐27
☐18 × 6 = ___ ÷ 6 = ♘	☐24 × 3 = ___ ÷ 8 = 3
(×6 ♘, ÷6/♘) ☐18	(×3/8, ÷8/3) ☐24
☐21 × 7 = ___ ÷ 3 = 7	☐12 × 4 = ___ ÷ 4 = 3
(×7/3, ÷3/7) ☐21	(×4 ♗, ÷4/3) ☐12

Mom! I Learn Division Using Math-Chess-Puzzles Connection

Ho Math Chess　何数棋谜　妈!我会棋谜式除法啦!

Frank Ho, Amanda Ho © 2004 − 2017, all rights reserved.

Student's Name _____   Date _____

From multiplication to division

Fill in the following ☐ with a number.

☐30   ☐30
___   ÷ ♖
× 5   6
  6

☐54   ☐54
___   ÷ 6
× 6   ♕
  9

☐48   ☐48
___   ÷ 6
× 6   8
  8

☐56   ☐56
___   ÷ 7
× 7   8
  8

☐42   ☐42
___   ÷ 7
× 6   6
  7

☐24   ☐24
___   ÷ 6
× 6   4
  4

Page 211

Multiplication and division facts

Use 2, 7, 14 to write the following multiplication and division facts.

☐ × ☐ = ☐   ☐ × ☐ = ☐

☐ ÷ ☐ = ☐   ☐ ÷ ☐ = ☐

$2 \times 7 = 14, \ 7 \times 2 = 14, \ 14 \div 2 = 7, \ 14 \div 7 = 2$

Use 3, 8, 24 to write the following multiplication and division facts.

☐ × ☐ = ☐   ☐ × ☐ = ☐

☐ ÷ ☐ = ☐   ☐ ÷ ☐ = ☐

$3 \times 8 = 24, \ 8 \times 3 = 24, \ 24 \div 3 = 8, \ 24 \div 8 = 3$

Use 4, 9, 36 to write the following multiplication and division facts.

☐ × ☐ = ☐   ☐ × ☐ = ☐

☐ ÷ ☐ = ☐   ☐ ÷ ☐ = ☐

$4 \times 9 = 36, \ 9 \times 4 = 36, \ 36 \div 4 = 9, \ 36 \div 9 = 4$

Mom! I Learn Division Using Math-Chess-Puzzles Connection

Use 5, 7, 35 to write the following multiplication and division facts.

☐ × ☐ = ☐   ☐ × ☐ = ☐
☐ ÷ ☐ = ☐   ☐ ÷ ☐ = ☐

$5 \times 7 = 35$, $7 \times 5 = 35$, $35 \div 5 = 7$, $35 \div 7 = 5$

Use 6, 8, 48 to write the following multiplication and division facts.

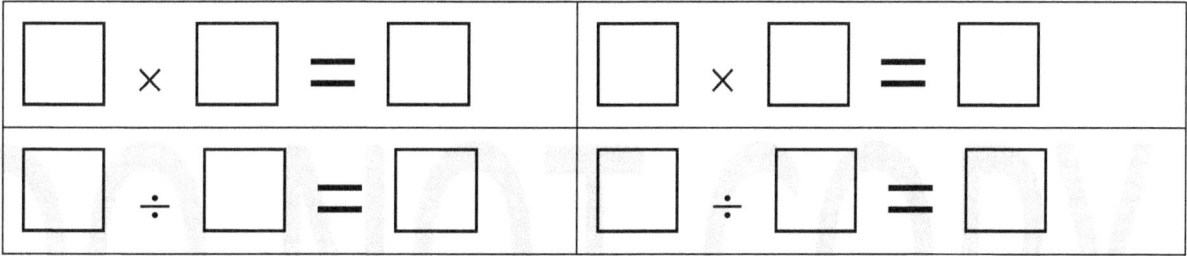

$6 \times 8 = 48$, $8 \times 6 = 48$, $48 \div 6 = 8$, $48 \div 8 = 6$

Use 7, 9, 63 to write the following multiplication and division facts.

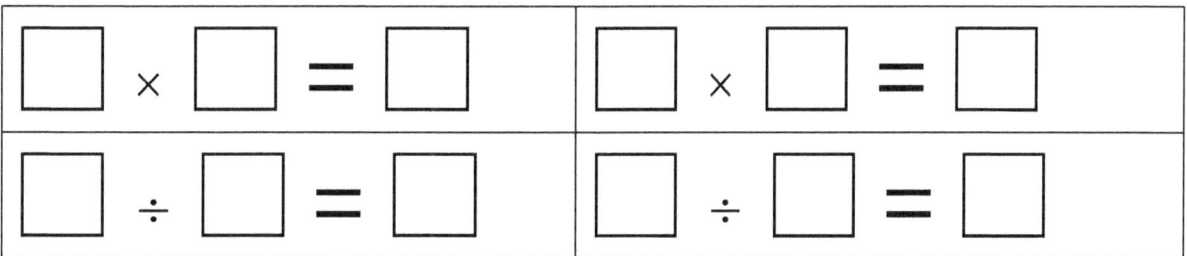

$7 \times 9 = 63$, $9 \times 7 = 63$, $63 \div 9 = 7$, $63 \div 7 = 9$

Mom! I Learn Division Using Math-Chess-Puzzles Connection

Ho Math Chess 何数棋谜 妈!我会棋谜式除法啦!

Frank Ho, Amanda Ho © 2004 − 2017, all rights reserved.

Student's Name _____ Date _____

Use the following array

• • • • • •
• • • • • •

to write the following multiplication and division facts.

□ × □ = □   □ × □ = □

□ ÷ □ = □   □ ÷ □ = □

2 × 6 = 12,   6 × 2 = 12,   12 ÷ 2 = 6,   12 ÷ 6 = 2

Use the following array

• • • • • •
• • • • • •
• • • • • •

to write the following multiplication and division facts.

□ × □ = □   □ × □ = □

□ ÷ □ = □   □ ÷ □ = □

3 × 6 = 18,   6 × 3 = 18,   18 ÷ 3 = 6,   18 ÷ 6 = 3

Mom! I Learn Division Using Math-Chess-Puzzles Connection

Ho Math Chess 何数棋谜 妈!我会棋谜式除法啦!

Frank Ho, Amanda Ho © 2004 − 2017, all rights reserved.

Student's Name _____ Date _____

Use the following array

• • • • • • •
• • • • • • •
• • • • • • •
• • • • • • •

to write the following multiplication and division facts.

□ × □ = □	□ × □ = □
□ ÷ □ = □	□ ÷ □ = □

$4 \times 7 = 28$, $7 \times 4 = 28$, $28 \div 7 = 4$, $28 \div 4 = 7$

Use the following array

• • • • • • • • •
• • • • • • • • •
• • • • • • • • •

to write the following multiplication and division facts.

□ × □ = □	□ × □ = □
□ ÷ □ = □	□ ÷ □ = □

$3 9 \times = 27$, $9 \times 3 = 27$, $27 \div 3 = 9$, $27 \div 9 = 3$

Mom! I Learn Division Using Math-Chess-Puzzles Connection

Ho Math Chess 何数棋谜 妈!我会棋谜式除法啦!

Frank Ho, Amanda Ho © 2004 – 2017, all rights reserved.

Student's Name_____ Date_____

Division math minutes

18 ÷ 6 =3	15 ÷ ♗ =5	12 ÷ 4 =3	8 ÷ 2 =4
14 ÷ 2 =7	16 ÷ 8 =2	27 ÷ 9 =3	81 ÷ 9 =9
32 ÷ 4 =8	45 ÷ 5 =9	21 ÷ ♗ =7	28 ÷ 7 =4
25 ÷ ♖ =5	35 ÷ 7 =5	48 ÷ 4 =12	58 ÷ 2 =29
64 ÷ 8 =8	76 ÷ 4 =19	87 ÷ ♗ =29	99 ÷ ♕ =11
82 ÷ 2 =41	75 ÷ ♖ =15	63 ÷ 3 =21	64 ÷ 8 =8
58 ÷ 2 =29	45 ÷ 9 =5	32 ÷ 4 =8	28 ÷ 2 =14
16 ÷ 8 =2	24 ÷ 8 =3	33 ÷ ♘ =11	45 ÷ 9 =5
55 ÷ 5 =11	65 ÷ 5 =13	72 ÷ 4 =18	68 ÷ 4 =17
98 ÷ 2 =49	15 ÷ 5 =3	42 ÷ 2 =21	44 ÷ 4 =11
54 ÷ ♗ =18	66 ÷ 6 =11	76 ÷ 4 =19	84 ÷ 4 =21
96 ÷ 8 =12	45 ÷ ♕ =5	32 ÷ 8 =4	35 ÷ 7 =5
24 ÷ 6 =4	55 ÷ 5 =11	42 ÷ 6 =7	68 ÷ 2 =34
75 ÷ 3 =25	46 ÷ 2 =23	27 ÷ 3 =9	81 ÷ ♗ =27
32 ÷ 8 =4	45 ÷ 9 =5	21 ÷ 7 =3	28 ÷ 4 =7
18 ÷ ♘ =6	15 ÷ 3 =5	12 ÷ ♘ =4	8 ÷ 4 =2
14 ÷ 7 =2	16 ÷ 2 =8	27 ÷ 3 =9	72 ÷ 9 =8
32 ÷ 8 =4	45 ÷ 9 =5	21 ÷ 7 =3	32 ÷ 4 =8

Mom! I Learn Division Using Math-Chess-Puzzles Connection

Ho Math Chess 何数棋谜 妈!我会棋谜式除法啦!

Frank Ho, Amanda Ho © 2004 − 2017, all rights reserved.

Student's Name _____ Date _____

Division math minutes

24 ÷ 6 =4	45 ÷ 3 =15	48 ÷ 4 =12	18 ÷ 2 =9
38 ÷ 2 =19	56 ÷ 8 =7	54 ÷ 9 =6	72 ÷ 9 =8
24 ÷ 4 =6	50 ÷ 5 =10	24 ÷ ♘ =8	56 ÷ 7 =8
30 ÷ ♖ =6	42 ÷ 7 =6	56 ÷ 4 =14	72 ÷ 2 =36
40 ÷ 8 =5	36 ÷ 4 =9	72 ÷ 6 =12	90 ÷ 9 =10
96 ÷ 6 =16	65 ÷ 5 =13	72 ÷ ♕ =8	72 ÷ 8 =9
84 ÷ 7 =12	54 ÷ ♕ =6	36 ÷ 4 =9	34 ÷ 2 =17
24 ÷ 8 =3	32 ÷ 8 =4	66 ÷ 3 =22	18 ÷ 9 =2
65 ÷ 5 =13	70 ÷ 5 =14	80 ÷ 4 =20	96 ÷ 4 =24
86 ÷ 2 =43	25 ÷ ♖ =5	44 ÷ 2 =22	60 ÷ ♖ =12
57 ÷ ♘ =19	72 ÷ 6 =12	84 ÷ 7 =12	96 ÷ 4 =24
64 ÷ 8 =8	54 ÷ 9 =6	40 ÷ 8 =5	42 ÷ 7 =6
30 ÷ 6 =5	65 ÷ 5 =13	48 ÷ 6 =8	72 ÷ 2 =36
45 ÷ 3 =15	98 ÷ 2 =49	18 ÷ 3 =6	27 ÷ ♕ =3
40 ÷ 8 =5	54 ÷ ♕ =6	28 ÷ 7 =4	36 ÷ 4 =9
18 ÷ 3 =6	48 ÷ 6 =8	75 ÷ 5 =15	96 ÷ 8 =12
21 ÷ 7 =3	16 ÷ 2 =8	27 ÷ ♘ =9	72 ÷ 9 =8
45 ÷ ♕ =5	54 ÷ 9 =6	28 ÷ 7 =4	35 ÷ ♖ =7

No part of this publication can be copied, duplicated, or reproduced.

Mom! I Learn Division Using Math-Chess-Puzzles Connection

Ho Math Chess   何数棋谜   妈!我会棋谜式除法啦!

Frank Ho, Amanda Ho © 2004 – 2017, all rights reserved.

Student's Name _____   Date _____

dd ÷ d with 2-digit quotient and no remainder

Step 1: Do ☐ × 2 ≤ 6

× ☐☐ 33 ← step 2: 3 × 2 = 6

2) 66

− ☐ ↓ ← step 3: 6 − 6 = 0

☐ ← step 4: bring down 6, 6 ÷ 2 = 3

− ☐ ← step 5: 3 × 2 = 6

0 ← Remainder = 0

Step 1: Do ☐ × 3 ≤ 4 [the remainder must be ≤ divisor (the outside number)]

× ☐☐ 16 ← step 2: 1 × 3 = 3

3) 48

− ☐ ↓ ← step 3: 4 − 3 = 1

☐☐ ← step 4: bring down 8, 18 ÷ 3 = 6

− ☐☐ ← step 5: 6 × 3 = 18

0 ← Remainder = 0

Step 1: Do ☐ × 5 ≤ 7

× ☐☐ 15 ← step 2: Do multiplication

5) 75

− ☐ ↓ ← step 3: Do subtraction

☐☐ ← step 4: bring down one more digit

− ☐☐ ← step 5: Do multiplication

0 ← Remainder = 0

Step 1: Do ☐ × 3 ≤ 7 4 [the remainder must be ≤ divisor (the outside number)]

× ☐☐ 25 ← step 2: Do multiplication

3) 75

− ☐ ↓ ← step 3: Do subtraction

☐☐ ← step 4: bring down one more digit

− ☐☐ ← step 5: Do multiplication

0 ← Remainder = 0

Mom! I Learn Division Using Math-Chess-Puzzles Connection

Ho Math Chess　何数棋谜　妈!我会棋谜式除法啦!

Frank Ho, Amanda Ho © 2004 − 2017, all rights reserved.

Student's Name _____ Date _____

dd ÷ d with 2-digit quotient and no remainder

Step 1: Do ☐ × 6 ≤ 6

× ☐☐₁₀ ← step 2: 1 × 6 = 6

$6 \overline{)60}$

− ☐ ↓ ← step 3: 6 − 6 = 0

☐ ← step 4: bring down 0, 0 ÷ 6 = 0

− ☐ ← step 5: 0 × 6 = 0

0 ← Remainder = 0

Step 1: Do ☐ × 9 ≤ 9

× ☐☐₁₀ ← step 2: 1 × 9 = 9

$9 \overline{)90}$

− ☐ ↓ ← step 3: 9 − 9 = 0

☐ ← step 4: bring down 0, 0 ÷ 9 = 0

− ☐ ← step 5: 0 × 9 = 0

0 ← Remainder = 0

Step 1: Do ☐ × 5 ≤ 5

× ☐☐₁₀ ← step 2: Do multiplication

$5 \overline{)50}$

− ☐ ↓ ← step 3: Do subtraction

☐ ← step 4: bring down one more digit

− ☐ ← step 5: Do multiplication

0 ← Remainder = 0

Step 1: Do ☐ × 3 ≤ 3

× ☐☐₁₀ ← step 2: Do multiplication

$3 \overline{)30}$

− ☐ ↓ ← step 3: Do subtraction

☐ ← step 4: bring down one more digit

− ☐ ← step 5: Do multiplication

0 ← Remainder = 0

Mom! I Learn Division Using Math-Chess-Puzzles Connection

dd ÷ d with 2-digit quotient and no remainder

□₁ × 2 ≤ ♗	□₆ × 2 ≤ 12	× □□ 16 2)32 −□↓ □□ −□□ 0
□₁ × 2 ≤ 3	□₉ × 2 ≤ 18	× □□ 19 2)38 −□↓ □□ −□□ 0
□₁ × ♗ ≤ 4	□₆ × 3 ≤ 18	× □□ 16 3)48 −□↓ □□ −□□ 0

Mom! I Learn Division Using Math-Chess-Puzzles Connection

Ho Math Chess 何数棋谜 妈!我会棋谜式除法啦!

Frank Ho, Amanda Ho © 2004 – 2017, all rights reserved.

Student's Name _____ Date _____

dd ÷ d with 2-digit quotient and no remainder

$\square_2 \times 4 \leq 8$	$\square_1 \times 4 \leq 4$	$4\overline{)84}$ quotient 21
$\square_1 \times 5 \leq \text{♛}$	$\square_8 \times \text{♖} \leq 40$	$5\overline{)90}$ quotient 18
$\square_1 \times 6 \leq 9$	$\square_6 \times 6 \leq 36$	$6\overline{)96}$ quotient 16

Mom! I Learn Division Using Math-Chess-Puzzles Connection

dd ÷ d with 2-digit quotient and no remainder

3)96 = 32	2)52 = 26	4)72 = 18
4)84 = 21	4)52 = 13	2)34 = 17
4)84 = 21	4)52 = 13	4)64 = 16

Mom! I Learn Division Using Math-Chess-Puzzles Connection

dd ÷ d with 2-digit quotient and no remainder

$7\overline{)84}$ = 12	$6\overline{)72}$ = 12	$7\overline{)91}$ = 13
$9\overline{)99}$ = 11	$8\overline{)88}$ = 11	$6\overline{)66}$ = 11
$8\overline{)96}$ = 12	$6\overline{)78}$ = 13	$6\overline{)90}$ = 15

Mom! I Learn Division Using Math-Chess-Puzzles Connection

Ho Math Chess 何数棋谜 妈!我会棋谜式除法啦!

Frank Ho, Amanda Ho © 2004 − 2017, all rights reserved.

Student's Name _____ Date _____

dd ÷ d with 2-digit quotient and remainder

4)69 r 17 ... 1
4)79 r 19 ... 3
4)86 r 21 ... 2

5)69 r 13 ... 4
6)79 r 13 ... 1
8)89 r 11 ... 1

5)99 r 19 ... 4
6)85 r 14 ... 1
3)37 r 12 ... 1

Page 224

Mom! I Learn Division Using Math-Chess-Puzzles Connection

Ho Math Chess 何数棋谜 妈!我会棋谜式除法啦!

Frank Ho, Amanda Ho © 2004 – 2017, all rights reserved.

Student's Name _____ Date _____

4)59 = 14 r 3	5)62 = 12 r 2	2)23 = 11 r 1
6)73 = 12 r 1	4)55 = 13 r 3	6)69 = 11 r 3
5)67 = 13 r 2	7)97 = 13 r 6	4)47 = 11 r 3

Page 225

Mom! I Learn Division Using Math-Chess-Puzzles Connection

Ho Math Chess　何数棋谜　妈!我会棋谜式除法啦!

Frank Ho, Amanda Ho © 2004 − 2017, all rights reserved.

Student's Name _____ Date _____

ddd ÷ d with three-digit quotient and no remainder

1. ☐ × 7 ≤ 8

2. ☐ × 7 ≤ 14

```
       × ☐☐☐  120
    7)  8 4 0
      − ☐ ↓ ↓
        ─────
        ☐☐ ↓
      − ☐☐ ↓
        ─────
          ☐
        − ☐
        ─────
          0
```

1. ☐ × 6 ≤ ♕

6. ☐ × 6 ≤ 36

```
       × ☐☐☐  160
    6)  9 6 0
      − ☐ ↓ ↓
        ─────
        ☐☐ ↓
      − ☐☐ ↓
        ─────
          ☐
        − ☐
        ─────
          0
```

Page 226

Mom! I Learn Division Using Math-Chess-Puzzles Connection

Ho Math Chess 何数棋谜 妈!我会棋谜式除法啦!

Frank Ho, Amanda Ho © 2004 − 2017, all rights reserved.

Student's Name _____ Date _____

ddd ÷ d with three-digit quotient and no remainder

605 ÷ ♜ = ____ 121

5)605

786 ÷ 6 = ____ 131

6)786

987 ÷ 7 = ____ 141

7)987

968 ÷ 8 = ____ 121

8)968

Mom! I Learn Division Using Math-Chess-Puzzles Connection

Ho Math Chess 何数棋谜 妈!我会棋谜式除法啦!

Frank Ho, Amanda Ho © 2004 – 2017, all rights reserved.

Student's Name _____ Date _____

ddd ÷ d with three-digit quotient and no remainder

652 ÷ 2 = ____326

2)652

963 ÷ ♗ = ____321

3)963

981 ÷ ♘ = ____327

3)981

648 ÷ 6 = ____108

6)648

Page 228

Mom! I Learn Division Using Math-Chess-Puzzles Connection

Ho Math Chess 何数棋谜 妈!我会棋谜式除法啦!

Frank Ho, Amanda Ho © 2004 － 2017, all rights reserved.

Student's Name _____ Date _____

ddd ÷ d with three-digit quotient and no remainder

526 ÷ 2 = _____ 263

696 ÷ ♘ = _____ 232

981 ÷ ♕ = _____ 109

636 ÷ 6 = _____ 106

Page 229

Mom! I Learn Division Using Math-Chess-Puzzles Connection

Ho Math Chess 何数棋谜 妈!我会棋谜式除法啦!

Frank Ho, Amanda Ho © 2004 − 2017, all rights reserved.

Student's Name _____ Date _____

ddd ÷ d with three-digit quotient and remainder

982 ÷ ♕ = _____ 109

9)982

637 ÷ 6 = _____ 106

6)637

967 ÷ ♘ = _____ 322

3)967

929 ÷ ♗ = _____ 309

3)929

Page 230

Mom! I Learn Division Using Math-Chess-Puzzles Connection

Ho Math Chess 何数棋谜 妈!我会棋谜式除法啦!

Frank Ho, Amanda Ho © 2004 − 2017, all rights reserved.

Student's Name _____ Date _____

ddd ÷ d with two-digit quotient and remainder

253 ÷ 8 = _____ 31	196 ÷ ♗ = _____ 65
8)253 ... □5	3)196 ... □1
629 ÷ 7 = _____ 89	537 ÷ 6 = _____ 89
7)629 ... □6	6)537 ... □3

Mom! I Learn Division Using Math-Chess-Puzzles Connection

Ho Math Chess 何数棋谜 妈!我会棋谜式除法啦!

Frank Ho, Amanda Ho © 2004 − 2017, all rights reserved.

Student's Name _____ Date _____

dddd ÷ d

1234 ÷ 2 = _____ 617

2) 1234

1876 ÷ 2 = _____ 938

2) 1876

3612 ÷ 4 = _____ 903

4) 3612

41228 ÷ 4 = _____ 10307

4) 41228

Mom! I Learn Division Using Math-Chess-Puzzles Connection

Ho Math Chess   何数棋谜   妈!我会棋谜式除法啦!

Frank Ho, Amanda Ho © 2004 – 2017, all rights reserved.

Student's Name _____ Date _____

Short Division

☐☐☐617 2)123^{1}4	☐☐☐938 2)187^{1}6
☐☐☐903 4)3612	☐☐☐☐☐10307 4)41228
5 3 7 5 6 0 R1 4)2150241	8 8 8 2)1776
3 5 7 R4 5)1789	2 6 8 7)1876
4 4 4 R2 3)1334	3 2 9 R2 6)1976

Mom! I Learn Division Using Math-Chess-Puzzles Connection

Ho Math Chess　何数棋谜　妈!我会棋谜式除法啦!

Frank Ho, Amanda Ho © 2004 – 2017, all rights reserved.

Student's Name _____ Date _____

Short Division

137 R1 9)1234	234 R4 8)1876
928 R1 4)3713	12804 R2 4)51218
430048 R1 5)2150241	355 R1 5)1776
298 R1 6)1789	234 R4 8)1876
333 R2 4)1334	247 8)1976

Mom! I Learn Division Using Math-Chess-Puzzles Connection

Ho Math Chess 何数棋谜 妈!我会棋谜式除法啦!

Frank Ho, Amanda Ho © 2004 – 2017, all rights reserved.

Student's Name _____ Date _____

Rounding whole number (5 up, 4 down)

Rounding is a method of giving an approximate value to a number. The procedure of rounding a whole number is the same as the procedure of rounding a decimal number; only the place value is different. For example, round $29 to the nearest tens, it means to get an estimated number whose value is as close to the tens position of $29 as possible.

When $29 is rounded to the nearest tens position, there will be two answers: $20 or $30.

Is $29 closer to $20 or is $29 closer to $30? $29 is closer to $30, so the nearest tens value will be $30. The rule of rounding is as follows:

Question: Round the following numbers to the nearest tens (underlined)	Step 1: Point to the place value to be rounded by circling it.	Step 2: Look at the digit (single number) to the right of the circled number.	Step 3: **5 up, 4 down** If it is 5 or more the add 1 to the circled number (round up); if it is less than 5 do not add 1 to the circled number (round down).	Step 4: All digits to the right of the circle number should be changed to 0.	Final answer
41<u>2</u>8	41②8	8	41③8	41③0	4130
<u>2</u>9	②9	9	③9	③0	30
<u>2</u>5	②5	5	③5	③0	30
<u>2</u>4	②4	4	②4	②0	20
<u>3</u>5	③	5	④5	④0	40
<u>3</u>9	③	9	④9	④0	40
<u>3</u>4	③	4	③4	③0	30
3<u>5</u>5	⑤	5	⑥5	⑥0	360
4<u>1</u>2	①	2	①2	①0	410
4<u>0</u>0	⓪	0	⓪0	⓪0	400
5<u>5</u>0	⑤	0	⑤0	⑤0	550

No part of this publication can be copied, duplicated, or reproduced.

Mom! I Learn Division Using Math-Chess-Puzzles Connection

Ho Math Chess 何数棋谜 妈!我会棋谜式除法啦!

Frank Ho, Amanda Ho © 2004 – 2017, all rights reserved.

Student's Name _____ Date _____

Rounding whole number

Question: Round the following numbers to the nearest hundreds	Step 1: Point to the place value to be rounded by circling it.	Step 2: Look at the digit (single number) to the right of circled number.	Step 3: If it is 5 or more then add 1 to the circled number; if it is less than 5, do not add 1 to the circled number.	Step 4: All digits to the right of the circle number should be changed to 0.	Final answer
219999	9	9	10		220000
200099	0	9	1		200100
200051	0	5	1		200100
200150	1	5	2		200200
209951	5	5	6		210000
209949	9	4	9		209900
209940	9	4	9		209900
299999	9	9	10		300000

Question: Round the following numbers to the nearest thousands	Step 1: Point to the place value to be rounded by circling it.	Step 2: Look at the digit (single number) to the right of circled number.	Step 3: If it is 5 or more then add 1 to the circled number; if it is less than 5 do not add 1 to the circled number.	Step 4: All digits to the right of the circle number should be changed to 0.	Final answer
99999	9	9	10		100000
88888	8	8	9		89000
12699	2	6	3		13000
49999	9	9	10		50000
43111	3	1	3		43000
45959	5	9	6		46000

Mom! I Learn Division Using Math-Chess-Puzzles Connection

Ho Math Chess 何数棋谜 妈!我会棋谜式除法啦!

Frank Ho, Amanda Ho © 2004 − 2017, all rights reserved.

Student's Name _____ Date _____

Round the following numbers to the nearest place values indicated.

Standard form	10000	1000	100	10	Total place value underlined
99999	10000	10000	10000	10000	Ten thousands
55555	60000	56000	55600	55560	Hundreds
54545	50000	55000	54500	54550	Thousands
50	N/A	N/A	100	50	unit

Insert digits in the ☐ so that the following rounding would make sense.

5☐9 rounds to 600, _____ 9

99☐ rounds to 1000, _____ 5 or 6 or 7 or 8 or 9

123☐4 rounds to 12300, _____ 0 or 1 or 2 or 3 or 4

55☐55 rounds to 56000, _____ 9

49☐99 rounds to 50000, _____ 9

No part of this publication can be copied, duplicated, or reproduced.

Mom! I Learn Division Using Math-Chess-Puzzles Connection

Write the place value to which each number has been rounded.

Number rounded	Place value rounded
3590 ⇒ 3600	hundreds
3590 ⇒ 4000	_____ thousands
43995 ⇒ 44000	_____ thousands
43995 ⇒ 40000	_____ ten thousands
3590 ⇒ 4000	_____ thousands
135910 ⇒ 135900	_____ hundreds
135910 ⇒ 136000	_____ thousands

Mom! I Learn Division Using Math-Chess-Puzzles Connection

Ho Math Chess   何数棋谜   妈!我会棋谜式除法啦!

Frank Ho, Amanda Ho © 2004 − 2017, all rights reserved.

Student's Name _____ Date _____

Trailing zeros in the dividend

$1 \overline{)7}$ with □ above and □ below	7 tens ← $1 \overline{)7\,tens}$ ↑ (Just bring up 0's) **7 tens**	7 hundreds $1 \overline{)7\,hundreds}$ **7 hundreds**
	□□70 $1 \overline{)70}$ □0	□□□700 $1 \overline{)700}$ □□□
$1 \overline{)9}$ with □ above and □ below	□□90 $1 \overline{)90}$ □□	□□□900 $1 \overline{)900}$ □□□

Mom! I Learn Division Using Math-Chess-Puzzles Connection

Ho Math Chess 何数棋谜 妈!我会棋谜式除法啦!

Frank Ho, Amanda Ho © 2004 − 2017, all rights reserved.

Student's Name _____ Date _____

Trailing zeros in the dividend and divisor

Crossing out 1 zero in divisor and dividend.	Crossing out 1 zero in divisor and dividend.	Crossing out 2 zeros in divisor and dividend. (Cross out equal number of 0's in divisor and dividend)
10) 60 with □ on top and □ below	60) 6000 with □□□100 on top and □□ below	600) 600000 with □□□□1000 on top and □□□□ below
20) 1200, quotient 60	300) 1800, quotient 6	120) 240000, quotient 2000
3) 240, quotient 80	3) 2400, quotient 800	30) 480000, quotient 16000

Mom! I Learn Division Using Math-Chess-Puzzles Connection

Ho Math Chess 何数棋谜 妈!我会棋谜式除法啦!

Frank Ho, Amanda Ho © 2004 − 2017, all rights reserved.

Student's Name _____ Date _____

Dividend with trailing 0's (with no remainder)

$8100 \div 81$

```
       1 0 0  ← (Just bring up the 0's straight up as the quotient)
   _____
81 ) 8 1 0 0  ↑
     8 1 0 0
```

$810 \div 81 = 10$	$8100 \div 81 = 100$	$81000 \div 81 = 1000$
$480 \div 6 = 80$	$4800 \div 60 = 80$ Think as $480\cancel{0} \div 6\cancel{0} = 480 \div 6$	$48000 \div 6000 = 8$ Think as $48\cancel{000} \div 6\cancel{000} = 48 \div 6$
$490 \div 7 = 70$	$49000 \div 70 = 700$ Think as $4900\cancel{0} \div 7\cancel{0} = 4900 \div 7$	$490000 \div 7000 = 70$ Think as $490\cancel{000} \div 7\cancel{000} = 490 \div 7$
$640 \div 4 = 160$	$64000 \div 40 = 1600$	$640000 \div 4000 = 160$
$250 \div ♖ = 50$	$25000 \div 500 = 50$	$250000 \div 5000 = 50$

Mom! I Learn Division Using Math-Chess-Puzzles Connection

Trailing zeros in the dividend and divisor

120 ÷ ♗ = 40	12000 ÷ 300 = 40	120000 ÷ 3000 = 40
240 ÷ ♘ = 80	24000 ÷ 300 = 80	240000 ÷ 3000 = 80
840 ÷ 24 = 35	84000 ÷ 2400 = 35	840000 ÷ 24000 = 35
750 ÷ 25 = 30	75000 ÷ 2500 = 30	750000 ÷ 25000 = 30
240 ÷ 12 = 20	24000 ÷ 1200 = 20	240000 ÷ 12000 = 20
390 ÷ 13 = 30	39000 ÷ 1300 = 30	390000 ÷ 13000 = 30
280 ÷ 14 = 20	28000 ÷ 1400 = 20	14000 ÷ 280 = 50

Mom! I Learn Division Using Math-Chess-Puzzles Connection

Ho Math Chess 何数棋谜 妈!我会棋谜式除法啦!

Frank Ho, Amanda Ho © 2004 − 2017, all rights reserved.

Student's Name _____ Date _____

50 ÷ 25 = 2	50 × 2 = 100 100 ÷ 25 = 4
200 ÷ 25 = 8	200 × 2 = ____400 400 ÷ 25 = _____16
60 ÷ 30 = 2	60 × 2 = ____120 120 ÷ 30 = _____4
240 ÷ 30 = 8	240 × 2 = ____480 480 ÷ 30 = ____16
600 ÷ 40 = 15	120 ÷ 40 = _____3
120 ÷ 20 = 6	120 × 2 = ____240 20 × 2 = ____40 240 ÷ 40 = _____6
160 ÷ 40 = 4	320 ÷ 80 = _____4
160 ÷ 80 = 2	320 ÷ 160 = _____2
240 ÷ 30 = 8	480 ÷ 60 = _____8
240 ÷ 60 = 4	240 ÷ 120 = _____2

Mom! I Learn Division Using Math-Chess-Puzzles Connection

Ho Math Chess 何数棋谜 妈!我会棋谜式除法啦!

Frank Ho, Amanda Ho © 2004 – 2017, all rights reserved.

Student's Name _____ Date _____

Zeros in the middle of quotient

1) 2)212 = 106

2) 3)921 = 307

3) 4)424 = 106

4) 4)1236 = 309

5) 5)153505 = 30701

6) 6)1236 = 206

Page 244

Mom! I Learn Division Using Math-Chess-Puzzles Connection

Zeros in the middle of quotient

$$4\overline{)12036} = 3009$$

$$5\overline{)1503505} = 300701$$

$$6\overline{)12036} = 2006$$

$$4\overline{)16032} = 4008$$

$$5\overline{)20035015} = 4007003$$

$$6\overline{)120042} = 20007$$

Mom! I Learn Division Using Math-Chess-Puzzles Connection

Quotient with leading, middle, and training zeros

1) 4) 36040 = 9010

2) 3) 70040 = 23346

3) 5) 140050 = 28010

4) 4) 130040 = 32510

5) 6) 17040240 = 2840040

6) 7) 2100490 = 300070

Mom! I Learn Division Using Math-Chess-Puzzles Connection

Ho Math Chess 何数棋谜 妈!我会棋谜式除法啦!

Frank Ho, Amanda Ho © 2004 − 2017, all rights reserved.

Student's Name _____ Date _____

d0… d0.. ÷ d0… with no remainder

6006 ÷ ♘ = 2002 2002 (Bring up 0's) 3)6006 **6006**	60006 ÷ 3 = _____ 20002	600006 ÷ 3 = _____ 200002
220000 ÷ 11 = 20000	220022 ÷ 11 = 20002	220000 ÷ 1100 = 200
660066 ÷ 33 = 20002	66006600 ÷ 330 = 200020	6600066̸0̸0̸ ÷ 33̸0̸0̸ = 6600066 ÷ 33 = 200002
88880088 ÷ 44 = 2020002	8888008800 ÷ 440 = 20200020	88880088000 ÷ 44000 = 2020002
100000 ÷ 100 = 1000	10000000 ÷ 1000 = 10000	1000000000000 ÷ 100000 = 10000000

Mom! I Learn Division Using Math-Chess-Puzzles Connection

÷ **by 10's power (equivalent to × by power of 0.1)**

$810 \div 10 = 810. \div 10 = 81$ (move the invisible decimal point of the dividend to the left as many as zeros in the divisor, in this case, it is 1 zero in 10.)	$8100 \div 10 = 810$
$8100 \div 100 = 8100. \div 100 = 81$ (move the invisible decimal point to the left 2 places because there are 2 zeros in 100.)	$8100 \div 100 = 81$
$10000 \div 10 = $ _____ 1000	$120 \div 10 = 12$
$10000 \div 100 = 100$	$1200 \div 100 = 12$
$10000 \div 1000 = 10$	$12000 \div 1000 = 12$
$10000 \div 10000 = 1$	$120000 \div 10000 = 12$
$100000 \div 10000 = 10$	$120000 \div 10000 = 12$

Mom! I Learn Division Using Math-Chess-Puzzles Connection

Estimating quotient of ddd ÷ dd

Step1: Round 21 as 20 (multiple of 10), estimate quotient by dividing 64 ÷ 20 = 3. $$\begin{array}{r}3\\20\overline{)640}\\60\end{array}$$ Step 2: Compare 64 > 60, so 3 is the estimated quotient.	Think 64 ÷ 20 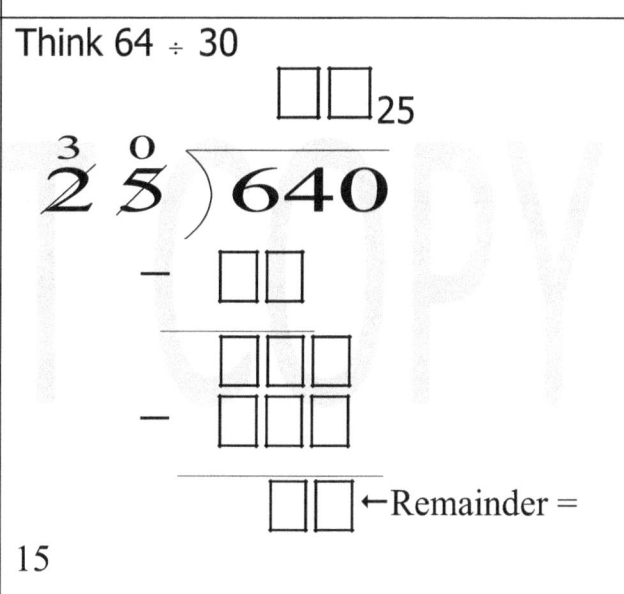 Remainder = 10
Step1: Round 25 as 30 (multiple of 10), estimate quotient by dividing 64 ÷ 30 = 2. $$\begin{array}{r}2\\30\overline{)640}\\60\end{array}$$ Step 2: Compare 64 > 50, so 2 is the estimated quotient. $$\begin{array}{r}4\\30\overline{)140}\\120\end{array}$$ Compare 140 > 120, so 4 is the estimated quotient. Try it, it is too small, so try 5	Think 64 ÷ 30 Remainder = 15

Mom! I Learn Division Using Math-Chess-Puzzles Connection

Ho Math Chess 何数棋谜   妈!我会棋谜式除法啦!

Frank Ho, Amanda Ho © 2004 – 2017, all rights reserved.

Student's Name _____ Date _____

ddd ÷ dd with 2-digit quotient

2□ × 42 ≤ 84	42□ × 2 ≤ 84	× □□20 42)840 −□□ ↓ □ −□ □0
2□ × 48 ≤ 96	48□ × 2 ≤ 96	× □□ 20 48)960 −□□ ↓ □ −□ □0

Page 250

Mom! I Learn Division Using Math-Chess-Puzzles Connection

ddd ÷ dd with 2-digit quotient

```
      ×☐☐10                    ×☐☐                      ×☐☐
   10)100              12                       12
                          10)120                    11)132
     −☐☐ ↓
     ─────                  −☐☐ ↓                    −☐☐ ↓
        ☐                  ─────                    ─────
      − ☐                    ☐☐                      ☐☐
        ☐                   −☐☐                     −☐☐
                            ─────                   ─────
                              ☐                       ☐


      ×☐☐16                    ×☐☐                      ×☐☐
   40)640              12                       32
                          51)612                    28)896
     −☐☐ ↓
     ─────                  −☐☐ ↓                    −☐☐ ↓
      ☐☐☐                  ─────                    ─────
     −☐☐☐                    ☐☐☐                     ☐☐
     ─────                  −☐☐☐                    −☐☐
        ☐                   ─────                   ─────
                              ☐                       ☐☐
```

Page 251

Mom! I Learn Division Using Math-Chess-Puzzles Connection

ddd ÷ dd with 2-digit quotient

13 r 24, 12 r 16, 15 r 45, 11 r 13, 11 r 47, 11 r 21

Mom! I Learn Division Using Math-Chess-Puzzles Connection

Ho Math Chess 何数棋谜 妈!我会棋谜式除法啦!

Frank Ho, Amanda Ho © 2004 – 2017, all rights reserved.

Student's Name _____ Date _____

ddd ÷ dd with 2-digit quotient

11 r 33, 12 r 2, 12 r 23, 14 r 7, 12 r 16, 11 r 31

Mom! I Learn Division Using Math-Chess-Puzzles Connection

ddd ÷ dd with 2-digit quotient

57) 697 × □□12 −□□ ↓ □□ −□□ □□13	19) 278 × □□14 −□□ ↓ □□ −□□ □□12	72) 747 × □□10 −□□ ↓ □□ −□□ □□27
29) 345 × □□11 −□□ ↓ □□ −□□ □□26	37) 451 × □□12 −□□ ↓ □□ −□□ □□7	62) 670 × □□10 −□□ ↓ □□ −□□ □□50

Page 254

Mom! I Learn Division Using Math-Chess-Puzzles Connection

Ho Math Chess 何数棋谜 妈!我会棋谜式除法啦!

Frank Ho, Amanda Ho © 2004 − 2017, all rights reserved.

Student's Name _____ Date _____

ddd ÷ dd with 2-digit quotient

×□□12 29)349 −□□ ↓ ──── □□ −□□ ──── □□1	×□□11 49)570 −□□ ↓ ──── □□ −□□ ──── □□31	×□□12 35)427 −□□ ↓ ──── □□ −□□ ──── □□7
×□□12 37)447 −□□ ↓ ──── □□ −□□ ──── □□3	×□□11 67)743 −□□ ↓ ──── □□ −□□ ──── □□6	×□□11 57)629 −□□ ↓ ──── □□ −□□ ──── □□2

Page 255

Mom! I Learn Division Using Math-Chess-Puzzles Connection

Ho Math Chess 何数棋谜 妈!我会棋谜式除法啦!

Frank Ho, Amanda Ho © 2004 − 2017, all rights reserved.

Student's Name _____ Date _____

ddd ÷ dd with 2-digit quotient

Page 256

Mom! I Learn Division Using Math-Chess-Puzzles Connection

Ho Math Chess 何数棋谜 妈!我会棋谜式除法啦!

Frank Ho, Amanda Ho © 2004 – 2017, all rights reserved.

Student's Name _____ Date _____

ddd ÷ dd with 2-digit quotient

49) 588 quotient □□12

79) 869 quotient □□ × 11

37) 481 quotient □□13

39) 546 quotient □□14

68) 952 quotient □□14

67) 930 quotient 13R59

Page 257

Mom! I Learn Division Using Math-Chess-Puzzles Connection

Ho Math Chess 何数棋谜 妈!我会棋谜式除法啦!

Frank Ho, Amanda Ho © 2004 – 2017, all rights reserved.

Student's Name _____ Date

Estimating ddd ÷ dd with 1-digit quotient

Step 1: Round 83 as 80 (multiple of 10), estimate quotient by dividing 412 ÷ 80 = 5. $$80\overline{)412}$$ $$400$$ Step 2: Try quotient 5. Compare 415 > 412, so 5 is over estimated. Try 4, 332 < 412, so 4 is the right quotient.	Think 412 ÷ 80 □4 $8\overset{0}{3}\overline{)412}$ − □□□ □□ 80 ← Remainder = 80
Step 1: Round 86 as 90 (multiple of 10), estimate quotient by dividing 441 ÷ 90 = 4. $$90\overline{)441}$$ $$360$$ Step 2: Compare 441 > 360, so 4 is the estimated quotient. 4 times 86 = 344 < 441. So the quotient 4 is underestimated. Try 5.	Think 441 ÷ 90 □5 $\overset{9}{8}\overset{0}{6}\overline{)441}$ − □□□ □□ 11 ← Remainder = 11

Page 258

Mom! I Learn Division Using Math-Chess-Puzzles Connection

dd ÷ dd with 1-digit quotient

$_9\square \times 12 \leq$ 108	▢9 12)108 ▢▢▢	▢9R1 12)109 ▢▢▢ ▢
$_7\square \times 21 \leq$ 147	▢7 21)147 ▢▢▢	▢7R10 21)157 ▢▢▢ ▢▢
$_6\square \times 33 \leq$ 198	▢6 32)192 ▢▢▢	▢6R11 33)209 ▢▢▢ ▢▢

Mom! I Learn Division Using Math-Chess-Puzzles Connection

Ho Math Chess　何数棋谜　妈!我会棋谜式除法啦!

Frank Ho, Amanda Ho © 2004 − 2017, all rights reserved.

Student's Name _____　Date _____

ddd ÷ dd with 1-digit quotient

$8\square \times 19 \leq 152$	$\square 8$ $19\overline{)152}$ $\square\square\square$	$\square$ 8R17 $19\overline{)169}$ $\square\square\square$ $\square\square$
$5\square \times 25 \leq 147$	$\square 8$ $25\overline{)200}$ $\square\square\square$	$\square 8R17$ $25\overline{)217}$ $\square\square\square$ $\square\square$
$6\square \times 37 \leq 222$	$\square 6$ $37\overline{)222}$ $\square\square\square$	$\square 6R17$ $37\overline{)239}$ $\square\square\square$ $\square\square$

Mom! I Learn Division Using Math-Chess-Puzzles Connection

Ho Math Chess 何数棋谜 妈!我会棋谜式除法啦!

Frank Ho, Amanda Ho © 2004 – 2017, all rights reserved.

Student's Name _____ Date _____

ddd ÷ dd with 1-digit quotient

$8\square \times 42 \leq 336$	$\square 8$ $42 \overline{)336}$ $\square\square\square$	$\square$ 8R13 $42 \overline{)349}$ $\square\square\square$ $\square\square$
$7\square \times 53 \leq 371$	$\square 7$ $53 \overline{)371}$ $\square\square\square$	$\square 7R16$ $53 \overline{)387}$ $\square\square\square$ $\square\square$
$7\square \times 67 \leq 469$	$\square 7$ $67 \overline{)469}$ $\square\square\square$	$\square 7R43$ $67 \overline{)512}$ $\square\square\square$ $\square\square$

8, 8 r 16, 7, 7 r 16, 7, 7 r 43

Mom! I Learn Division Using Math-Chess-Puzzles Connection

Ho Math Chess 何数棋谜 妈!我会棋谜式除法啦!

Frank Ho, Amanda Ho © 2004 – 2017, all rights reserved.

Student's Name _____ Date _____

ddd ÷ dd with 1-digit quotient

₄□ × 83 ≤ 332	□4 83)332 □□□	□4R21 83)353 □□□ □□
₇□ × 97 ≤ 679	□7 97)679 □□□	□7R8 97)687 □□□ □
₈□ × 78 ≤ 624	□8 78)624 □□□	□8R33 78)657 □□□ □□

4, 4 r 21, 7, 7 r 8, 8, 8 r 33

Mom! I Learn Division Using Math-Chess-Puzzles Connection

Ho Math Chess 何数棋谜 妈!我会棋谜式除法啦!

Frank Ho, Amanda Ho © 2004 – 2017, all rights reserved.

Student's Name _____ Date _____

ddd ÷ dd with 1-digit quotient and remainder

7□ × 24 ≤ 173	24)173 7R5 □□□ □□	47)299 6R17 □□□ □□
4□ × 48 ≤ 200	48)200 4R8 □□□ □□	12)123 10R3 □□□ □□
7□ × 48 ≤ 348	48)348 7R12 □□□ □□	78)667 8R43 □□□ □□

4, 4 r 21, 7, 7 r 8, 8, 8 r 33

Mom! I Learn Division Using Math-Chess-Puzzles Connection

Ho Math Chess 何数棋谜 妈!我会棋谜式除法啦!

Frank Ho, Amanda Ho © 2004 – 2017, all rights reserved.

Student's Name _____ Date _____

ddd ÷ dd with 1-digit quotient and remainder

8☐ × 25 ≤ 213	8R3 25)213	6R25 37)247
9☐ × 87 ≤ 850	9R67 87)850	9R14 97)887
6☐ × 58 ≤ 404	6R56 58)404	8R33 78)657

4, 4 r 21, 7, 7 r 8, 8, 8 r 33

Page 264

Mom! I Learn Division Using Math-Chess-Puzzles Connection

Ho Math Chess 何数棋谜 妈!我会棋谜式除法啦!

Frank Ho, Amanda Ho © 2004 − 2017, all rights reserved.

Student's Name _____   Date _____

ddd ÷ dd with 1-digit quotient and remainder

$_4\square \times 83 \leq$ 532	83)532 6R34 □□□	63)253 4R1 □□□ □□
$_7\square \times 37 \leq$ 279	37)279 7R20 □□□	77)687 8R71 □□□ □
$_7\square \times 68 \leq$ 524	68)524 7R48 □□□	58)557 9R35 □□□ □□

4, 4 r 21, 7, 7 r 8, 8, 8 r 33

Page 265

Mom! I Learn Division Using Math-Chess-Puzzles Connection

Ho Math Chess 何数棋谜 妈!我会棋谜式除法啦!

Frank Ho, Amanda Ho © 2004 − 2017, all rights reserved.

Student's Name _____ Date _____

ddd ÷ dd with 1-digit quotient and remainder

$7\boxed{} \times 43 \leq 332$	7R31 43)332 ☐☐☐	7R12 63)453 ☐☐☐ ☐☐
$8\boxed{} \times 76 \leq 679$	8R71 76)679 ☐☐☐	9 43)387 ☐☐☐ ☐
$\boxed{} \times 38 \leq 424$	11R6 38)424 ☐☐☐	11R29 48)557 ☐☐☐ ☐☐

4, 4 r 21, 7, 7 r 8, 8, 8 r 33

Page 266

Mom! I Learn Division Using Math-Chess-Puzzles Connection

Estimating of 2-digit(s) quotient by rounding

Step1: Round 53 as 50 (multiple of 10), estimate quotient by dividing 202 ÷ 50 = 4.

```
        4
   _____
50 ) 2021
     200
```

Step 2: Try quotient 4. Compare 212 > 202, so 4 is over estimated. Try 3, 159 < 202, so 3 is the right quotient.

Use 431 divided by 50, the estimated quotient is 8.

```
        8
   _____
50 ) 431
     400
```

Step1: Round 56 as 60 (multiple of 10), estimate quotient by dividing 202 ÷ 60 = 3.

```
        3
   _____
60 ) 2021
     180
```

Step 2: Compare 180 < 202, so 3 is the estimated quotient. 3 times 56 = 198 < 202. So 3 is the quotient.
Step 3: 341 divided by 60, the estimated quotient is 5.
5 times 56 = 280, 341 − 280 = 61 which is > 56. So the quotient should be 6.

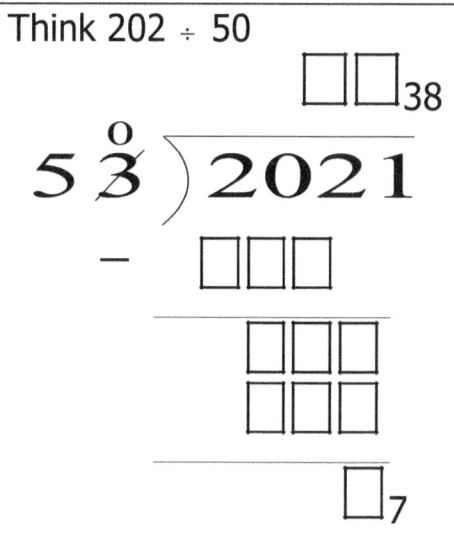

Think 202 ÷ 50

Think 202 ÷ 60

Mom! I Learn Division Using Math-Chess-Puzzles Connection

Ho Math Chess 何数棋谜 妈!我会棋谜式除法啦!

Frank Ho, Amanda Ho © 2004 – 2017, all rights reserved.

Student's Name _____ Date _____

Estimating quotient of 2-digit or more divisors by rounding

7R29 30)239	8R5 40)325	9R33 50)483
7R41 60)461	5R15 70)365	5R65 80)465
(Think 239 ÷ 30) 7R22 31)239	(Think 195 ÷ 40) 4R31 41)195	(Think 475 ÷ 50) 9R16 51)475
(Think 281 ÷ 40) 8R1 35)281	(Think 405 ÷ 50) 8R37 46)405	(Think 445 ÷ 60) 7R46 57)445

7 r 29, 8 r 5, 9 r 33, 7 r 41, 5 r 15, 5 r 65, 7 r 22, 4 r 31, 9 r 16, 8 r 1, 8 r 37, 7 r 46

Mom! I Learn Division Using Math-Chess-Puzzles Connection

Ho Math Chess 何数棋谜 妈!我会棋谜式除法啦!

Frank Ho, Amanda Ho © 2004 – 2017, all rights reserved.

Student's Name _____ Date _____

Estimating quotient of 2-digit or more divisors by rounding

5R39 40)239	59R31 40)2391	597R31 40)23911
(Think 361 ÷ 70) 5R31 66)361	(Think 3614 ÷ 70) 54R50 66)3614	(Think 36140 ÷ 70) 547R38 66)36140
(Think 239 ÷ 20) 12R11 19)239	(Think 2391 ÷ 20) 125R16 19)2391	(Think 23913 ÷ 20) 1258R11 19)23913

5 r 39, 59 r 31, 597 r 31, 5 r 31, 54 r 50, 547 r 38, 12 r 11, 125 r 16, 1258 r 11

Mom! I Learn Division Using Math-Chess-Puzzles Connection

ddd ÷ dd = q with no remainder

105 ÷ 21 = □5	110 ÷ 22 = □5	115 ÷ 23 = □5
126 ÷ 21 = □6	132 ÷ 22 = □6	138 ÷ 23 = □6
144 ÷ 24 = □6	175 ÷ 25 = □7	208 ÷ 26 = □8
200 ÷ 25 = □8	216 ÷ 36 = □6	188 ÷ 47 = □4
156 ÷ 26 = □6	185 ÷ 37 = □5	288 ÷ 48 = □6
243 ÷ 27 = □9	342 ÷ 38 = □9	294 ÷ 49 = □6
224 ÷ 28 = □8	273 ÷ 39 = □7	400 ÷ 50 = □8
203 ÷ 29 = □7	320 ÷ 40 = □8	255 ÷ 51 = □5
150 ÷ 30 = □5	246 ÷ 41 = □6	416 ÷ 52 = □8
186 ÷ 31 = □6	294 ÷ 42 = □7	371 ÷ 53 = □7
224 ÷ 32 = □7	172 ÷ 43 = □4	216 ÷ 54 = □4
264 ÷ 33 = □8	220 ÷ 44 = □5	220 ÷ 55 = □4
306 ÷ 34 = □9	270 ÷ 45 = □6	504 ÷ 56 = □9
315 ÷ 35 = □9	414 ÷ 46 = □9	456 ÷ 57 = □8

5, 5, 5, 6, 6, 6, 6, 7, 8, 8, 6, 4, 6, 5, 6, 9, 9, 6,
8, 7, 8, 7, 8, 5, 5, 6, 8, 6, 7, 7, 7, 4, 4, 8, 5, 4,
9, 6, 9, 9, 9, 8

Mom! I Learn Division Using Math-Chess-Puzzles Connection

Ho Math Chess 何数棋谜 妈!我会棋谜式除法啦!

Frank Ho, Amanda Ho © 2004 − 2017, all rights reserved.

Student's Name _____ Date _____

ddd ÷ dd = qq with no remainder

231 ÷ 11 = □ 21	792 ÷ 22 = □ 36	897 ÷ 23 = □ 39
441 ÷ 21 = □ 21	990 ÷ 22 = □ 45	943 ÷ 23 = □ 41
864 ÷ 24 = □ 36	850 ÷ 25 = □ 34	754 ÷ 26 = □ 29

21, 36, 39, 21, 45, 41, 36, 34, 29

Mom! I Learn Division Using Math-Chess-Puzzles Connection

Ho Math Chess 何数棋谜 妈!我会棋谜式除法啦!

Frank Ho, Amanda Ho © 2004 – 2017, all rights reserved.

Student's Name _____ Date _____

ddd ÷ dd = qq with no remainder

875 ÷ 25 = □ 35	828 ÷ 36 = □ 23	987 ÷ 47 = □ 21
910 ÷ 26 = □ 35	592 ÷ 37 = □ 16	912 ÷ 48 = □ 19
702 ÷ 27 = □ 26	874 ÷ 38 = □ 23	539 ÷ 49 = □ 11

35, 23, 21, 35, 16, 19, 26, 23, 11

Mom! I Learn Division Using Math-Chess-Puzzles Connection

Student's Name _____ **Date** _____

ddd ÷ dd = qq with no remainder

224 ÷ 28 = □ 8	273 ÷ 39 = □ 7	400 ÷ 50 = □ 8
203 ÷ 29 = □ 7	320 ÷ 40 = □ 8	255 ÷ 51 = □ 5
150 ÷ 30 = □ 5	246 ÷ 41 = □ 6	416 ÷ 52 = □ 8

8, 7, 8, 7, 8, 9, 5, 6, 8

Mom! I Learn Division Using Math-Chess-Puzzles Connection

ddd ÷ dd = qq with no remainder

186 ÷ 31 = □ 6	294 ÷ 42 = □ 7	371 ÷ 53 = □ 7
224 ÷ 32 = □ 7	172 ÷ 43 = □ 4	216 ÷ 54 = □ 4
264 ÷ 33 = □ 8	220 ÷ 44 = □ 5	265 ÷ 53 = □ 5

6, 7, 7, 7, 4, 4, 8, 5, 5

Mom! I Learn Division Using Math-Chess-Puzzles Connection

Ho Math Chess 何数棋谜 妈!我会棋谜式除法啦!

Frank Ho, Amanda Ho © 2004 – 2017, all rights reserved.

Student's Name _____ Date _____

ddd ÷ dd = qq with no remainder

306 ÷ 34 = □ 9	270 ÷ 45 = □ 6	504 ÷ 56 = □ 9
315 ÷ 35 = □ 9	414 ÷ 46 = □ 9	456 ÷ 57 = □ 8
315 ÷ 35 = □ 9	414 ÷ 46 = □ 9	456 ÷ 57 = □ 8

9, 6, 9, 9, 9, 8, 9, 9, 8

Mom! I Learn Division Using Math-Chess-Puzzles Connection

ddddd ÷ ddd

133 618)82194	602 121)72842	140 533)74620
256 318)81408	161 307)49427	354 256)90624
23 799)18377	133 618)82194	24 596)14304

Mom! I Learn Division Using Math-Chess-Puzzles Connection

96 368)35328	37 419)15503	39 297)11583
4406 12)52872	1526 38)57988	954 71)67734
1411 33)46563	408 56)22848	668 47)31396

Mom! I Learn Division Using Math-Chess-Puzzles Connection

1062 67)71154	1611 11)17721	3117 31)96627
210 79)16590	811 50)40590	1064 92)97888

Mom! I Learn Division Using Math-Chess-Puzzles Connection

Ho Math Chess 何数棋谜 妈!我会棋谜式除法啦!

Frank Ho, Amanda Ho © 2004 − 2017, all rights reserved.

Student's Name _____ Date _____

Addition and subtraction

Fill in 2 circles with 2 consecutive natural numbers having a difference of 1

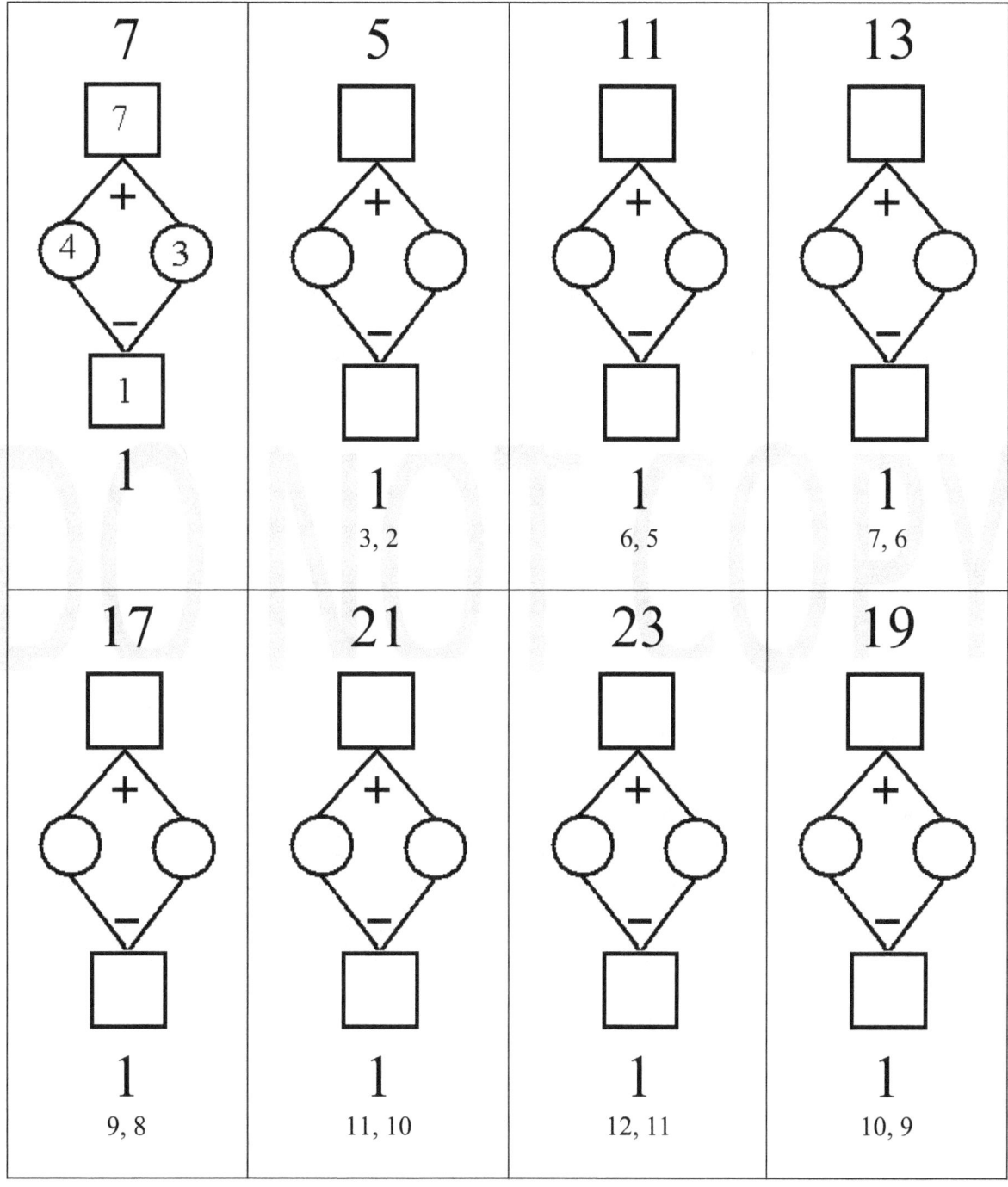

Mom! I Learn Division Using Math-Chess-Puzzles Connection

Addition and subtraction

Fill in 2 circles with 2 consecutive natural numbers having a difference of 1

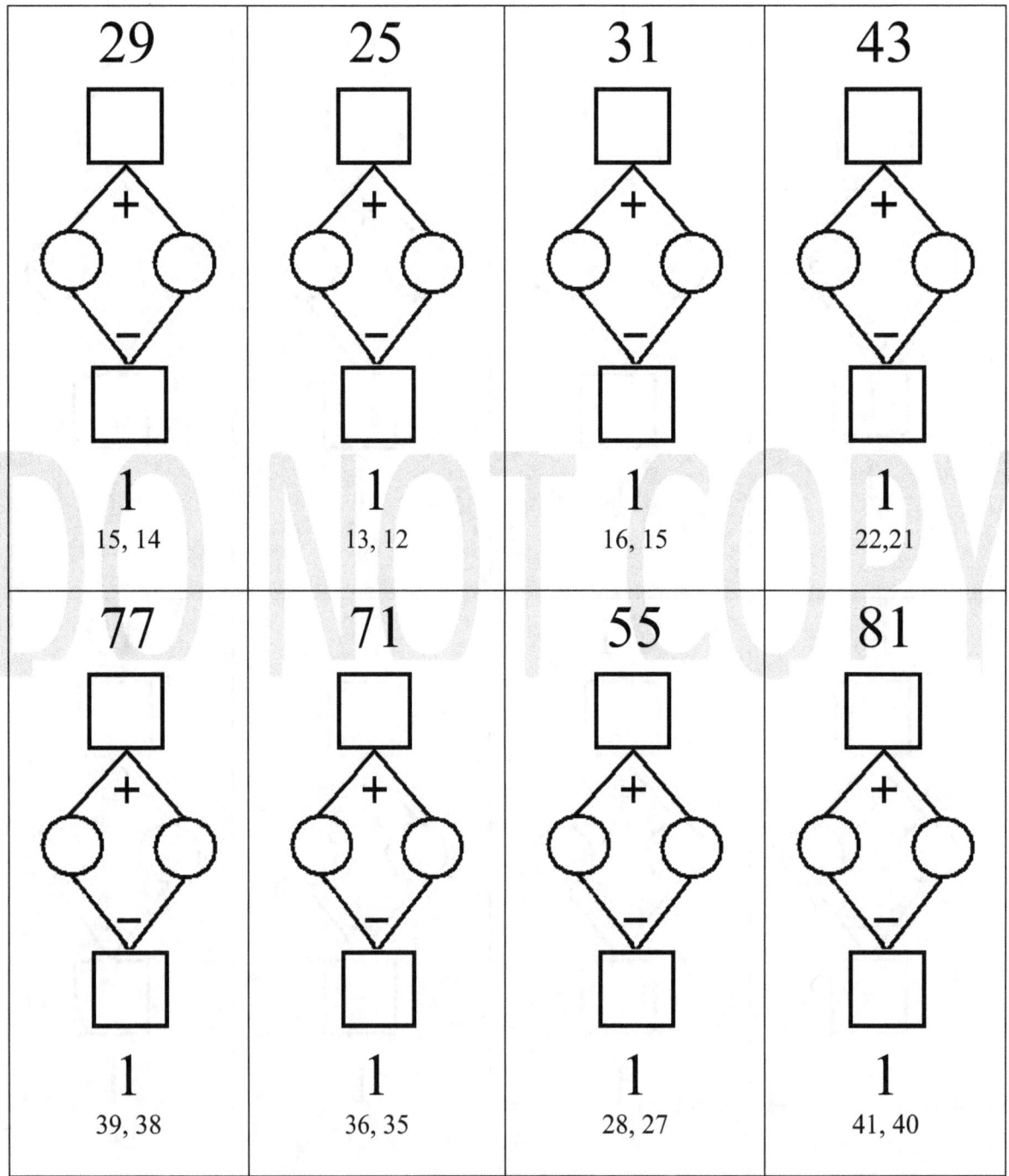

Mom! I Learn Division Using Math-Chess-Puzzles Connection

Ho Math Chess 何数棋谜 妈!我会棋谜式除法啦!

Frank Ho, Amanda Ho © 2004 − 2017, all rights reserved.

Student's Name _____ Date _____

Addition and subtraction

Fill in 2 circles with 2 consecutive natural numbers having a difference of 1

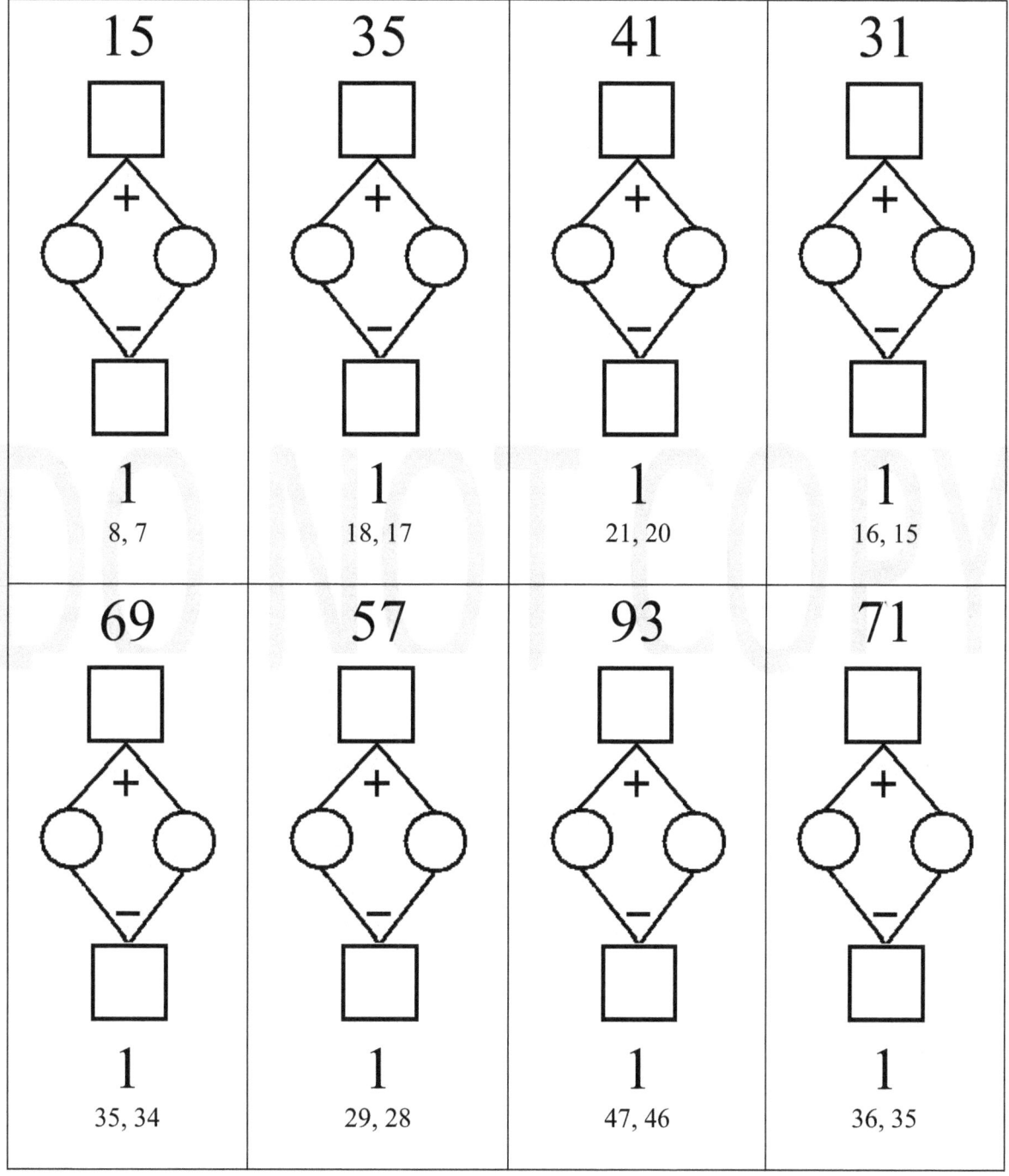

Page 281

Mom! I Learn Division Using Math-Chess-Puzzles Connection

Addition and subtraction

Fill in 2 circles with 2 consecutive natural numbers having a difference of 2

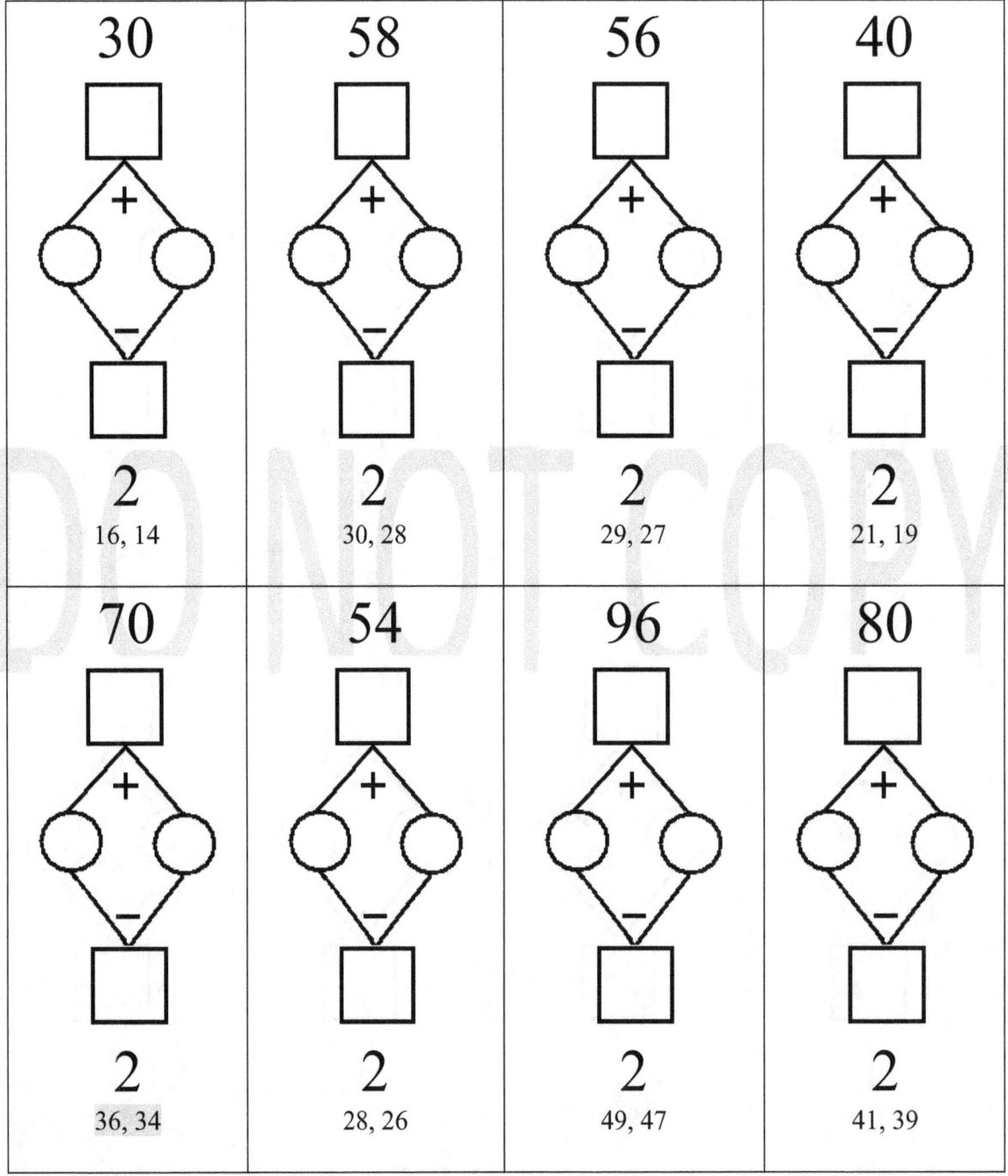

Mom! I Learn Division Using Math-Chess-Puzzles Connection

Addition and subtraction

Fill in 2 circles with 2 consecutive natural numbers having a difference of 2

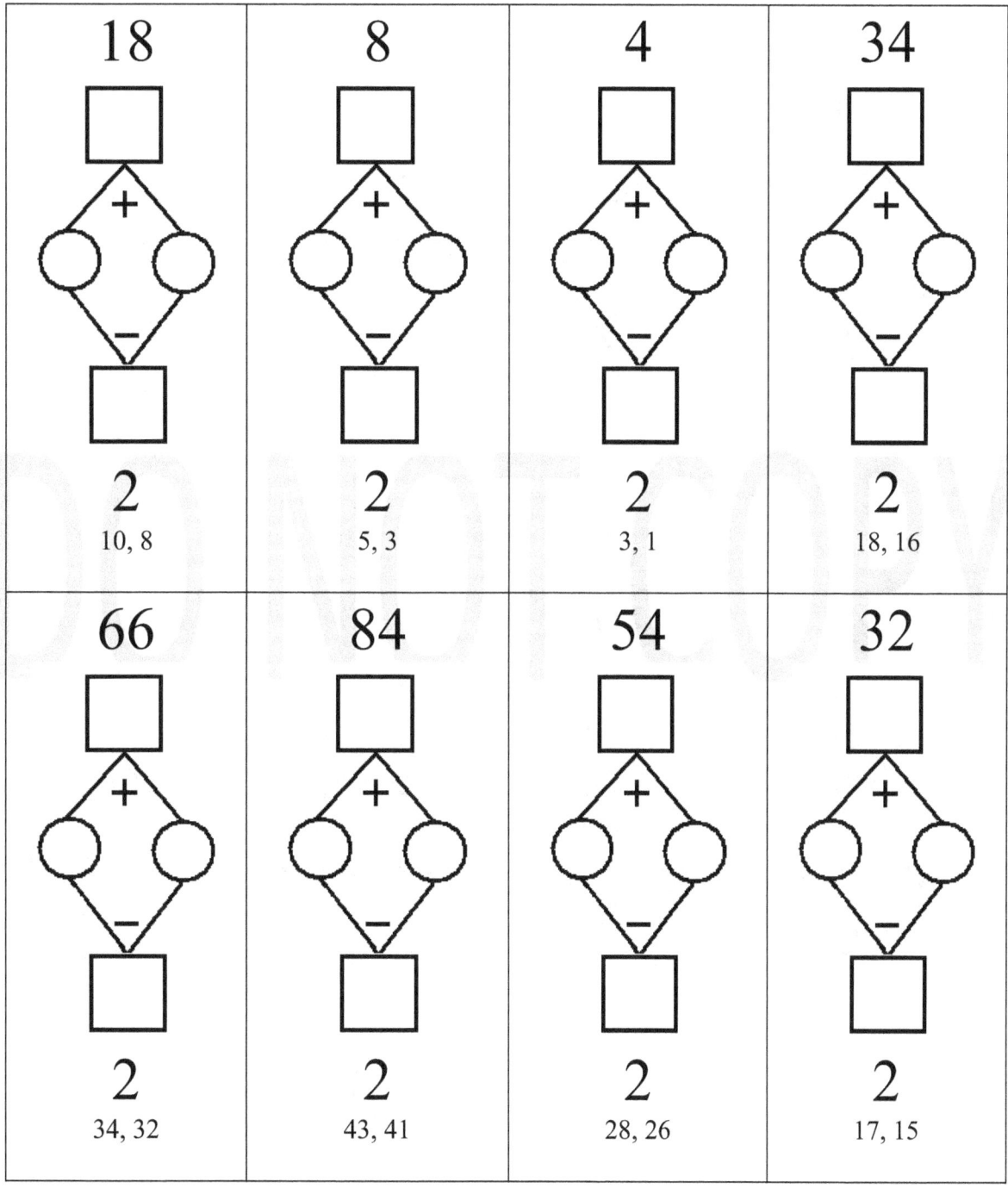

Mom! I Learn Division Using Math-Chess-Puzzles Connection

Ho Math Chess 何数棋谜 妈!我会棋谜式除法啦!

Frank Ho, Amanda Ho © 2004 – 2017, all rights reserved.

Student's Name _____ Date _____

Addition and subtraction

Fill in 2 circles with 2 consecutive natural numbers having a difference of 2

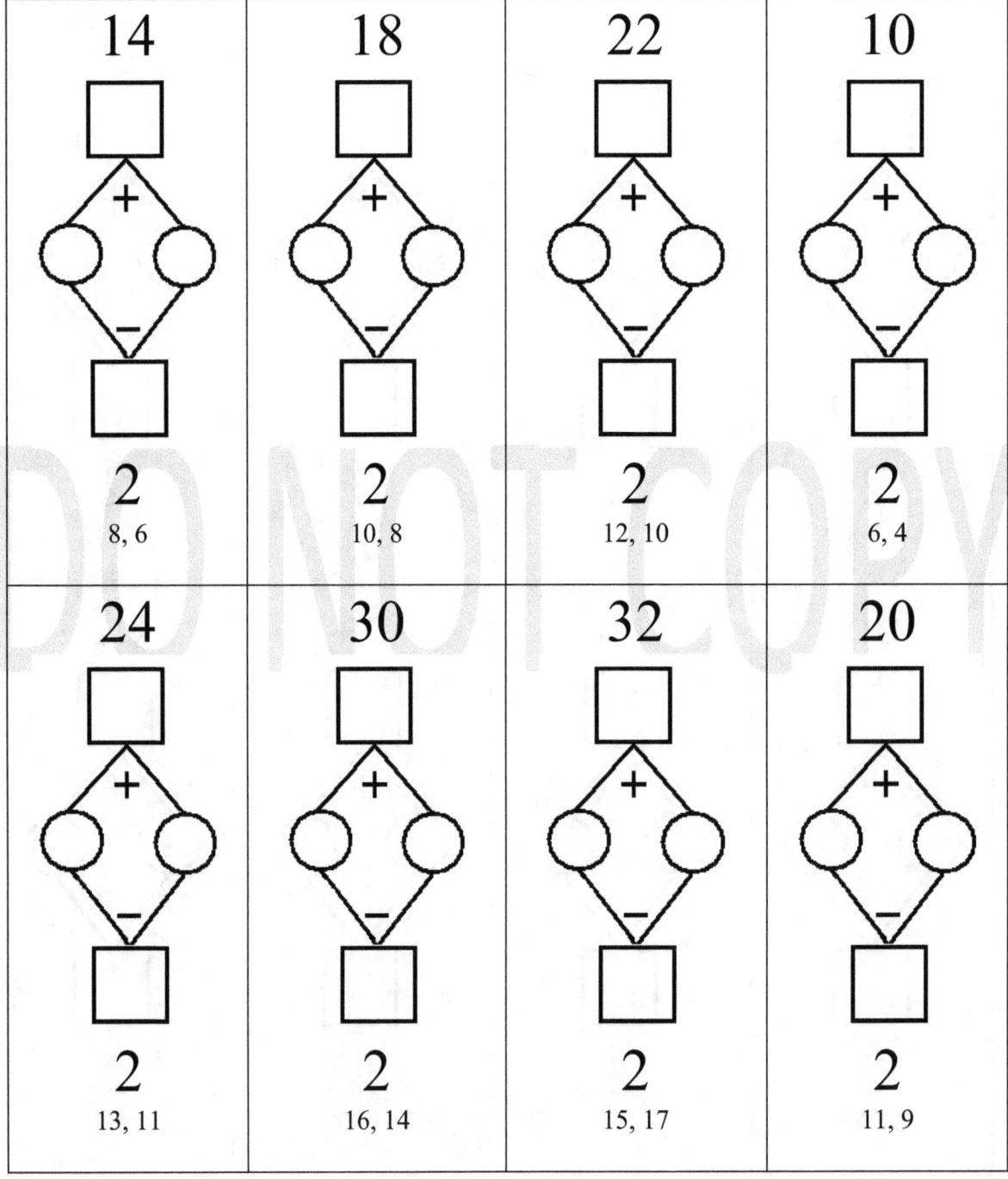

Page 284

Mom! I Learn Division Using Math-Chess-Puzzles Connection

Ho Math Chess 何数棋谜 妈!我会棋谜式除法啦!

Frank Ho, Amanda Ho © 2004 – 2017, all rights reserved.

Student's Name _____ Date _____

Multiplication and addition

Fill in one natural number in each circle.

2 / 3 (1, 2)	7 / 8 (1, 7)	12 / 8 (2, 6)	18 / 9 (3, 6)
3 / 4 (1, 3)	6 / 5 (2, 3)	5 / 6 (1, 5)	4 / 5 (1, 4)

Mom! I Learn Division Using Math-Chess-Puzzles Connection

Ho Math Chess 何数棋谜 妈!我会棋谜式除法啦!

Frank Ho, Amanda Ho © 2004 – 2017, all rights reserved.

Student's Name _____ Date _____

Multiplication and addition

Fill in one natural number in each circle.

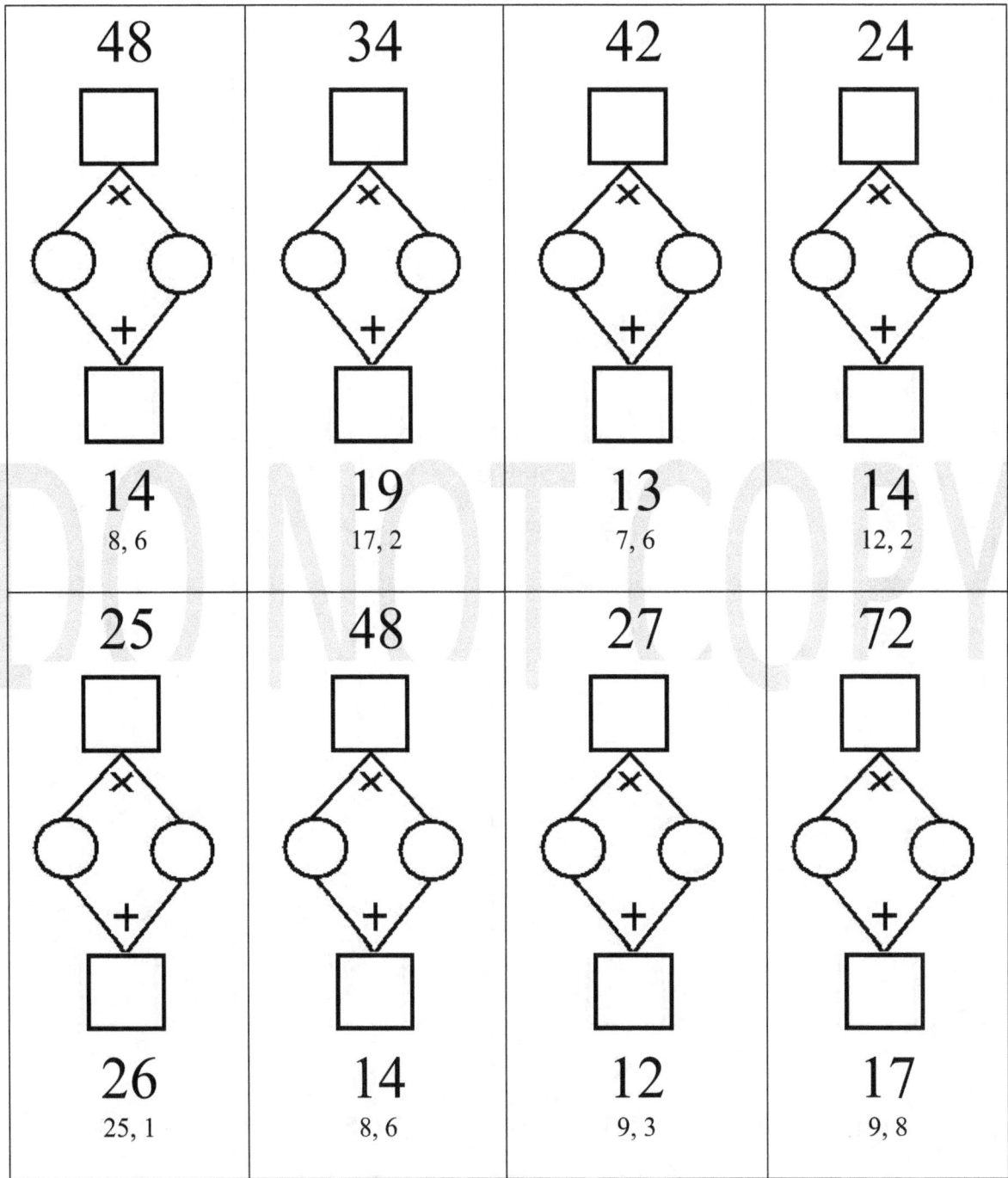

Mom! I Learn Division Using Math-Chess-Puzzles Connection

Ho Math Chess   何数棋谜   妈!我会棋谜式除法啦!

Frank Ho, Amanda Ho © 2004 − 2017, all rights reserved.

Student's Name _____   Date _____

Multiplication and addition

Fill in one natural number in each circle.

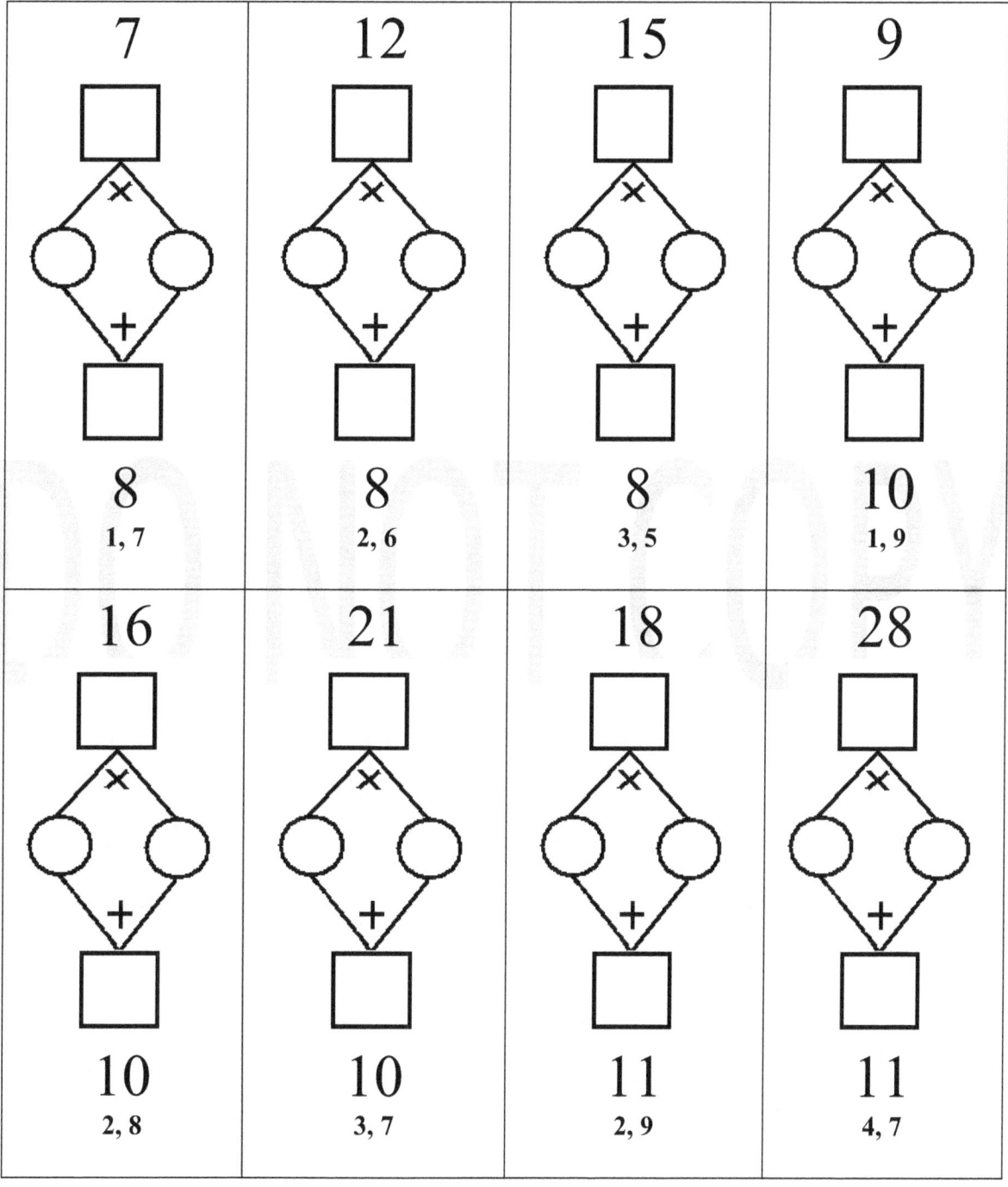

Mom! I Learn Division Using Math-Chess-Puzzles Connection

Ho Math Chess 何数棋谜 妈!我会棋谜式除法啦!

Frank Ho, Amanda Ho © 2004 − 2017, all rights reserved.

Student's Name _____ Date _____

Multiplication and addition

Fill in one natural number in each circle.

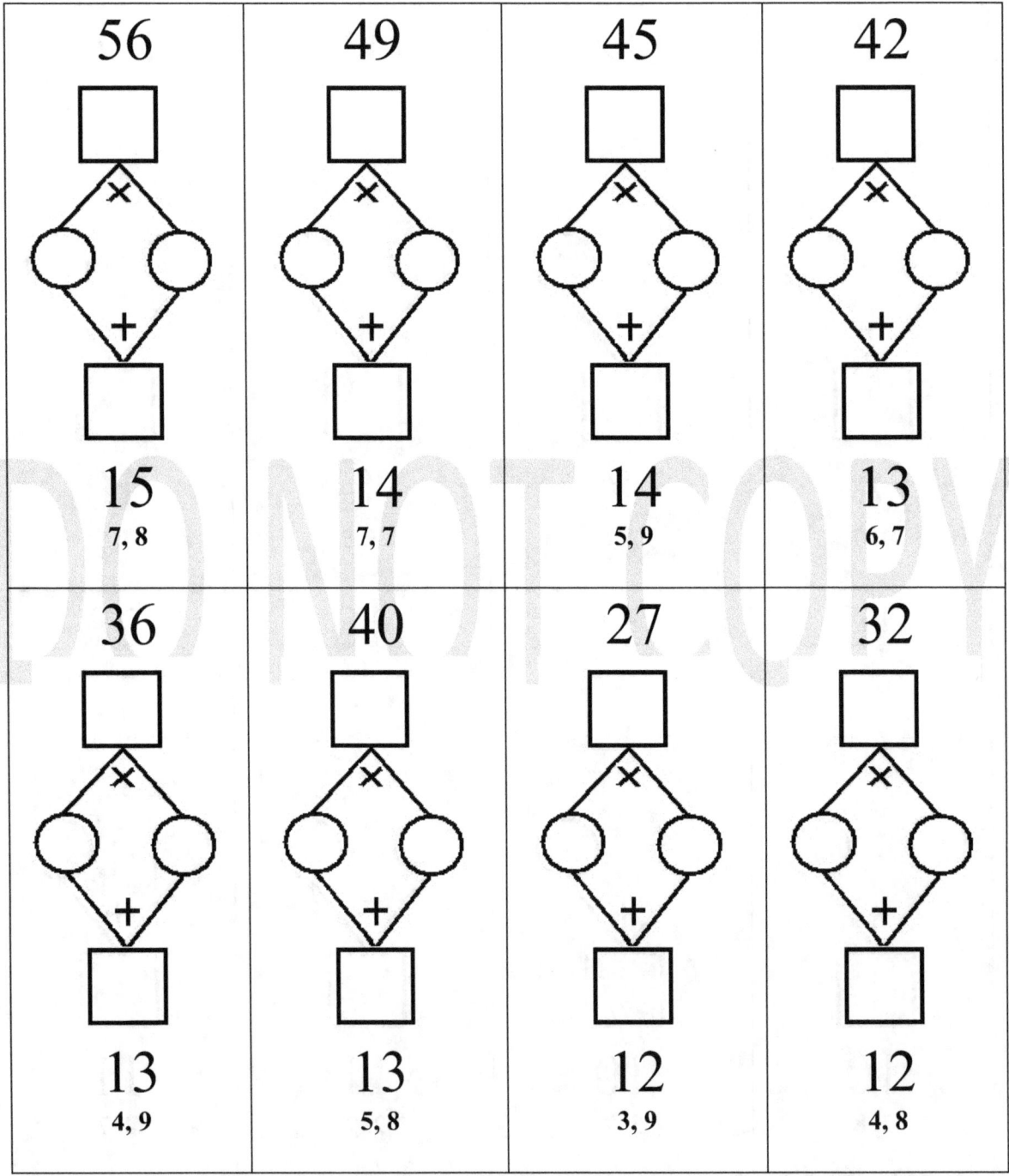

Mom! I Learn Division Using Math-Chess-Puzzles Connection

Ho Math Chess 何数棋谜 妈!我会棋谜式除法啦!

Frank Ho, Amanda Ho © 2004 – 2017, all rights reserved.

Student's Name _____ Date _____

Multiplication and subtraction

Fill in one natural number in each circle.

5 ... 4 5, 1	12 ... 4 6, 2	21 ... 4 7, 3	32 ... 4 8, 4
45 ... 4 9, 5	6 ... 5 6, 1	24 ... 5 8, 3	36 ... 5 9, 4

No part of this publication can be copied, duplicated, or reproduced.

Mom! I Learn Division Using Math-Chess-Puzzles Connection

Multiplication and subtraction

Fill in one natural number in each circle.

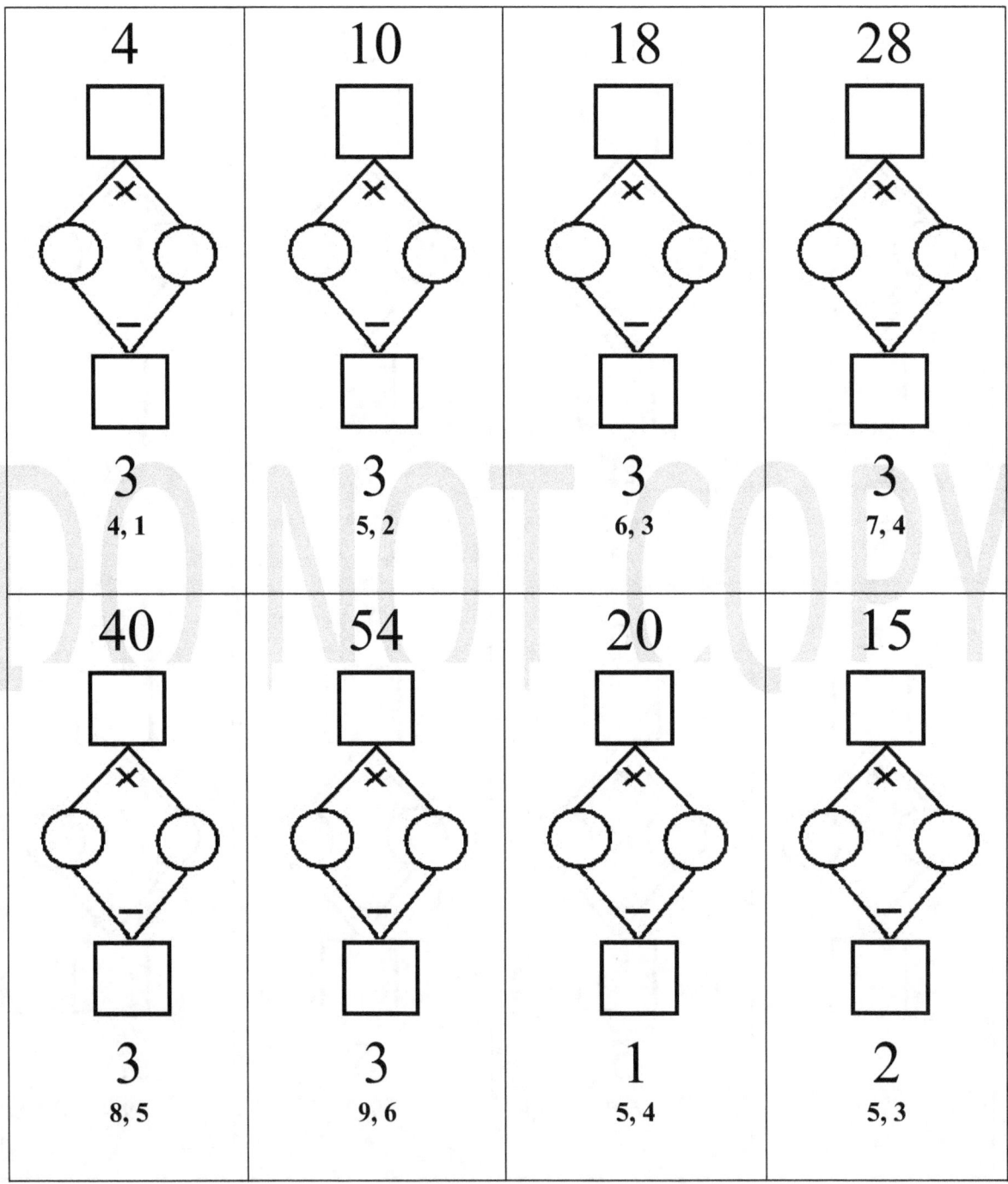

Mom! I Learn Division Using Math-Chess-Puzzles Connection

Multiplication and subtraction

Fill in one natural number in each circle.

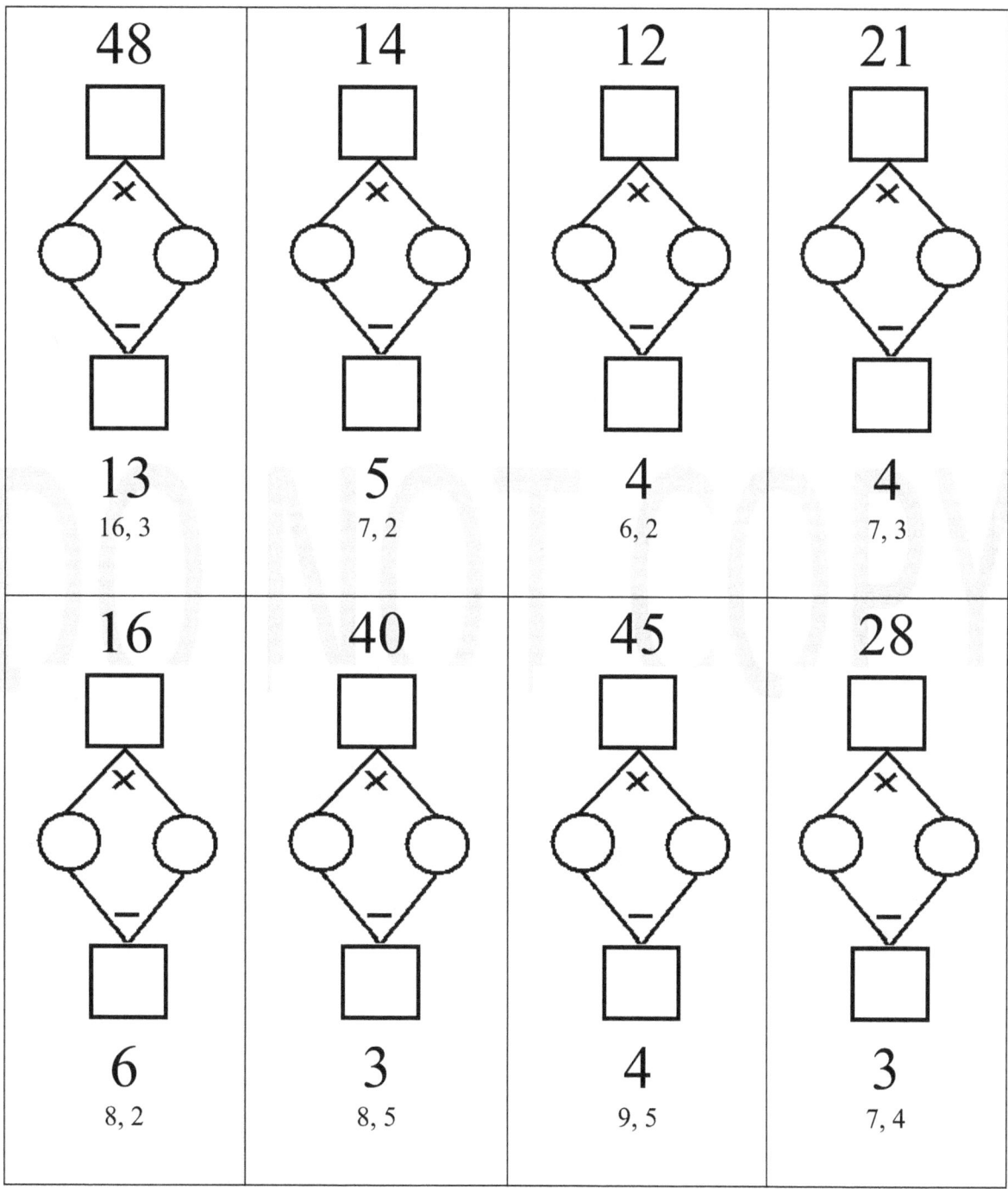

Mom! I Learn Division Using Math-Chess-Puzzles Connection

Ho Math Chess 何数棋谜 妈!我会棋谜式除法啦!

Frank Ho, Amanda Ho © 2004 – 2017, all rights reserved.

Student's Name_____ Date_____

Division and addition

Fill in one natural number in each circle.

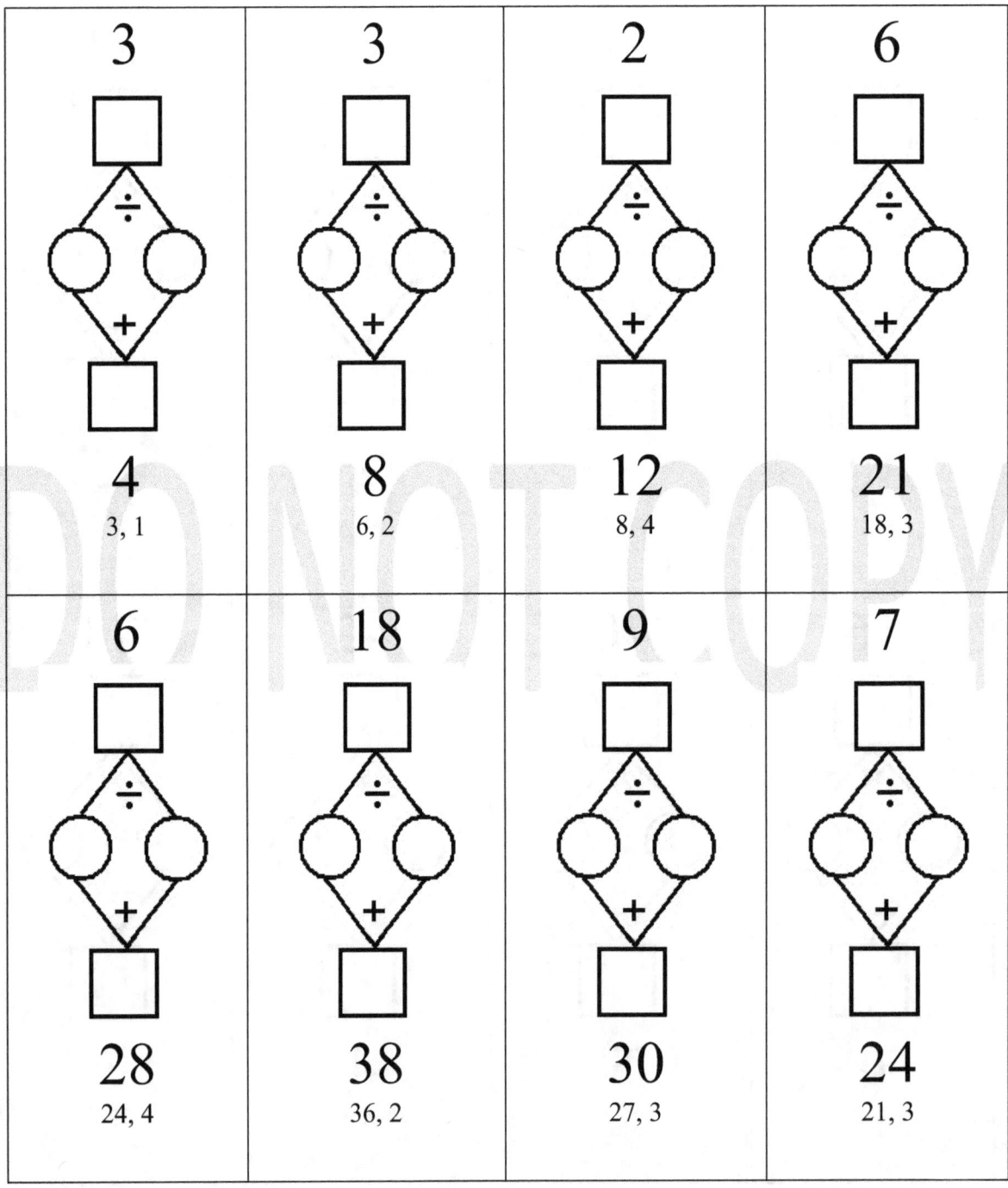

Mom! I Learn Division Using Math-Chess-Puzzles Connection

Division and addition

Fill in one natural number in each circle.

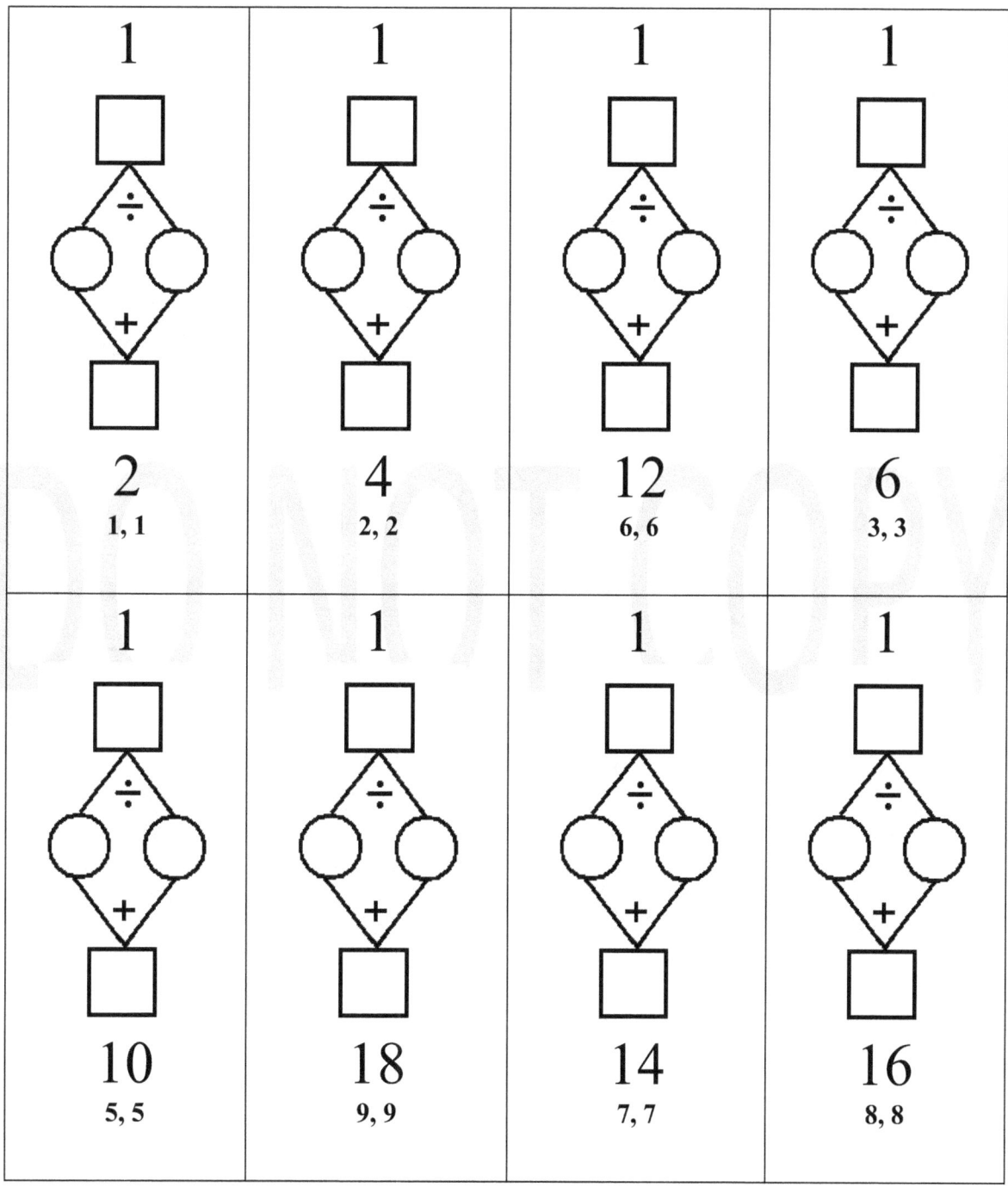

Mom! I Learn Division Using Math-Chess-Puzzles Connection

Ho Math Chess 何数棋谜 妈!我会棋谜式除法啦!

Frank Ho, Amanda Ho © 2004 – 2017, all rights reserved.

Student's Name_____ Date_____

Division and addition

Fill in one natural number in each circle.

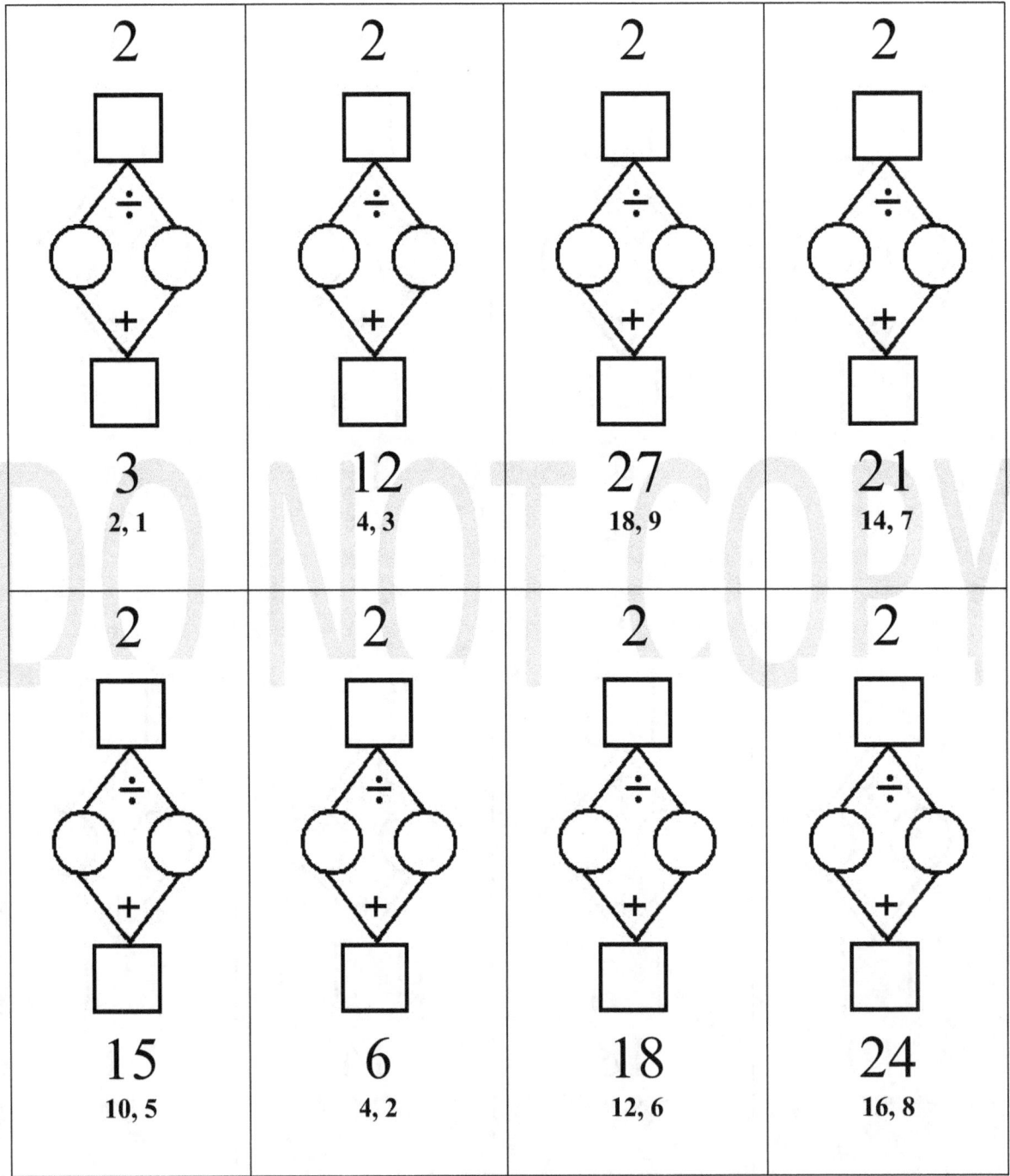

Mom! I Learn Division Using Math-Chess-Puzzles Connection

Ho Math Chess 何数棋谜 妈!我会棋谜式除法啦!

Frank Ho, Amanda Ho © 2004 − 2017, all rights reserved.

Student's Name _____ Date _____

Division and addition

Fill in one natural number in each circle.

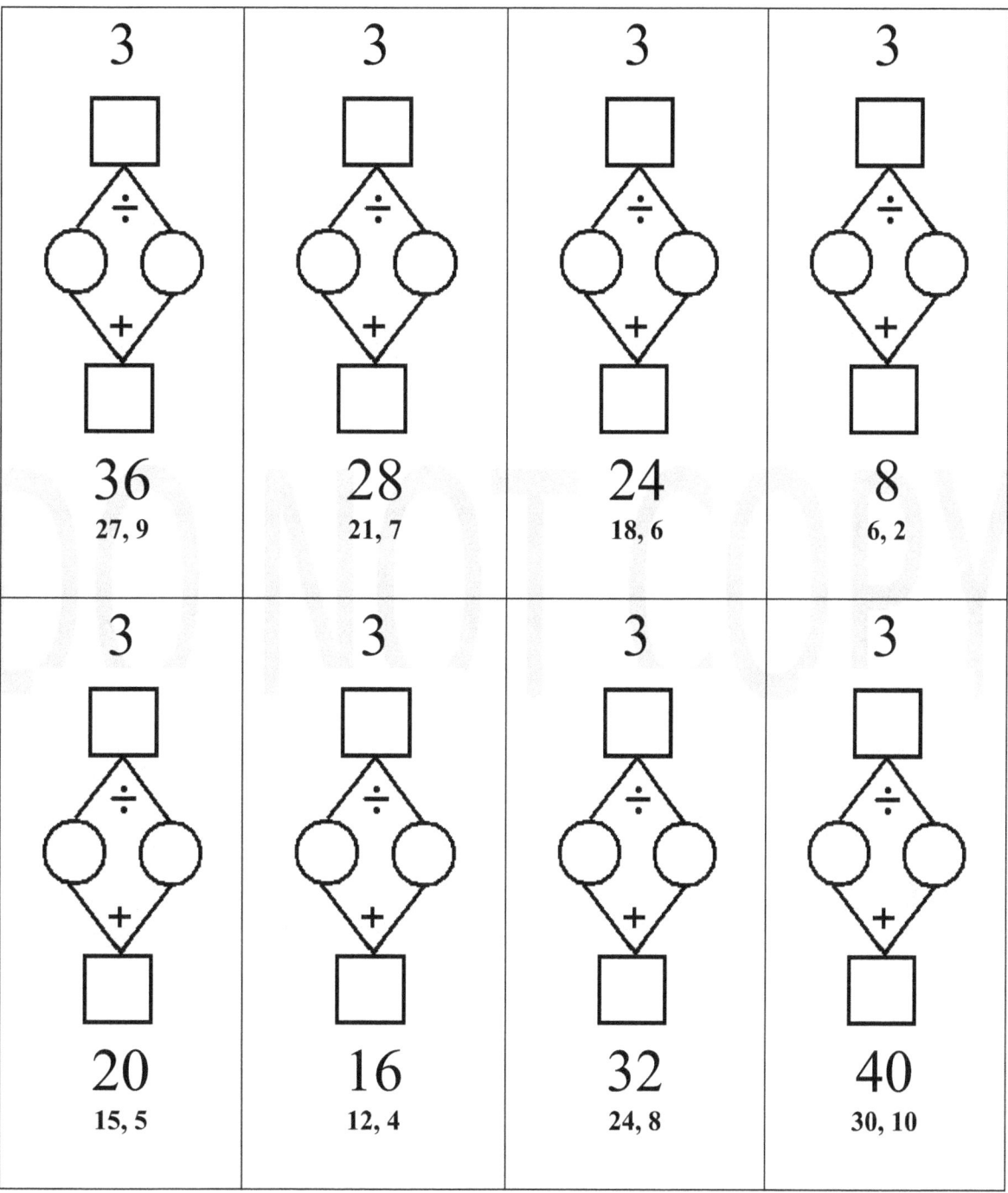

Mom! I Learn Division Using Math-Chess-Puzzles Connection

Ho Math Chess 何数棋谜 妈!我会棋谜式除法啦!

Frank Ho, Amanda Ho © 2004 — 2017, all rights reserved.

Student's Name_____ Date_____

Division and addition

Fill in one natural number in each circle.

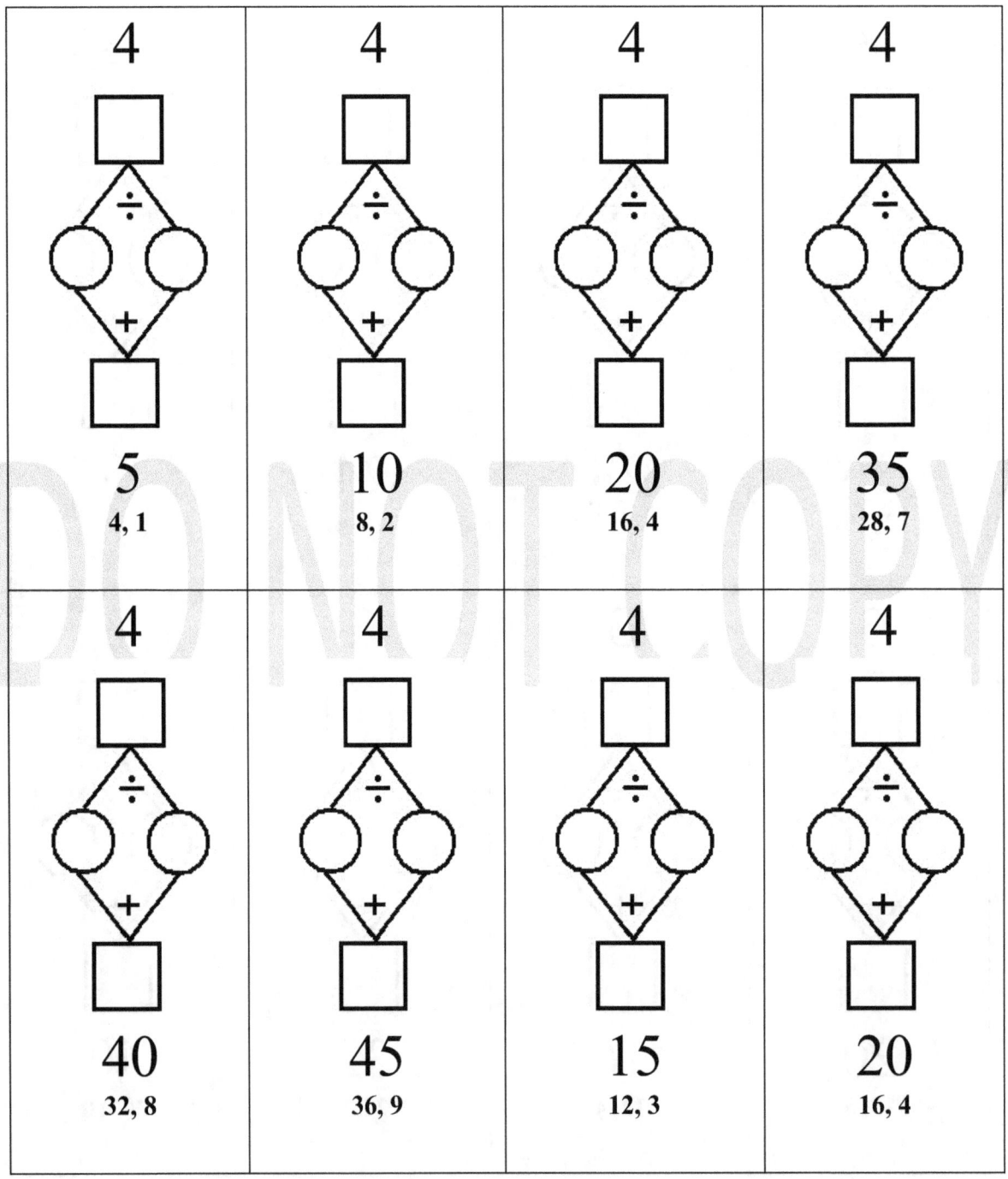

Mom! I Learn Division Using Math-Chess-Puzzles Connection

Ho Math Chess 何数棋谜 妈!我会棋谜式除法啦!

Frank Ho, Amanda Ho © 2004 – 2017, all rights reserved.

Student's Name _____ Date _____

Division and addition

Fill in one natural number in each circle.

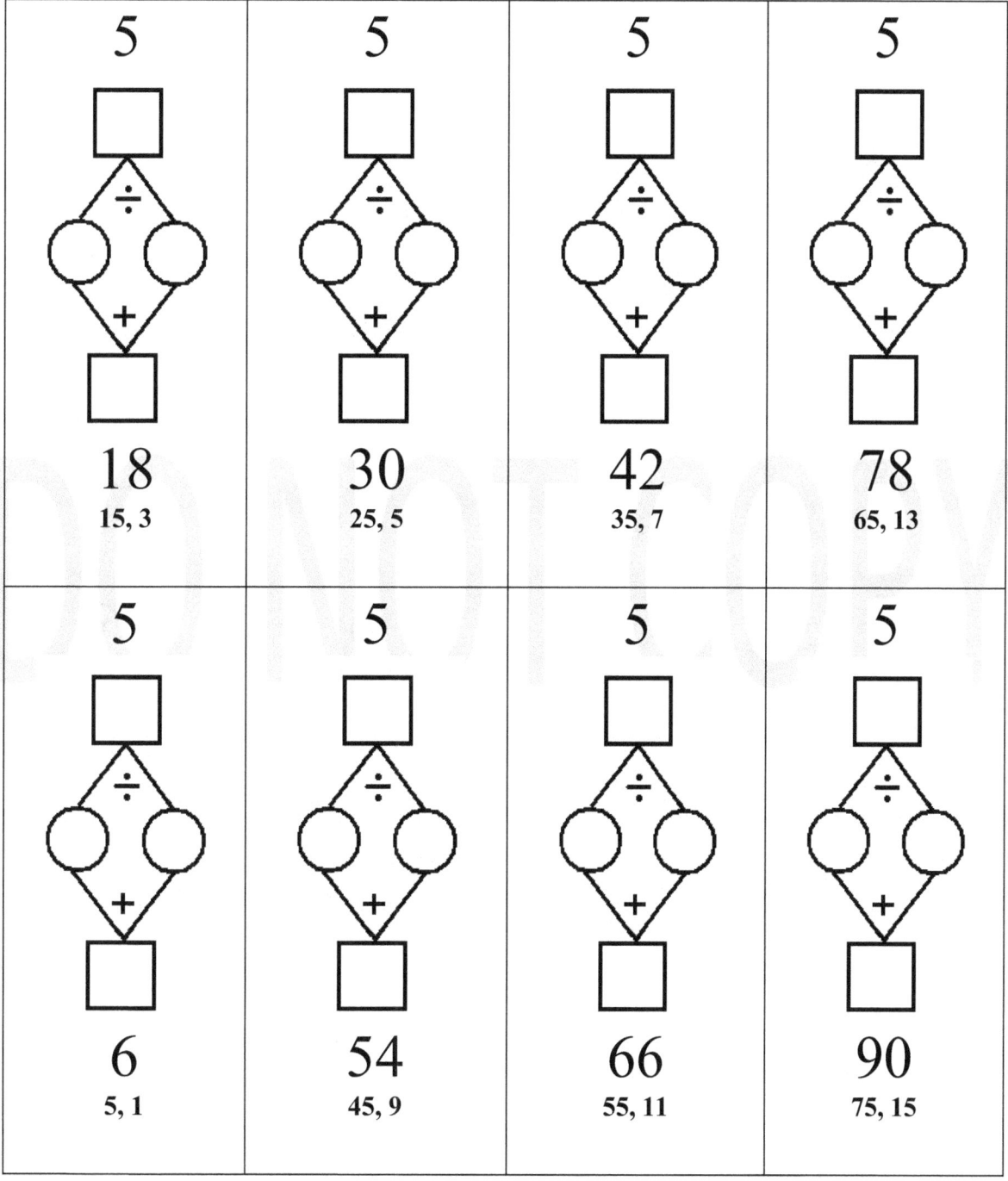

Mom! I Learn Division Using Math-Chess-Puzzles Connection

Ho Math Chess 何数棋谜 妈!我会棋谜式除法啦!

Frank Ho, Amanda Ho © 2004 – 2017, all rights reserved.

Student's Name _____ Date _____

Division and addition

Fill in one natural number in each circle.

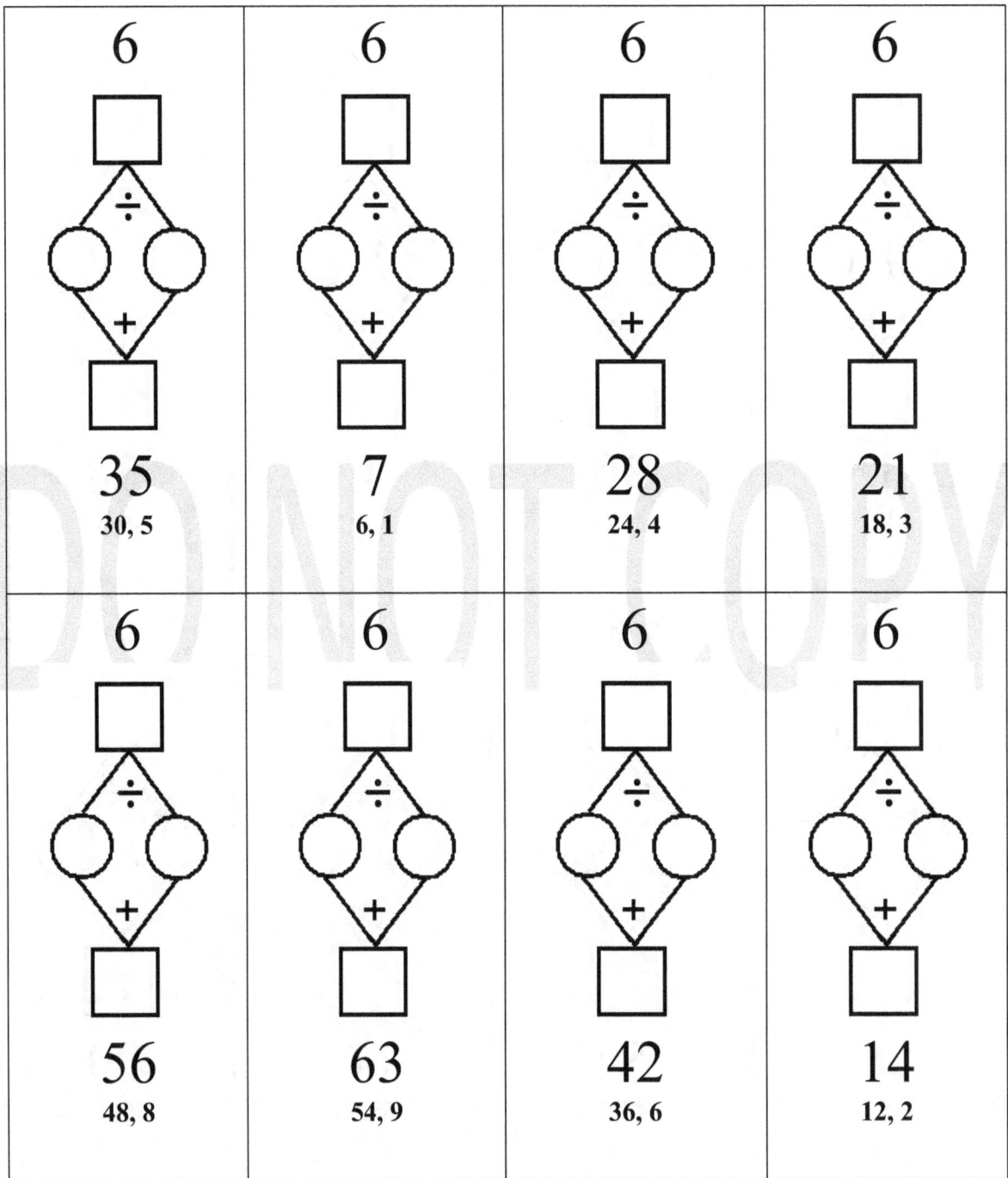

Mom! I Learn Division Using Math-Chess-Puzzles Connection

Ho Math Chess 何数棋谜 妈!我会棋谜式除法啦!

Frank Ho, Amanda Ho © 2004 – 2017, all rights reserved.

Student's Name _____ Date _____

Division and addition

Fill in one natural number in each circle.

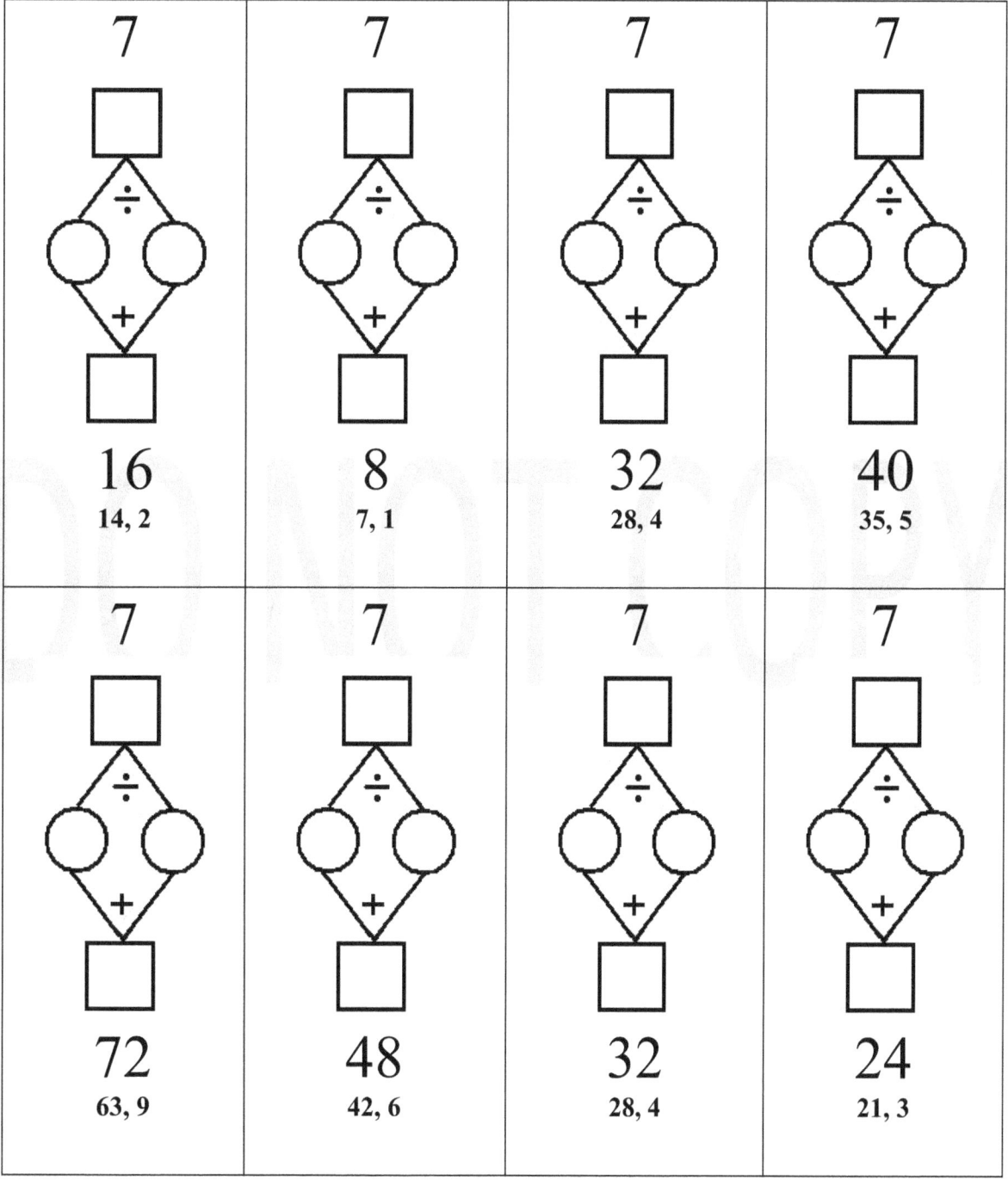

Mom! I Learn Division Using Math-Chess-Puzzles Connection

Ho Math Chess　何数棋谜　妈!我会棋谜式除法啦!

Frank Ho, Amanda Ho © 2004 – 2017, all rights reserved.

Student's Name _____ Date _____

Division and addition

Fill in one natural number in each circle.

8 → □ ÷ ○○ + → □ = 18	8 → □ ÷ ○○ + → □ = 54	8 → □ ÷ ○○ + → □ = 36	8 → □ ÷ ○○ + → □ = 27
16, 2	**48, 6**	**32, 4**	**24, 3**
8 → □ ÷ ○○ + → □ = 9	8 → □ ÷ ○○ + → □ = 81	8 → □ ÷ ○○ + → □ = 63	8 → □ ÷ ○○ + → □ = 45
8, 1	**72, 9**	**56, 7**	**40, 5**

No part of this publication can be copied, duplicated, or reproduced.　Page 300

Mom! I Learn Division Using Math-Chess-Puzzles Connection

Ho Math Chess 何数棋谜 妈!我会棋谜式除法啦!

Frank Ho, Amanda Ho © 2004 − 2017, all rights reserved.

Student's Name _____ Date _____

Division and addition

Fill in one natural number in each circle.

9 ☐ ÷ ○ ○ + ☐ 70 **63, 7**	9 ☐ ÷ ○ ○ + ☐ 20 **18, 2**	9 ☐ ÷ ○ ○ + ☐ 40 **36, 4**	9 ☐ ÷ ○ ○ + ☐ 30 **27, 3**
9 ☐ ÷ ○ ○ + ☐ 40 **36, 4**	9 ☐ ÷ ○ ○ + ☐ 60 **54, 6**	9 ☐ ÷ ○ ○ + ☐ 30 **27, 3**	9 ☐ ÷ ○ ○ + ☐ 10 **9, 1**

Mom! I Learn Division Using Math-Chess-Puzzles Connection

Ho Math Chess 何数棋谜 妈!我会棋谜式除法啦!

Frank Ho, Amanda Ho © 2004 – 2017, all rights reserved.

Student's Name _____ Date _____

Division and subtraction

Fill in one natural number in each circle.

9 ÷ ○ ○ − = 8	34 ÷ ○ ○ − = 66	12 ÷ ○ ○ − = 88	14 ÷ ○ ○ − = 26
9, 1	68, 2	96, 8	28, 2
16 ÷ ○ ○ − = 45	18 ÷ ○ ○ − = 34	13 ÷ ○ ○ − = 36	9 ÷ ○ ○ − = 64
48, 3	36, 2	39, 3	72, 8

Mom! I Learn Division Using Math-Chess-Puzzles Connection

Ho Math Chess 何数棋谜 妈!我会棋谜式除法啦!

Frank Ho, Amanda Ho © 2004 − 2017, all rights reserved.

Student's Name _____ Date _____

Multiplication and division

Fill in one natural number in each circle.

4 ... 1 (2, 2)	8 ... 2 (4, 2)	44 ... 11 (22, 2)	32 ... 2 (8, 4)
48 ... 3 (12, 4)	49 ... 1 (7, 7)	16 ... 4 (8, 2)	27 ... 3 (9, 3)

Mom! I Learn Division Using Math-Chess-Puzzles Connection

Ho Math Chess 何数棋谜 妈!我会棋谜式除法啦!

Frank Ho, Amanda Ho © 2004 – 2017, all rights reserved.

Student's Name_____ Date_____

***** Part 4 Decimal division *****

Divide ddd by dd. Round to the nearest hundredth.

[Four long-division puzzle grids:
- 16) 282
- 70) 974
- 29) 485
- 36) 543]

17.63   13.91   17r10, 13r64
16.72   15.08333   16r21, 15r3

Page 304

Mom! I Learn Division Using Math-Chess-Puzzles Connection

Ho Math Chess 何数棋谜 妈!我会棋谜式除法啦!

Frank Ho, Amanda Ho © 2004 – 2017, all rights reserved.

Student's Name _____ Date _____

Divide ddd by ddd. Round to the nearest hundredth.

$120 \overline{)586}$

$241 \overline{)876}$

$322 \overline{)564}$

$224 \overline{)453}$

4.88,   3.63   4r106, 3r153
1.75,   2.02   1r242   2r5

Mom! I Learn Division Using Math-Chess-Puzzles Connection

Ho Math Chess 何数棋谜 妈!我会棋谜式除法啦!

Frank Ho, Amanda Ho © 2004 – 2017, all rights reserved.

Student's Name _____ Date _____

Divide dddd by ddd. Round to the nearest hundredth.

462) 1234

421) 6843

364) 2718

583) 7492

2.6709,   16.25   2r310, 16r107
7.47,   12.85   7r170, 12r496

Page 306

Mom! I Learn Division Using Math-Chess-Puzzles Connection

Ho Math Chess 何数棋谜 妈!我会棋谜式除法啦!

Frank Ho, Amanda Ho © 2004 – 2017, all rights reserved.

Student's Name _____ Date _____

ddd ÷ dd. Round the answers to the nearest hundredth.

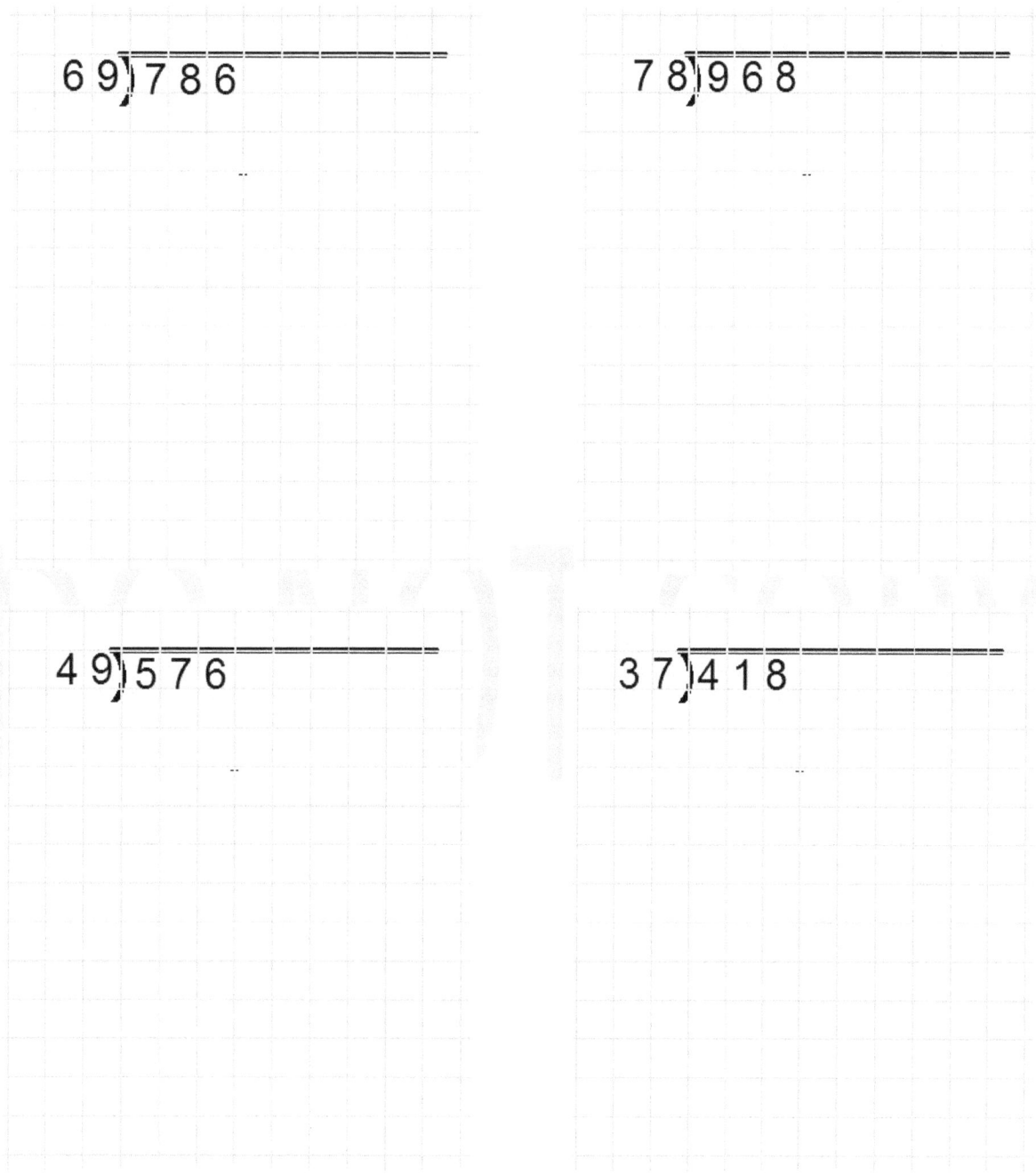

11.39, 12.41
17.76, 11.30

Mom! I Learn Division Using Math-Chess-Puzzles Connection

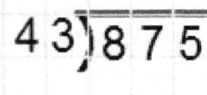 Math Chess   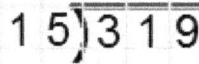 数棋谜   妈!我会棋谜式除法啦!

Frank Ho, Amanda Ho © 2004 – 2017, all rights reserved.

Student's Name _____ Date _____

ddd ÷ dd. Round the answers to the nearest hundredth.

43)875

15)319

63)874

13)278

20.35, 21.23
13.87, 21.38

Mom! I Learn Division Using Math-Chess-Puzzles Connection

Ho Math Chess 何数棋谜 妈!我会棋谜式除法啦!

Frank Ho, Amanda Ho © 2004 – 2017, all rights reserved.

Student's Name _____ Date _____

dddd÷ dd. Round the answers to the nearest hundredth.

185.65, 134.82
106.16, 117.71

No part of this publication can be copied, duplicated, or reproduced.   Page 309

Mom! I Learn Division Using Math-Chess-Puzzles Connection

dddd ÷ dd. Round the answers to the nearest hundredth.

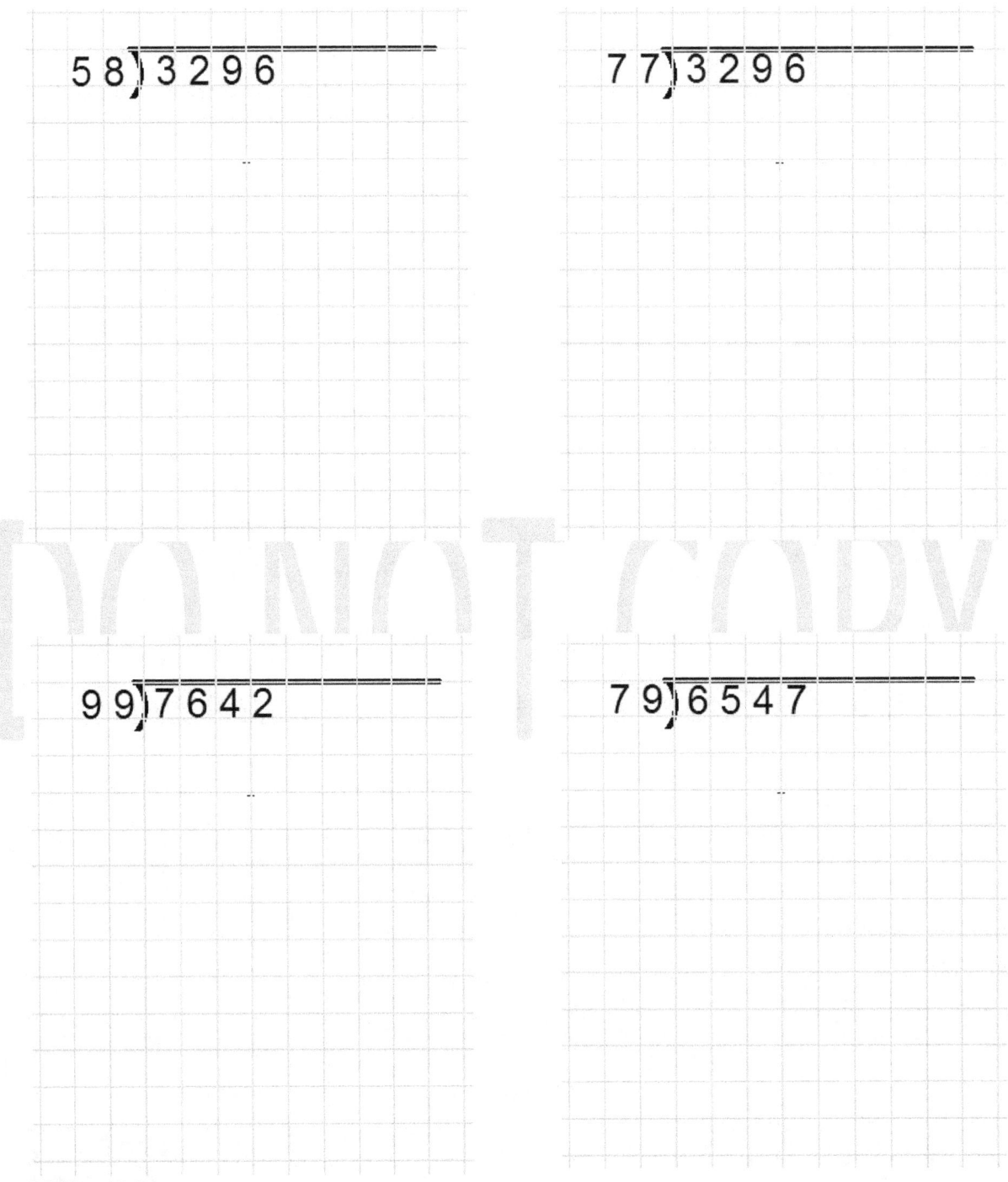

56.83, 42.81
77.20, 82.87

Mom! I Learn Division Using Math-Chess-Puzzles Connection

Ho Math Chess 何数棋谜 妈!我会棋谜式除法啦!

Frank Ho, Amanda Ho © 2004 – 2017, all rights reserved.

Student's Name _____ Date _____

ddd ÷ ddd. Round the answers to the nearest hundredth.

2.02, 1.48
1.81, 1.57

No part of this publication can be copied, duplicated, or reproduced.   Page 311

Mom! I Learn Division Using Math-Chess-Puzzles Connection

Ho Math Chess　何数棋谜　妈!我会棋谜式除法啦!

Frank Ho, Amanda Ho © 2004 – 2017, all rights reserved.

Student's Name _____　Date _____

dddd ÷ ddd. Round the answers to the nearest hundredth.

5.54, 9.38
6.32, 5.15

Mom! I Learn Division Using Math-Chess-Puzzles Connection

Ho Math Chess　何数棋谜　妈!我会棋谜式除法啦!

Frank Ho, Amanda Ho © 2004 − 2017, all rights reserved.

Student's Name _____　Date _____

介紹何数棋谜

何数棋谜=奧数棋谜 + 思唯腦力開發
英文教材，中英双语教学

什麼是何数棋谜？

上百篇科學論文已發表國際象棋可以提高兒童問題解答能力．並且訓練他們的專心及耐力．所以我們已經知道下國際象棋對兒童有好處．但是因為國際象棋與計算能力並無直接關係，所以如何讓兒童能在一個歡樂的環境下也能利用下棋來提高數學的計算呢？何老師首創並發明有版权的幾何棋藝符號並利用此符號發明了世界第一的独特結合數學与棋谜教材．何数棋谜讓兒童能利用幾何棋藝符號進行邏輯推理及數字的運算．棋藝與算術的綜合題含蓋了整數，幾何，集合，抽象數，對比異同，函數，座標，多空間圖形資料，及規則性數字分析．並且把棋藝的趣味性和數學的知識性結合在一起．

何数棋谜如何幫助兒童腦力思唯的開發？

很簡單的一個道理就是讓學生自願地去用腦，何数棋谜首創獨一無二的融合數學與棋谜的独特趣味寓教於樂教材，利用國際象棋訓練右腦的座標，空間分析及圖形處理，並利用發明了整合棋子與數學的圖形語言，讓兒童能利用符號圖形訓練左腦進行邏輯推理及數字的運算．國際象棋與算術的綜合題含蓋了整數，幾何，集合，抽象數，對比異同，函數，多空間圖形資料．所以枯燥無味的計算題變成了謎題，學生需要通過更多的思考．能讓腦去思考愈多則腦力也愈開發．處里訊息，分析資料才能發掘出題目．做這些謎題式數學時可以訓練學生比較會專心及有耐心．

何数棋谜融合數學與國際象棋的教學理論已在 BC 省數學教師刊物上發表．科研報告已經證實何数棋谜教學法不但可以提高兒童數學解題及思維能力，還可以開發兒童的腦力，及分析問題的能力並且增加兒童學習的耐力，學生的探索創造精神及求知欲．判斷力，及自信心等，啟發思維訓練機警靈巧及加強手腦眼的靈活運用．

Mom! I Learn Division Using Math-Chess-Puzzles Connection
Ho Math Chess 何数棋谜 妈!我会棋谜式除法啦!
Frank Ho, Amanda Ho © 2004 – 2017, all rights reserved.
Student's Name _____ Date _____

Introducing Ho Math Chess™

Ho Math Chess™ = math + puzzles + chess

Frank Ho, a Canadian math teacher, intrigued by the relationships between math and chess after teaching his son chess started **Ho Math Chess™** in 1995. His long-term devotion of research has led his son to become a FIDE chess master and Frank's publications of over 20 math workbooks. Today **Ho Math Chess™** is the world largest and the only franchised scholastic math, chess and puzzles specialty learning center with worldwide locations. **Ho Math Chess™** is a leading research organization in the field of math, chess, and puzzles integrated teaching methodology.

There are hundreds of articles already published showing chess benefits children and that math puzzles are a very good way of improving brainpower. So, by integrating chess and mathematical chess puzzles together, the learning effect is more significant.

Parents send their children to **Ho Math Chess™** because of they like **Ho Math Chess™** teaching philosophy – offering children problem-solving questions in a variety of formats. The questions could be pure chess, chess puzzles or mathematical chess puzzles in nature of logic, pattern, tree structure, Venn diagram, probability and many more math concepts.

Ho Math Chess™ has developed a series of unique and high-quality math, chess, and puzzles integrated workbooks. **Ho Math Chess™** produced the world's first workbook **Learning Chess to Improve Math.** This workbook is not only for learning chess but also for enriching math ability. This sets **Ho Math Chess** apart from other math learning centers, chess club, or chess classes.

The teaching method at **Ho Math Chess™** is to use math, chess, and puzzles integrated workbooks to teach children fun math. The purposes of **Ho Math Chess™** teaching method and workbooks are to:

- Improve math marks.
- Develop problem-solving and critical thinking skills.
- Improve logic thinking ability.
- Boost brainpower.

Testimonials, sample worksheets, reports, and franchise information can be found at www.homathchess.com.

More information about **Ho Math Chess™** can also be found from the following publications:

1. Why Buy a **Ho Math Chess™** Learning Centre Franchise: A Unique Learning Centre?
2. **Ho Math Chess™** Sudoku Puzzles Sample Worksheets
3. Introduction to **Ho Math Chess™** and its Founder Frank Ho

The above publications can be purchased from www.amazon.com.

www.ingramcontent.com/pod-product-compliance
Lightning Source LLC
Chambersburg PA
CBHW080543230426
43663CB00015B/2691